Date Due

THE POLITICS OF FREIGHT RATES

THE POLITICS OF FREIGHT RATES

The Railway Freight Rate Issue in Canada

Howard Darling

Canada in Transition Series
McCLELLAND AND STEWART

McClelland and Stewart Limited
The Canadian Publishers
25 Hollinger Road
Toronto, Ontario
M4B 3G2

CANADIAN CATALOGUING IN PUBLICATION DATA

Darling, Howard J.
  The politics of freight rates

(Canada in transition series)
Includes index.
ISBN 0-7710-2554-8 bd.   ISBN 0-7710-2555-6 pa.

1. Railroads — Canada — Rates — History.
I. Title.   II. Series.

HE2135.D37   385'.12   C80-094682-0

Printed and bound in Canada

Contents

Editors' Foreword

The volumes in this series, *Canada in Transition: Crisis in Political Development,* attempt to place our current national dilemma in historical perspective. As a country embedded from the outset in the political and economic fortunes of powerful neighbours, Canada has encountered unique social, economic, and political obstacles to unity and cohesion. Indeed, the term "crisis" denotes for us the central features of the Canadian experience: a fascinating mix of dangers and opportunities in a rapidly changing international environment.

The issue of transportation policy has always been a major feature of the Canadian experience, and railways have been at the centre of transportation controversies. Enshrined in the consciousness as part of our "national dream," written into the British North America Act as part of the federal bargain, incorporated into the language of Western discontent in the emotive phrase "freight rates," railway politics have historical roots and substantive breadth unique to Canada.

That so timeless a topic should be analysed by so skilful and experienced a writer as Howard Darling is a fortunate achievement for the *Canada in Transition* Series and for Canadian scholarship in general. Although his untimely death prevented Mr. Darling from putting his personal touch on the final manuscript, the essence of his tough-minded approach is well-preserved in the pages that follow. Everyone familiar with the elements of this issue and the extent of Mr. Darling's personal involvement in and knowledge of it, will recognize instantly the importance and worth of this book. To the uninitiated, it will provide both a fascinating introduction and a pointed critique. Thus both experts and general readers will welcome Howard Darling's fresh, penetrating views on this perennial topic, which remains a focal point of contemporary Canadian politics and economics – particularly in Western and Atlantic Canada – where it serves as a continuing source of friction and alienation.

In contrast to the vast polemical literature on the freight rate question Mr. Howard Darling's immense experience in the transport field at both federal and provincial levels has permitted an analysis of unparalleled scholarly authority. There is a total absence of sacred cows; conventional views of this explosive issue are all critically examined (and many dismissed for lack of evidence); and everywhere the stages of the debate are examined in their institutional setting. It is not too much to say that Mr. Darling's work contributes an entirely new focus: freight rates will not be the same again.

David V. J. Bell
Edgar J. E. Dosman

Preface

Although he is best known for his work in the field of marine transport, the subjects of railway freight rates and railway transportation policy were dear to the heart of the late Howard Darling. He spent most of his career in transportation economics and contributed directly to all sides of the railway freight rate issue, having worked for the Canadian Pacific Railway, the Province of Alberta (preparing its briefs on various rate increase applications and to the Turgeon Royal Commission), the Transportation Economics Bureau, and the federal Department of Transport. In 1965 he was appointed Chairman of the Canadian Maritime Commission, and with the absorption of that body into the Canadian Transport Commission in 1967, became the first Chairman of its Water Transport Committee. He was also Chairman of the Commodity Pipeline Committee and a member of the Railway Transport Committee of the CTC. He retired from the Commission in 1970 to enter private consulting.

Based on his personal experience, his contacts with many of the participants, and his wide range of expertise, Mr. Darling first developed his analysis of the freight rate issue in "Transportation Policy in Canada: The Struggle of Ideologies versus Realities," delivered as the keynote address at a Conference on Canadian National Transportation Policy held at York University in 1972, and subsequently published in K.W. Studnicki-Gizbert (ed.), *Issues in Canadian Transportation Policy*. The theme of that paper was that transportation policy, from the Crow's Nest Pass Agreement in 1897 to the passage of the National Transportation Act in 1967, was the story of the growth, decline, and fall of what Mr. Darling calls the Railway Age Ideology. This was a collection of public attitudes and objectives, held mainly outside of the Central Provinces, which identified the main regional economic problem as transportation – a railway problem – and which rejected the assumption that the railways were just like any other business and should be free, within limits, to make their own business decisions. The paper ended on a note of optimism, suggesting that the passage of the National Transportation Act had issued the death certificate for the Railway Age Ideology, despite an attempt to revive it by Saskatchewan Premier Ross Thatcher in 1969. But there was also a note of caution lest there develop a Competitive Age Ideology that could be "as persistent or rigid as was the Railway Age Ideology."

Somewhat later, after having read the freight rates issue paper, one

1

of Mr. Darling's correspondents wrote approvingly, "I don't think anyone will ever surpass it for a succinct summary of the freight rate story in Canada and where we are now. Unfortunately, there seems to be indications that the RAI is trying to be reborn." Howard was still optimistic, replying, "I hope that there is to be no sequel, 'The son of RAI'!"

By the end of 1973, after being approached by the Canadian Institute of Guided Ground Transport to undertake further research on freight rates, Howard was of a different mind. He wrote that, "I would propose a full-length study of the history and consequences – economic, political and social – of public attitudes towards rail transport and particularly rail freight rates as they have developed and become crystalized over the past one hundred years. This is a matter of widespread interest, and even urgency, at the present time as governments become increasingly captive to the logical consequences of stereotyped attitudes." The result was this book, supported jointly by Canadian Pacific Limited, Canadian National, the Canadian Institute of Guided Ground Transport, and Transport Canada.

Work was interrupted in 1974 and 1975 when Mr. Darling held a Senior Transportation Development Agency Fellowship at York University to refine work he had done for the Canadian Transport Commission on subsidies. This research, *The Structure of Railroad Subsidies in Canada*, published by the York University Transport Centre, touched on many of the topics covered in this book. In fact, some of the research done for this book was used in *The Structure of Railroad Subsidies*. During this period, he also wrote a major study of the Canadian Merchant Marine.

By the end of 1976, work on *The Politics of Freight Rates* was well in hand, there being three hundred pages of typed manuscript. On the day of his untimely death in January of 1977, Mr. Darling had intended to come to Kingston to deliver the manuscript on events leading to the MacPherson Commission and discuss the completion of the final chapters of the book. Although the manuscript was incomplete, I made the decision to put the book in order for publication. Mr. Darling was an efficient writer. Having done his research and assembled his data, he would write out whole chapters or sections in longhand with very few interlineations or changes. A few quotations and reference material might be added later. He worked from a basic outline, but the flow of the book took its actual form as he wrote. Every so often Howard would bring chapters to Kingston for typing. This was rough typing at best, set up for convenience in editing, with blanks being left wherever the typist could not follow Howard's writing. Unfortunately, since he was always pressing forward on new chapters and on other research, he was unable to go back and edit much of the typescript.

Mr. Darling's writing style was unique, with long rambling sentences, and metaphors drawn from his wide reading. This complicated the editing, and, after a few false starts, the manuscript was restructured and unclear passages interpreted. As far as possible, however, it is Howard Darling's style, and the reader will have to progress carefully to understand the full significance of the subtleties. While the book is for the general reader, not just specialists in transportation economics, a background in Canadian history will help.

The Introduction and first eight chapters of this book are essentially as Howard wrote them, with a minimum of editing. Chapter Nine has been taken from his first handwritten draft and has required more extensive editing. Chapter Ten of the history of the freight rate issue is not entirely Howard Darling's. This was put together from his notes, clippings, and bits and pieces of existing manuscript, enhanced with other papers he had written on freight rates. The concluding chapter, "Freight Rates and the Constitutional Issue," while not written specifically for this book, makes the points Mr. Darling had intended to make as his conclusion, and was written by him.

A number of other chapters dealing with transportation economics and regulation are lost forever. While some of this material was originally intended to be appendices to *The Politics of Freight Rates*, it is more likely that, unknown to us, a companion book was also under way. The notes for this material have been catalogued and are preserved at CIGGT.

The bulk of the editing has been done by Charles Schwier of the Canadian Institute of Guided Ground Transport and myself, assisted by an editorial steering committee composed of George A. Scott, recently retired Senior Assistant Deputy Minister of Transport, W.G. Scott, General Manager, Pricing Economics, CP Rail, Colin J. Hudson, Senior Policy Advisor, Canadian National Railways, and J. Andrew Macdonald, until recently, Chief of Policy Development in Transport Canada's Strategic Planning Group.

It should be emphasized that the goal of the steering committee was to preserve Mr. Darling's wording, style, and viewpoint as far as possible. The opinions expressed are therefore essentially Howard Darling's and do not necessarily reflect the opinions of the sponsors, or the personal views of the individual committee members.

Professor Cecil E. Law
Executive Director
Canadian Institute of Guided Ground Transport

Introduction

A book on railway freight rates is bound to provoke widely different reactions in different parts of the country. In Montreal, in Toronto, and perhaps today also in Vancouver, it is likely to be regarded as a boring business that thankfully can be left to the economists – a dismal subject in a dismal science. But in the Prairie and Maritime Provinces, freight rates can be a matter of passion, an ever-timely issue and a most appropriate subject for parlour conversation, because all will regard it as important and all are informed on the basic outline of the argument, having absorbed it at an early age as thoroughly as any church catechism. Statements on the importance of railway freight rates for the country, or for particular regions or provinces, can be found in wholesale quantities in almost any period in our history since the advent of the railways. There is no point in compiling an anthology of them here. I shall simply select from the early beginnings of the issue and from contemporary sources.

The reason for writing about freight rates is self-evident. But this study is not concerned with freight rates as such, but rather, as its title indicates, with the railway freight rate issue in Canadian economics and politics. Why in the 1970's and 1980's are freight rates a more politically sensitive issue than they were in 1905? How is it possible that the same language of denunciation can be carried, essentially unmodified, over so long a period, in spite of the labours of successive Royal Commissions and the regulatory body in its three incarnations – the Board of Railway Commissoners 1904-1937, the Board of Transport Commissioners 1937-1967, and the Canadian Transport Commission 1967 to date? Has there been some obstinate resistance to a removal of grievances? Or have they persisted in spite of the best efforts of the authorities to cope with them? Or have the complaints hardened into a ritual stance, a regional litany, and become as much a part of Canadian life as Hockey Night in Canada?

Next, we must ask ourselves why an issue that is perceived to be of such great importance over such a long time has, as far as I have been able to ascertain, not only never been subjected to an examination in depth, but also has remained largely neglected. Since the publication of the report of the MacPherson Royal Commission on Transportation in 1961, there has been an almost continuous procession of important events in the field of transportation policy, to say nothing of the chain of events that led to the appointment of that Commission. Yet until the

4

mid-1970's, in the leading journals of economic discussion, there had been only one article referring to these matters: a short review, in 1961, on the Commission Report by John Meyer of Harvard University – some polite comments from an outsider. And until the policy review initiated in 1974, there was nothing that could be called a serious debate on the matter, either in Parliament or in the press. For the most part, the impassioned outcries of East and West have gone unexamined and unanswered. The Central Canadian press has for the most part been content either to let the issue go by default or to try to demonstrate a broad-minded attitude by arguing that "freight rate discrimination" should be removed. Even the recent furore over transportation policy, in which the old issues have been brought back to life, does not seem to have provoked much serious discussion on either side but rather a series of ritualistic poses as though there were some reluctance and distaste for coming to grips with the actual problem. The Minister of Transport is simply told to produce a new policy.

In part, the neglect of any serious study of the problem and, therefore, the persistence of stereotyped attitudes and responses may be due to the compartmentalization of the problems themselves. Economists, sociologists, and psychologists have tried to occupy exclusive domains, avoiding encroaching upon or being encroached upon by neighbouring disciplines. This process has been carried further by a subdivision within the major disciplines, so that everyone is left to his own specialty with a theory and field of action appropriate and distinctive to it. The consequences are seen in the selection of problems for research, with a preference for the simple technical or statistical, and in the inability to handle problems that refuse to be categorized after the manner of the disciplines themselves.

Thus in the railway freight rate issue, economists have felt qualified only to analyse freight rates and trace their effects on the parties concerned–carrier, shipper, producer, and consumer. They may have become discouraged by the barrenness of the results of such analyses. The more one strives for precision in analysis, the more the road leads to particular cases and circumstances. Factors insignificant to the overall problem crowd into the picture, complicate the analysis, and rule out the possibility of arriving at any conclusions of even the slightest generality. Yet it is broad, sweeping conclusions that are demanded by the freight rate patient. He is not too concerned with the minutiae of particular cases, his complaint is that "he hurts all over." At the same time, the sociologist or the social psychologist is likely to take the attitude that the problem is obviously a technical one, requiring a thorough knowledge of the subject of freight rates, and to hand it back to the economist.

The historian has more successfully resisted compartmentalization, since history would have no subject matter if it respected the boundaries laid down by the other social sciences. But the historian is likely to respect modern conventions and rely on special disciplines for technical facts and knowledge. If he were to go to the economist for this, however, he would receive little more than bundles of freight tariffs and an account of the freight rate structure and how it has changed over the years and who was for and who was against the change.

In short, we have so equipped ourselves academically that some basic problems of great importance and persistence continually escape the nets of the investigators even if they can be persuaded to dip their nets into these troubled waters. At best they are treated superficially and in a manner that yields few general conclusions of any significance or validity and which fails to yield an understanding of the problem since it cannot escape the narrow context in which it is considered.

There have been many histories of transportation and texts on the economics of transportation produced in Canada, but such attention as is given to the freight rate issue tends to consist largely of a recital of the decisions and recommendations of the regulatory authorities and the royal commissions and of a description of the principal legislation. The emphasis is invariably on the building of the transcontinental railways, the extension of the branch line networks, and the issues of nationalization and highway competition, all of which are treated in a very general way. Of course, these are useful and interesting in themselves, but they do not touch on the problems arising from the freight rate issue.

There are two opposite approaches that might be used in evaluating the railway freight rate issue in Canada. First, one can regard it as strictly a matter of transportation economics, which is the way most of those who are aroused by the issue would claim that it should be regarded. In other words, one can play it straight, taking the economic problem at its face value. Thus, it should be possible to establish a level of freight rates for specific commodities, by government subsidy if necessary, which would encourage regional development, particularly industrialization, thereby relieving the worst of regional disparities. For those who follow this view, the gist of the issue is that this has never been done. Furthermore, it is either stated or implied that in the constitution and the various terms of union, this is a direct federal obligation. Certain federal actions since Confederation, such as making the essential part of the Crow's Nest Pass agreement statutory and the passage of the Maritime Freight Rates Act, seem to bear this out. Such an economic approach is necessary in any case, but it cannot be content to treat freight rates in a purely theoretical fashion and isolate their effects from the great number of other factors with which regional disparities are associated in real life. This approach must be examined critically, since the manipulation of freight rates in the past seems to have produced singularly meagre results compared with what was expected. Here we have the basis for suspicion that more than a problem of freight rates is involved. The disparities between cause and effect, and between the evidence of detriment and the scale of treatment or remedy sought, should warn us that the issue is of much greater complexity than we are asked to believe.

At the other extreme one might regard the issue as purely a political one, kept alive by the politicians because it is a risk-free form of agitation since responsibility for action lies with the railway companies and the federal government. The enthusiastic response an appeal to the issue still arouses in some parts of the country is of great assistance in mobilizing provincial opinion against Ottawa whatever the real points at issue. The political aspects can no more be overlooked than the economic ones, but it would be evading any attempt to arrive at a serious understanding of the issue to dismiss these political agitations as rhetoric and be content to wait for the passage of time until they finally peter out. Even a cursory examination of freight rates as a cost of production would indicate that they *could* be a critical factor, but what has yet to be determined is to what extent they *are* critical.

Having bounded the extremes of approach, either of which would regard the other as being of zero value, we are driven to find answers in the vast middle ground where it is largely impossible to segregate the effects of different factors in the total picture. This approach allows us to concede that neither the economic nor the political explanations can be disregarded, although each by itself fails to supply an adequate explanation.

My general line of argument is that the issue originated in an economic situation in which railway prices and costs were an important part. The existing political philosophy derived from the experience of a small country – the United Kingdom – was difficult to adapt to the continental scale of the Canadian situation, or rather, there was no awareness of the degree of adaptation that might be required. The growth of the economy, the enlarged role of government in economic decisions, the cumulative adjustments to the freight rate structure, inflation, and the presence of competition have largely removed the substance from the long-standing complaints about freight rates. But this has not altered the relative disparities in development between the principal regions of the country, of which there has been a heightened consciousness, nor has there been sufficient progress in removing other regional grievances that stem from the limited role some regions play in making decisions at the national level.

The prolonged struggle to realize these economic and political objectives, which had so much to do with transportation, cut deeply certain patterns in the minds of people in the regions affected. It is at this point that the issue departs from its economic base and becomes an ideology obeying a logic all its own. The pattern unfortunately has hardened into a regional stance that can survive the weakening or the disappearance of the evidence on which it was originally based. This leaves us in the position of maintaining that there did exist a genuine freight rate problem having a diversity of origins. Today, regional discontents are neither ideology nor fiction, but they have little to do with freight rates. It is thus a result of the accidents of history that transportation economics and transportation economists should be looked upon as having the panaceas for these deeply-rooted ills. It is time that we rediagnosed the case, for the transportation doctor is at his wit's end.

PART I
History of the Freight Rate Issue: From Problem to Ideology

We are now embarking on a rather lengthy journey through the past of the freight rate issue, seeking to trace through the tangled course of events the gradual evolution of the issue into a regional ideology, based on the characteristics and problems typical of the railway age. The actual record of events has been set forth elsewhere.[1] However, as far as I have been able to discover, no study having objectives similar to this one has ever been undertaken. Our purpose is not simply to expose a record of misconception and error, but rather to try to obtain a clear understanding of events and attitudes which so far seem to lack any adequate explanation. In this I agree with Joseph Schumpeter when he says, "Ideologies are not simply lies; they are truthful statements about what a man thinks and sees."[2] The problem, therefore, is to establish what people thought they had seen, to compare this with "reality," and finally to suggest explanations for the course of events and for any apparent divergence of ideas from realities. In so doing, there is the hope that transportation policy in Canada can be freed of this incubus to the extent it may be found to consist of ideological elements.

The plan is to deal first with the early history of the freight rate issue in Western Canada, then turn to the same issue in the Maritime Provinces. While the freight rate issue in the Maritimes started prior to its development in the West, the West provided the example at a time when the issue remained dormant elsewhere. The Maritime Provinces have always relied heavily on constitutional arguments – what the British North America Act says or may be deemed to have intended to say – and to extract and protect every right that could be inferred from the origin and existence of the Intercolonial Railway. Since the Inter-colonial Railway did not come under the jurisdiction of the Board of Railway Commissioners until its absorption into the Canadian National Railways in 1923, the Board's early involvement with regional rate problems was restricted to the West. It was the West, therefore, that was first concerned with the Railway Act and the Board, and set the

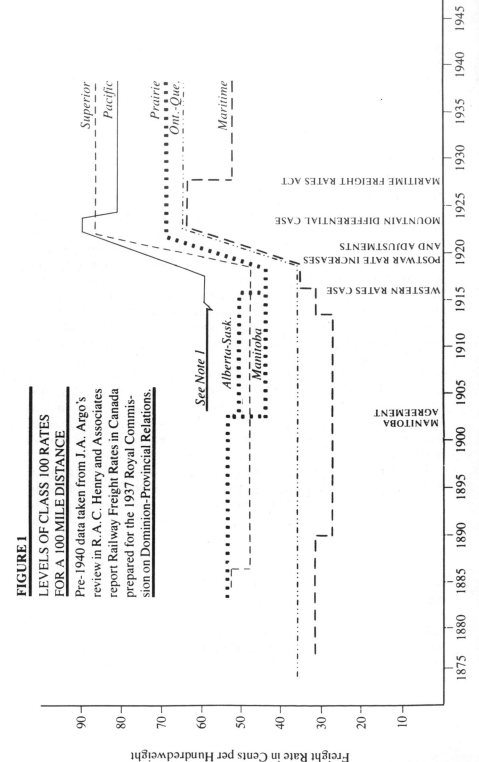

FIGURE 1

LEVELS OF CLASS 100 RATES
FOR A 100 MILE DISTANCE

Pre-1940 data taken from J.A. Argo's review in R. A. C. Henry and Associates report Railway Freight Rates in Canada prepared for the 1937 Royal Commission on Dominion-Provincial Relations.

Freight Rate in Cents per Hundredweight

NOTE 1 – Prior to September 1914, Pacific rates depended upon which 100 miles freight was moved over.

railways in hand-to-hand combat. It was the West that first developed the concept of equity in freight rates, discovering at the same time the peculiar political resonance that this issue possessed under the geography and conditions of Confederation.

Figure 1 plots the levels of Class 100 railway rates for a 100 mile distance as they developed from just after Confederation until the beginning of the Second World War. The figure shows the differences in the rates prevailing in the various parts of the country. These differences form much of the substance of the freight rate agitation described in the subsequent chapters.

CHAPTER 1

Prologue: The Political, Economic, and Social Significance of the Railway in Canada

The Railway Age came with startling suddenness, effecting a radical revolution in land transportation that had remained essentially the same from before the time of Julius Caesar until the time of Napoleon. Within a hundred years or so it had spent its force and had been superseded in many respects by highway and air transport. But its political, economic, and social effects were profound and they fundamentally conditioned the activities and ideas of all strata of the populations of the western and westernized industrial nations. The railway's advantage in speed, cost, and service over then existing modes was nothing short of miraculous, and hopes and ambitions of even the most isolated village rose sharply with the prospects of being located on a railway. The future possibilities, whether political, economic, or social, were unlimited. It is necessary to appreciate this, for faith in the power of the railway to work wonders did not easily disappear with the discovery of its first limitations. The failure to realize all the dreams inspired by the railway was long attributed – and to some extent still is – to the baneful effects of monopoly giving the railway the financial and economic power to extract the advantages of the mode at the expense of others who had no choice but to avail themselves of the railway's services.

There were, of course, good grounds for believing that the railway meant the difference between life and death for the numerous small settlements scattered throughout the back country in pre-Confederation Canada and the Maritime Provinces. In the Canadian West, unlike what happened in the American West, the railway preceded almost all settlement except in the Red River Valley and on the Pacific Coast. The towns, even those that are now great cities, were first of all railway stations, their location generally selected by the railway company. So universal was the connection between railway services and survival for all but the tiniest crossroads, that one is hard pressed to discover the rare exception. But there are at least two. Lanark in

Eastern Ontario, nine miles north of Perth, the nearest railway point, and Steinbach, in Manitoba, 33 miles southeast of Winnipeg, survived in isolation with their industries until the coming of the motor truck and highways restored the balance.

We are not primarily concerned with the general economic impact of the railway, however, because such information is available from many other sources and covers many facts that are either already well-known or can be easily surmised. Our concern here is with the situations existing in the Provinces of Canada, New Brunswick, and Nova Scotia on the eve of Confederation and then with the circumstances leading to the entry of British Columbia into Confederation and the building of the Canadian Pacific Railway across the Prairies. It is generally agreed that without the railway, the original Confederation could hardly have taken place at all, or would have been a much later and looser form of union.

While there were good water communications during the open season between the St. Lawrence Valley and the Maritime Provinces, this alone could hardly have been looked upon as the unifying factor the railway provided. Water communications, apart from linking the two areas, also provided the St. Lawrence with a direct connection overseas. In the winter when that connection was shut off, the connection with the Maritime Provinces was equally shut off. The Maritime ports of Halifax and Saint John thus would have had no chance of serving the trade of Ontario and Quebec without a railway, and in the summer any trade could have proceeded without the need of a political union. In other words, what economic link there was between the two areas was either based on the railway or on the hopes provided by the railway. Lacking any economic basis for union, the political reason of national defence included a railway connection, and the financial necessities for building a railway took precedence. The rest remained largely hopes, based upon the miraculous powers ascribed to the railway.

Economically, both in theory and practice, the railway's impact was revolutionary. Subsistence farming and production for local markets gave way to cash crops whose production was spread over the continent thanks to the new means of transport available. Industrial production was freed from its confinement to points contiguous to coastal and inland waterways and the growth of cities extended far beyond what would have been possible were they to be fed and supplied by the earlier, primitive means of transport. The railway network, built up within two or three decades, linked the remote areas to metropolitan centres. While it greatly extended the area of economic exploitation, it substantially increased the centripetal forces that were at work building up those metropolitan centres. There was connectedness where there had formerly been isolation, but there was also dependence, along lines roughly parallel to the main railway and water routes.

People were not prepared for this second effect. Attention was directed to the explosion of economic activity into isolated or uninhabited areas. The railway was seen as the great equalizer, offsetting the age-old advantages of ocean and inland ports, so that a city completely without water transport could expect to compete and even outdistance the older centres based on the pre-railway conditions. But the agglomerative effect, always present, now suddenly became strengthened. Some hard lessons were still to be learned about the economics of railway transport. The benefits of the railway were not necessarily shared equally by all users. By enlarging both markets and producing areas, the railway inherently became an instrument favouring the concentration of economic activity and control. That such a consolidation would likely have taken place to a certain degree in any case is entirely probable, but the railway undoubtedly hastened the process and widened the areas of influence of the growing units of industry and trade.

In Canada, at least, this process was accentuated by the fact that the cost of building railways made extreme demands on the federal treasury and had done so on the treasuries of the much weaker separate provinces. There quickly arose the familiar equation in Canadian public finance – investment in canals and railways had to be serviced by the then main source of revenue, the customs tariff. Tariff policy, epitomized by Sir John A. Macdonald's National Policy, of which Galt's policies in the Province of Canada had been a forerunner, thus became the means of paying for the enormous transportation plant that the new country had committed itself to, first in canals and then in railways. The customs tariffs on manufactured goods were a protection for the nascent industries in Ontario and Quebec and the railways enabled these industries to serve a national market. But for those living outside of these provinces, the combination of railway rates and tariffs was seen almost as a mechanism of enslavement, setting a pattern of regional attitudes that has not greatly changed to this day. The price of Canada's entrance into the Railway Age was thus an interrelated set of conditions that, in addition to the very substantial advantages over the pre-railway society, created alleged burdens on the unprotected and less developed parts of the national economy. The linking of the chains may be set forth as follows:

(1) Although water transport was able to retain the bulk of traffic accessible to it, the railway was vastly superior to most other means of

transport. In other words, the railway was an economic and national necessity.

(2) Railways required enormous investments of capital, much of which was lost due to failure of traffic to develop quickly and in large volume. Finances were first exhausted, and private capital was insufficient. Provincial and finally national governments had to intervene with capital grants, loans, and concessions of lands and resources.

(3) The railway, once in place, displayed monopoly characteristics. Competing lines were weakened by insufficient traffic, and competition conferred disproportionate advantages on competitive points and routes. As the railways became institutionalized within the economy, they ceased to compete with each other in rates and developed a common rate structure against attacks of shippers and consigners. This was solidified by the provisions of the earliest railway regulation, the United States Interstate Commerce Commission in 1887. The size of the initial railway investment made monopoly conditions inevitable, but in addition, the Canadian Pacific Railway had a monopoly clause in its Act. This was to have applied for a period of 25 years but was eliminated three years after the opening of its line.

(4) The scale of financial assistance extended by the federal government to the railways created a problem in public finance, for which the only available relief in the then existing tax system was the customs tariff.

(5) The customs tariff also encouraged "infant industries," which were located primarily in the most heavily populated Central Provinces. Domestic industries thus received protection in the entire Canadian market, first raising prices of manufactured goods and secondly requiring longer railway hauls and higher freight charges.

(6) The prevailing philosophy of government was one of laissez-faire, the government abstaining from any intervention in economic problems except in certain permitted directions. The railway and the problems it created were the first breach in the ramparts of the laissez-faire philosophy, requiring governments eventually, with much reluctance, to intervene more directly in the economic affairs of the nation. In the main, however, the government limited itself to certain tools in dealing with economic problems: financing the construction and operation of canals and railways, applying the customs tariff, and encouraging immigration.

(7) The rather lopsided sharing of the advantages of the new mode of transport was reinforced by the prevailing philosophy of government, which could not bring itself to make the necessary distinction between particular Canadian conditions and those of an advanced country like Great Britain, which remained the model for so long.

(8) The settlement of the West appears to have been regarded as in no way qualitatively different from the settlement of the old areas in Eastern Canada. Individualism was the ruling philosophy of settlers and government alike. Homesteaders went out to make their fortunes, which life in rural Eastern Canada no longer seemed to promise. The Prairies, however, were unsuitable for anything but the briefest period of subsistence farming that elsewhere only gradually broadened into serving a growing local market and finally reached into an export market. From the beginning, the Prairie farmer had to reach overseas markets or face ruin. Climate, topography, lack of forests, and distant sources of necessities of life and farming forced a concentration on a cash crop. The vital inbound movement of supplies and the outbound movement of grain could only take place on the railway.

(9) This direct dependence on foreign markets and domestic transportation and manufactured goods built an instability into the new Prairie agricultural economy which individual initiative and government laissez faire were quite unable to offset. The economic theories developed in other countries, and applied with some success in the more diversified economy of Central Canada, tied the hands of the individuals and governments in Western Canada, who faced novel problems.

(10) The inability to control the wide swings of the agricultural economic pendulum did not at first discredit laissez faire, but did inspire a search for culprits and scapegoats. Railways and tariffs became singled out as the main agents of Eastern aggrandizement at the expense of the producer and consumer in the West and the Maritimes.

(11) The vulnerability of the Prairie economy was demonstrated in the inflation and deflation following the First World War, when the issues became sharpened into a regional defensive position against neglect and misunderstanding. The Great Depression of the thirties provided the final impetus to the confrontation with Central Canada. The almost complete economic breakdown of the farming economy of the Prairies was handled with inadequate, makeshift measures that finally

discredited the laissez-faire stance of government. Belatedly, and emboldened by the circumstances of the Second World War, they began to develop a wider range of policies and tools, leading in the fifties and sixties to the recognition that in Canada there was a regional problem as such. From the point of view that we are looking at this problem, the significant thing is that patterns of thought have survived based on the conditions which originally produced them. A protest movement based on realities of the day has transformed itself into an ideology, unmindful of the changes in circumstances and thought that have since taken place.

(12) This gradual realization of the nature of the problem, however, has been paralleled by the growth of regional ideologies that reveal the time and circumstances of their origin by their concentration on transportation and, above all, on freight rates as the source of their discontents. The two have not been kept in contact but have each gone their own way, the one into an ideology that has based itself on outdated economics and a simplistic interpretation of Canadian economic history with neither interest nor regard for present facts; the other has gone into a maze of theories about the nature of and cure for regional disabilities, but it at least has tried to remain in contact with the facts.

It will be seen from this concatenation of causes and effects that conditions for the development of a concrete, factually based political protest movement were extremely favourable. Such a movement created positions that were anchored in regionally shared experiences, and were very quick to assume the form of a standardized regional outlook. The equating of the effects to the conscious scheming of the actual beneficiaries ensured its permanence as an ideology. The "conspiracy theory" explanation assumes a psychology on the part of the "conspirators" that is relatively constant in nature, only now consciously directed toward the maintenance of the advantages already gained. Thus, the beneficiaries are held capable of developing wholly new "tricks." But if they gained advantage through freight rates and tariffs, what is a more natural reaction than to seek to undercut those advantages at the source by lowering freight rates and tariffs? As a political ideology took over from the original protest movements, these objectives, particularly in freight rates, became ends in themselves.
There is another important set of factors, however, that provided spawning ground for ideology – the railway itself. The monopoly nature of railway operations, the nature of railway rates and costs, and the shadowy connection between them have left open a wide area of disagreement in which no one position can triumph over all others.

Despite endless argument, widely diverging positions continue to coexist, providing sustenance and shelter for a variety of possible ideologies. As we shall see later, these ideas prior to the initial launching period are in close touch with the facts, but quickly on becoming airborne they rely on some seemingly simple and self-evident theoretical propositions. Subsequent facts, if they cannot be fitted into the desired picture, are discarded.

In addition to its revolutionary effects on transportation and on life generally, the railway had a lasting, disturbing effect on economic theory. It was the first general application of the limited liability company and was the first major participation of government in business enterprises. It also soon became apparent that the railway was a natural monopoly. The railways in the beginning competed in rates between competitive points, but gradually abandoned this as unremunerative to all parties and combined to create "rate restrictions."

Economic theory in the minds of the classical economists had been based, however, on the assumptions of the perfect market through which the best possible results were held to have been obtained. The railway not only operated as a monopoly, but also had a product that was hard to classify. Oddly enough, while the practical problems of a railway rate structure were settled very quickly, the theoretically justifiable rate structure has remained a bone of contention. The most celebrated confrontation on this subject was that between Frank Taussig of Harvard University and A.G. Pigou of Cambridge. Despite the high level of acumen and the intensity of the investigation, the discussions did not result in a satisfactory decision. The problem was to give a satisfactory explanation of the discrimination in railway rates, that is, the different levels of rates that applied in different commodities carried similar distances, that could not be traced to differences in costs. Taussig claimed that the rates were the result of the jointness of costs between different services, but this seemed a less satisfactory explanation than the one offered by Pigou to the effect that all railway output was essentially similar and measurable in simple units such as ton-miles. From this Pigou went on to conclude that any discrimination was the result of monopoly. Neither developed a satisfactory theory of pricing because Pigou denied and Taussig failed to explore the differences in costs and demand conditions affecting the various traffic components.

Nevertheless, the value-of-service basis for rate-making was adopted, which is to charge what the traffic will bear on the basis of the demand for and the value of the commodities being transported. Notwithstanding the near universality of this method of pricing in all areas of business where direct price competition recedes in importance, it has not been wholeheartedly accepted by economists since it greatly complicates theoretical analysis. To the layman, the thought of "monopolists" involved in "charging what the traffic will bear" is quite intolerable. Fired up with these pejorative expressions, the public has developed a lasting distrust of this method of rate-making. It will be said that the railways are still monopolists with respect to large parts of their traffic, and that, in spite of more than seventy years of regulation in Canada, the railways are still practising discrimination. Today this has come to mean that the railways are adhering to arbitrary methods of establishing rates instead of making rates "based on cost." This latter point has been taken up as a slogan to express the objectives of those provinces who have been protesting about freight rates in general over many decades.

The earliest railway rate structures show a classification of commodities by level of rates. Bulky, low-priced raw materials such as coal bore lower rates than manufactured goods. Obviously, traffic managers readily understood that a uniform tariff on all commodities would either have to be so high as to dry up heavy volume traffic, or so low as to sacrifice needlessly a large amount of revenue that could be painlessly extracted from the higher-valued goods. The freight classification represented an attempt to maximize revenues and any precise relationship between costs and rates had to be disregarded.

From the very first, railways were subject to such controls as existed under common law. The common carrier obligations were significant in that the railways lost some control over what traffic they could accept and where they could accept it. A single carload hauled off a branch line through snowdrifts would have to be carried at the same rate as a car among hundreds of others carried in good weather between mainline points. While not strictly part of the common carrier obligation, the railway also was under pressure to own sufficient variety and quantity of equipment to handle peak traffic, even though this might mean idleness for the same equipment for most of the year. Nevertheless, the significant fact about the common carrier status was that it made it impossible to offer a "cost-oriented rate structure." With no assurance of forthcoming traffic volumes or the times and places of its appearance, the railway companies had to publish a schedule of rates in advance.

The rate structure in its simplest and most theoretical form is a list of all commodities in a classification distributed among different classes or levels of rates. When it is realized that class rate structures built up and put in effect on an *a priori* basis were intended to provide an underlying structure for the widest possible occasional movement of commodities, it will be recognized that the fit between the structure and reality will be a very crude one. It is possible with the class rate structure to find a rate for any commodity between any two points served by the railway. It will be obvious that the resulting rate may appear to be outrageously high for the normal movements of traffic, but still not unjustified for a single movement unlikely ever to be repeated. It will be equally evident that the class rates could never be expected to be used but for a small portion of the total traffic handled by the railways.

From theoretical precision, the *actual* rate structure represents successive erosions and assumes a most intricate shape. As the railways endeavoured to arrive at the rates that would encourage the movement of traffic, modifications occurred in the original structure. Lower levels of class rates were made applicable from cities and towns which generated a volume of secondary traffic. Movements of agricultural and industrial products were of such a volume and of such a low value that special scales were provided at lower rates.

The primary cause of the destruction of much of the symmetrical perfection of the theoretical rate structure was competition. Competition from water carriers, parallel to the railway lines, and market competition created great irregularities in rates. Most pervasive of all was truck competition. With the severity of competition from highway carriers, the railways were faced with the problem of knowing the costs of competitive traffic in order to know how far they could afford to reduce rates to meet competition. If competitive rates did not represent actual costs, they tended to be more and more cost-sensitive and to that extent depart from the basic principle on which the rate structure had been founded – the value of service. While being driven toward rate-making on a basis of costs in meeting competition, the cost principle alone would clearly be inadequate to yield sufficient revenues, since the railway rate structure is still subject to rigidities imposed both by law and custom that compel it to overlook what are often substantial differences in costs.

These common carrier obligations are more than merely a minimal legal requirement; they become more and more an instance of the application of a principle of fair and reasonable treatment which has come to apply to the railways as a consequence of their historical monopoly position. From this flows the requirement that rates must be published so that, unlike other industries, all can see what they and others will be charged, which leads in turn to a comparison of treatment of different shippers. This means that any concession made to one shipper, even where there may be competitive factors to justify it, will tend to be required by other shippers. Competitive rates themselves, instead of being related to local conditions and changes in them,

22

become standardized so that large areas may affect only a small area.

The ability to compare has meant increased sensitivity to freight rates not only on the part of the railways' customers, but also from outside observers such as governments, producers' associations, regional and local trade promotion bodies, and even the general public. The result is that railway rates cannot be adjusted in detail to costs even in competitive conditions. Rather, the rates become rigid. The demands for similar, identical, or even preferential treatment all restrict the carriers' ability to adjust rates according to their best judgement, and at the same time remove whatever justification there might be for rates made on a basis of cost.

The generalization of rates, whether it be done to give the railways themselves some logical foothold to withstand pressures for even greater reductions, or in the interests of less favoured regions, has forced a generalization of costs. Overhead cannot be applied uniformly to all rates, but it must be covered in total. Here again, the issue is beclouded by a tendentious term – cross-subsidization – which suggests that this generalization of costs involves some traffic paying for other traffic, or, more provocatively, subsidizing other traffic. This is defined as a bad thing and is accentuated by the fact that value-of-service rates survive mainly where competition has been insignificant. Therefore, it is possible to complain that these rates have not been made on the basis of costs and that other rates have, and in general are lower. From this chain of reasoning, we can see how the conclusion has been reached by some that a "cost-oriented rate structure" would remove discrimination.

Instead of meaning widespread rate competition, intermodal competition has had the effect over the years of sorting out the traffic, leaving each mode with that traffic which it has been proven more efficient to carry. Out of these developments, the value-of-service basis for freight rates has come off badly. From being the normal method of rate-making, it has declined in public favour until today it is regarded as the last stronghold of rate discrimination practised by the railway monopoly. To a great extent it has been rendered obsolete by the almost complete coverage of highway transport. At the other end of the scale, the movement of large volumes by railway has become more in the nature of a contract, often negotiated after extensive bargaining between carrier and shipper.

The outstanding features of the railway rate structure, such as the value-of-service principle where it still applies, the equalization or generalization of rate levels by commodities, areas, and particular areas and particular movements, and the common carrier obligations all conspire to draw a veil between railway costs and rates. Since the carriage of traffic involves a high degree of joint costs and requires some method of recovering overhead costs, it becomes a problem of allocation of both costs and revenues for which no single answer can be found. Any method of costing reveals merely the results of pursuing a given method of allocation and can hardly be taken as an unqualified judgement on how rates should be made. The result of this inability to decisively eliminate alternative methods means that arguments can continue indefinitely without any decision compelling assent.

In the past, cost studies have merely provoked further argument, and their inconclusive results, instead of reconciling people to living with uncertainties, have led to charges that not all the facts have been disclosed and that uncertainties will remain as long as shippers, or provincial governments speaking in their name, are prevented from full access to railway cost data. This is completely at variance with the pricing methods followed in industry generally. It indicates a type of cost-plus approach to railway rate-making, but with the "plus" minimized or left off on many occasions. What is a general practice in all business of charging what the traffic will bear, limited by the usual considerations of discretion and expediency based on an expected long-term presence in the market and a certain degree of public goodwill, has become in railway economics a never-failing source of public indignation – or at least attempts to portray itself as such. This in spite of continued regulation of the railways, equalization of class rates, and the full publicity that has been given to changes in rates.

Such a grey area between railway costs and rates provided as secure a base for an ideology as any Maquis for a guerrilla band. There seems to be no way of resolving it by logical argument because the means of settling the argument boils down to a question of how costs should be allocated to movements of traffic and how this should be rejected in rates. So long as there is no answer available, any system of ideas can continue unchecked and feel itself justified. In such a context it is not surprising that the introduction of public regulation, if anything, has served in the long run to keep the ideological fires burning rather than bringing relief. The existence and purpose of the Board of Railway Commissioners (and its successors) have led to the assumption that there is an answer to the question of what is a just rate.

We have thus far exposed some of the roots of the ideology that has grown up around the freight issue. It builds up into a very complex picture, strikingly different from the greatly over-simplified assumptions and conclusions of the ideology itself. But the ideology is not to be overcome by attempts to refute directly its simple propositions. Since it is an ideology, it has long immunized itself against such attacks, and is more likely to emerge strengthened. Only a painstaking analysis of the genesis and development of the ideology as an ideology, and a disentangling of the complaints and grievances from their increasingly irrelevant connection with the ideology, can restore a clear understanding of what is behind the exaggerated ideological posturing.

CHAPTER 2

The West to 1914

The Canadian Pacific Railway was built as one of the conditions of the union of British Columbia with the Dominion of Canada. The company was given a cash grant of $25 million and 25 million acres of land, most of it in the present Prairie Provinces, as well as municipal tax exemptions and a monopoly right in the area between its main line and the United States border. The fledgling Province of Manitoba was not a party to this agreement and Alberta and Saskatchewan had not yet been carved out of the largely uninhabited Northwest Territories. As a consequence, the population that poured into the Prairies during the first period of settlement from 1885 to 1914 found that the terms for the provision of their "lifeline"–a railway almost as important to them as the Nile is to Egypt–had already been settled between the central government and the railway company. Thus, early in its history, through the accidents of circumstance, the Prairie population did not have a share in the decision-making on a matter of the greatest importance to it. Early in the game they discovered that in order to change the picture into one that was more in line with their problems and aspirations, they had to buck the inertia of the majority in Central Canada, a majority well-entrenched behind the seemingly eternal virtues of laissez-faire economics.

Looking back now it is possible to recognize that the root of the deep-seated discontent in the Prairie Provinces is the combined maladaptation of the economic and political thought structures of the day to the realities of the new situation. The imposition of these systems of thought, unique to laissez-faire economic theory and British parliamentary traditions which had evolved over a long period in the compact economy of Great Britain, obscured or dismissed the new but very real problems of the Prairie economy, one which started from scratch on the empty landscape. Neither of these structures presented impenetrable barriers to the solution of the Prairie problems, but their response was often slow and reluctant. They offered themselves not as pragmatic solutions but more often as universal principles with little scope for dissent or modification. The resulting time-lag in the response served only to aggravate the problem requiring attention, which all too often had to assume the proportions of a catastrophe before sufficient support could be generated for what were regarded as "unorthodox" solutions.

This atmosphere of acute frustration must be credited for the development of some of the familiar characteristics of the Western social-psychological profile. Not the least of these characteristics was a strong sense of regional solidarity, paralleled by feelings of resentment and distrust toward the economic and political establishment in Central Canada. To round out this *Weltanschauung*, we are not surprised to see that conspiracy theories continually cropped up to offer their own explanatory versions, often being credible in inverse proportion to the amount of actual evidence available.

The economic relations of the Prairie homesteader were vastly different from those of the earlier settlers on the Eastern half of the continent. Whereas the latter went through a short period of establishment followed by a longer period at the subsistence level, only gradually reaching a stage of maturity with cash crops, the Western settler passed directly from establishment to producing a cash crop for the overseas market. The period of subsistence farming on the Prairies was quickly passed over if it occurred at all. The harsh climate and short season limited the farmer's ability to supply himself. He literally needed everything–food, fuel, clothing, tools, machinery, and all the consumer goods that comprised the minimum standard of living in his country of origin. There was a very small local market for produce, and the domestic market could not begin to absorb the growing volume of grain being produced. His necessities and supplies had only one means of getting to him – the railway – and his crop could only be marketed by rail. In all his economic transactions of any consequence the farmer found himself dealing with parties possessing superior bargaining power: grain elevator companies, banks, manufacturers, wholesalers, merchants, and of course the railway. In nearly all these cases the market was the final arbitrator. The idea of any regulatory intervention by the government was slow in gaining adherents. In fact, the farmer himself, at least in prosperous times, was one of the strongest advocates for freedom of the market.

This non-interventionist philosophy was not equipped to deal with extreme fluctuations in crops, weather, and market conditions that the farmer, at the end of the line, was exposed to and left largely defenceless against. Peaks of prosperity and speculation and troughs of depression and insolvency succeeded one another. Such experiences fostered a spirit of independence in good years and one of gloom and resentment in bad years. Throughout these fluctuations it seemed that the farmer's prices took the widest swings, while the costs of the goods and services he required went through much smaller changes or remained fixed. The laissez-faire economic philosophy preached to him on the one hand did not prevent the imposition of the national tariff policy on the other. It is not surprising, then, that the Western farmer, left to his own resources, should have developed a spirit of solidarity with his fellows in cooperative movements, and at a later stage, in political movements.

The small proportion that the population of the Western Provinces was to the national total also meant that a political avenue for solutions to Western problems was beset with obstacles, not the least of which was a two-party system where a solid base in Central Canada inevitably was necessary. The range of solutions in tariff, fiscal, and social policy tended to be narrowly confined to what could find acceptance with the majority of voters in Central Canada. Going beyond the maxims of the traditional laissez-faire economy was regarded as a lapse into favouritism or sectionalism. Circumstances made the Western voter more receptive to breaking new ground, with Western provincial legislatures pioneering many social and economic measures designed to rectify imperfections in the market economy.

The Liberal Party, with its professed devotion to free trade, at first seemed the natural home for the Prairie voter in national politics. Disillusionment first came during the economic upheavals triggered by the First World War, with the Western economy taking the full force of the unprecedented swings of the economic pendulum. When it came to the crunch, the Liberals cautiously avoided stepping outside the ring of the national consensus. At the very beginning we thus find the seeds of an inevitable regional confrontation – differences in the economies, control of the whole vested in one area, dependency of the West on one crop subject to wide variations in yield and market price, and, arising from these, a difference in basic attitudes accompanied by a certain amount of mutual miscomprehension.

As is often the case in a well-constructed play, where the very first lines may set forth the main theme of the plot, so in the drama of freight rates we are given our clues in the earliest years of the freight rate structure in Western Canada. Witness this report, written in the 1940's, about the railway system in the 1880's.

For a period of two years – 1881 to 1883 – the freight rates in Western Canada remained approximately the same as the winter rates of the Grand Trunk Railway in Eastern Canada except for the special rates referred to. It did not appear, however, that the Canadian Pacific which was then being extended across the prairies, could pay its way on the basis of the eastern rates, considering the sparse traffic and higher operating expenses in Western Canada, and on the recommendation of the Chief Engineer of the Government Railways to the Minister of Railways and Canals, a revised schedule for the Canadian Pacific's western lines was put into effect in the year 1883, on a basis approximately 50% higher than the Grand Trunk's eastern winter rates, except for some lower rates on coal and cordwood.[1]

This is interesting in that it shows that *at the very first* some principle of equity was employed in establishing the Western rate structure. After all, where else could one start but on a government-sponsored project? The period of "equalization," however, was brief, lasting only until the first financial results of the Canadian Pacific were available. Then it became obvious that if it were to be successfully operated as a private company – and no alternative seems to have been contemplated at that stage – the rates would have to be higher than those in Eastern Canada. The significance for future developments is that, from the beginning, a standard of comparison was at hand: an Archimedean point to provide the leverage through which the grievances and frustrations of the West could hope to move to the national sphere. The materials for the future were already assembled: a principle of equity; a departure from equity having an objective base of comparison (Eastern versus Western rates); and a candidate for a major contributing cause having suitably high negative connotations (the presence of monopoly). The story since has been largely one of continuing variations on these original themes, a contrapuntal composition yielding both seducing harmonies and discordant passages, depending perhaps upon the prior training or acculturation of the listener. So familiar have the themes become that even economists have been caught humming them absent-mindedly, as witness the following example: ". . . nevertheless freight rates were higher than the traffic could bear and undoubtedly tended to retard development."[2] It is tempting to regard such statements as examples of how readily freight rates may be singled out as the definitive cause of economic events and trends for which no objective evidence could be offered.

To establish the objective truth of a statement that "rates were higher than the traffic could bear" would require the identification of the volumes of traffic that did *not* move. With a subjective interpretation of the same statement there is less argument. Rates may indeed have been higher than people wanted to pay or thought they should be required to pay, but there is no way of definitely determining what would have been a reasonable rate in itself, apart from that suggested by available comparisons. One suspects that the basis for such statements is the knowledge that Western rates were higher than Eastern rates. Here is a theoretical cause looking about for, and available to be assigned to, a practical effect. The development of the West was subject to innumerable difficulties and setbacks proceeding from a variety of causes, many of which probably have long since been eroded by time and have thus escaped from everyday memory. On the other hand, the freight rate factor has resisted this weathering of time, becoming in the process increasingly isolated and conspicuous, much like a mesa left standing on a plain. The historical perspective has thus suffered some distortion.

The original rate structure gave ample grounds for making comparisons between rate levels and for trying to discover the logic behind these decisions. Not only were the Manitoba rate levels higher than those in Eastern Canada, but those of the Northwest Territories were higher still, and highest of all were those of British Columbia (the Mountain Differential). Compounding this were the unquestioned examples of service abuse due to monopoly. From the beginning the agitation for lower freight rates had these levers to work with. Concrete objectives did exist. The arguments were reinforced when the Canadian Pacific expanded into Eastern Canada to become a truly national railway, but one which charged different rates within each region even though revenues and expenses were pooled. The old argument that the railway had to derive its living from Western traffic was now turned against it with charges that the West was cross-subsidizing operations in other parts of the country. One can already discern the shape of the freight rate arguments to come.

The first rate structure in Western Canada was of extremely simple design, and like a ready-made suit of clothes picked at random off the rack, it provided a very crude fit. Alterations and adjustments were inevitable, and the story of Western freight rates is one of continuous bickering over tailoring, between the demands of the customer for a satisfactory piece of work and the demands of the tailor for an adequate price for his services. At the outset it will be useful to separate the two distinct types of rate grievances whose intermingling has greatly confused and complicated the freight rate issue. On the one hand, we have those pertaining to "unjust discrimination" in which the complainant was able to demonstrate "actual detriment" to the satisfaction of the Board of Railway Commissioners. The criteria here were practical and objective, with a minimum of hypothetical traffic and traffic conditions to be taken into account. This, to return to our metaphor, may be likened to the *fit* of the suit, which is determined by

30

actual measurements on which a degree of agreement can be reached. On the other hand, there are grievances based on the subjective principle of equity, whose application is not related to actual traffic and rate comparisons. That is to say, they attain the status of grievances only to the extent that some people *feel* they are unjust without being able to demonstrate any actual detriment to themselves or to anyone else. This type of grievance would be comparable to the *style* of the suit which is independent of the actual fit. It was the Western shipper's plea to have a suit like the one the fellow in Central Canada was wearing.

The later complaints about horizontal percentage increases fall somewhere in between. They generally were put forward in a purely theoretical manner but can be related by way of example to comparisons of actual traffic movements. They were the case where a new style actually involves a different fit. It is part of our story that as the judicial procedures of the Board of Railway Commissioners readily formed means for dealing with problems of fit (unjust discrimination) the rest of the problems became overwhelmingly composed of problems of style (appeals to some principle of equity). It is this class of problem that the regulatory body was least equipped to handle, particularly as the complaints took on more and more of an ideological colouring. Consequently, the regional opinion as to the Board's performance worsened and it was commonly regarded as having been an apologist for the railways and hopelessly bound by its own precedents.

In retrospect, the Crow's Nest Pass Agreement of 1897 may seem to have marked the first chapter of the story of the freight rate issue in Canada. This is not the way it appeared at the time, however. There is no need to give the details here, for they have already been repeated almost as many times as Dicken's *Christmas Carol*.[3] The agreement does mark the first major intervention by the federal government in the rate structure. Considering the "sacred" character some ascribed to it later, the agreement had a comparatively humble birth and it was not an occasion for unqualified rejoicing. It was complained that the rate concessions were small in comparison with the benefits granted to Canadian Pacific. Frank Oliver, member for the federal riding of Alberta, himself a doughty freight rate fighter whose career culminated many years later as a member of the Board of Railway Commissioners, was critical during the debate on the bill.

> The country gives $3,500,000 and gets the use of 330 miles of railway practically on the company's terms. The company gives slight reductions in certain freight rates–greater than which would have been secured from less money in other ways–and gets a further and more complete assurance of monopoly throughout the great Canadian

West. . . . The electors of Alberta sent me here to oppose railway monopoly.[4]

The failure to establish any termination date for the agreement would surprise anyone experiencing today's conditions, under which any such agreement would not only have had a termination date but also an escalation clause. In this, of course, it reflects the financial orthodoxy and confidence of the day, in which the gold standard was regarded as the permanent stabilizing factor, which, if it could not prevent swings of prices over the business cycle, would ensure that they at least revolved about a relatively constant point.

The early leader in the battle against railway rates and monopoly was the Manitoba government, whose presence had led to Canadian Pacific's surrendering of its legal monopoly in 1888. It continued to encourage the appearance of competition by whatever means available. The emergence of the Canadian Northern finally made this competition a reality. By amalgamating independently constructed lines with others leased from the province and with the aid of a provincial guarantee of bonds for the construction of the line connecting Winnipeg with the Lakehead, a second railway system was made available to the Western farmers. But it was limited in effectiveness because of the smallness of its original network.

The Manitoba Agreement of 1901 provided for a reduction in grain rates below that provided under the Crow's Nest Agreement and a 15 per cent reduction on westbound commodities. This reduction was achieved by the adoption of a "constructive mileage" of 290 miles between the Lakehead and Winnipeg in contrast with the actual distance of 410 miles. The class and commodity rates for the reduced mileage constituted a built-in advantage for Winnipeg over the more westerly Prairie distribution points because of the effect of the larger increments applied beyond 290 miles than those beyond 410 miles (resulting from the tapered structure of the rates). This provided fuel for intra-prairie rate-feuding. Winnipeg defended its advantage, and Calgary and Edmonton contested it, each with gradually decreasing vigour until the equalized class rate scale became effective in 1955.

In the meantime, federal thinking on rate policy had been evolving, prodded by the rising chorus of complaints of quality of service in monopoly areas and of discriminations and preferences in competitive areas. Professor S.L. McLean was authorized to make two inquiries between 1899 and 1902,[5] which provided the basis for the establishment of the Board of Railway Commissioners by an amendment to the Railway Act in 1903. McLean later served on the Board as Assistant Chief Commissioner for many years. His knowledge and experience contributed greatly to the development of the Board's jurisprudence.[6]

With the formation of the Board, we enter into a new period in freight rate history in Canada. There was now a permanent body to address rate complaints rather than the ad hoc sittings of the Railway Committee of the Privy Council. The Board had responsibilities regarding the rate structure that were contained in the statutes. We shall be looking in much greater detail at the implications of the Board's existence and activities at a later stage, but some of the immediate consequences must be pointed out. It was obvious that a regulatory body operating still within the economic philosophy of laissez-faire would be given and would assume very modest powers to intervene in the business of operating a railway. It would also protect itself against being flooded with irresponsible complaints by establishing criteria that could be applied to any action laid under any of the rate regulations. The word "shipper" seemed clearly to define the actual shipper of the goods, but certain organizations representative of shippers had to be admitted–boards of trade, shipper organizations, and so on–until ultimately provinces and groups of provinces became recognized as parties. Complaints about rates from any source had to establish "actual detriment," so that theoretical complaints or broader considerations of equity were generally dismissed. The existing situation was defended with whatever reasons seemed appropriate.

At the same time that the Board was being set up, the leadership of the fight for lower freight rates in Western Canada developed in the boards of trade of the main cities, which quickly evolved a body of expertise in all the contours in the rate structure. They represented the interests of the distributors in all sizeable Western towns, but in the early years concentrated in Winnipeg, from which they endeavoured to serve the entire West, hoping to create a Canadian Chicago. This meant an interest in "actual" or "concrete" rate problems that directly affected the competitive positions of the new Western cities, each eagerly seeking to carve out for itself a large distributing territory. During this period freight rates were mainly the concern of the distributing interests, while service shortcomings and the extension of branch lines were the farmers' main concern.

Apart from the problems of individual shippers in particular cases, there were some conspicuous targets to shoot at. As already noted, Manitoba rates were higher than comparable rates in Eastern Canada. Rates for Alberta and Saskatchewan were still higher and British Columbia's were the highest of all. Thus there was no unity among the Western cities. Winnipeg emerged as the point with the most to defend in the existing rate structure, while Alberta cities complained about the constriction of their territories due to the more favourable rates possessed by their longer-established and more powerful Winnipeg competitors. Calgary and Edmonton looked askance at any attempt by British Columbia to have the Mountain Differential reduced or abolished, fearing the improved competitive position this might give Vancouver. It was an era when theory and practice in rate-making fairly closely coincided. The railways were the only means of transport, and pricing was largely f.o.b. plant, so that rate differences tended to measure real differences. Many years away were the conflicts between theory and practice brought on by the differing service capabilities of highway carriers, the extension by Eastern manufacturing companies of their own means of distribution and pricing, and the growth of local centres of manufacture and supply. Because of the ease of their assembly and the illusion of preciseness they gave, however, the theoretical rate arguments developed during this period persisted long after the actual marketing and transportation conditions had changed. Rather than going out and badgering a busy and reluctant businessman for the facts, it was simpler to sit down with a railway tariff, which served as a do-it-yourself kit for discovering shipper disabilities. With the obligatory filing of railway tariffs, which made them available to everyone, the practice of looking at rate problems in a theoretical manner developed – rate mathematics as it were – in isolation from all other factors. We will suggest reasons for this later.

The early rate cases heard by the Board of Railway Commissioners had important effects on the rate structure, reducing rates in both Eastern and Western Canada. In 1905 a general reduction of rates was ordered on all export traffic from points in Eastern Canada to the Atlantic seaboard to a basis comparable with rates of American railways operating from southern Ontario to the coast.[7] Two years later a reduction in Eastern town tariff rates, averaging about 10 per cent, had the effect of reducing winter rates between points in that territory to almost as low as, and in some cases lower than, the summer rates.[8] Thus, early in the game, American railway competition was displacing water competition as the main factor in forcing lower rates in Eastern Canada, and the differences in levels between East and West were actually increased in the early years of the Board's operation.

By the beginning of the First World War, the main outlines of the plot and the characters of the principal actors in the freight rate issue in Western Canada were becoming established. The Prairie farmers, the distributors, the boards of trade who were their spokesmen, and the provincial governments had taken up positions fighting monopoly and discrimination. The peculiar nature of railway operations combined the disadvantages of monopoly in non-competitive areas with the giving of unconscionable preferences in competitive areas. The railway, always on the defensive, had no practical alternative but to fight a continuous action to preserve the status quo by making a minimum of concessions voluntarily and requiring all others to be ordered by the Board. In between, attempting to moderate the conflict, the Board was quickly developing its jurisprudence in a particular direction, treating the freight rate as a contract that might be subject to some modification to offset the unequal bargaining power of a single shipper with a railway monopoly. As a quasi-judicial body, the Board naturally assumed its function to be clarifying and interpreting the Railway Act, working toward the objective of complete clarification that would make further appeal unnecessary except as the statute might be amended. In this respect, the Board's jurisprudence on "unjust discrimination" was worked out in almost final form within the first decade of its existence. Cases of alleged unjust discrimination continued to be brought before it, but unless they possessed some new factual element of relevance they tended to be referred to the well-established precedents. Above all those parties there also existed a possible *deus ex machina* to resolve the unresolvable, the federal government, which was intent on shielding itself from the heat of the problem by hiding behind the Board.

The existence of regional rate differences, for which the only effective remedy under the Railway Act and the precedents of the Board was the proving of the existence of unjust discrimination, resulted in the building up of much frustration in the West. The West on one hand and the Board and railways on the other were talking past one another. The West was upset by the *existence* of different rate levels, but was told that it first must establish "actual detriment" in a specific case. Obviously such a condition made it practically impossible to establish the required case for equity. A great number of reasons, specious or otherwise, were always at hand to justify the status quo: alleged differences in costs, the carriers' needs for revenue, differing densities of traffic, and so on. To the West, none of these appeared to have any relevance. With some justification, the West regarded the general rate structure as having been constructed largely arbitrarily in the first place.

The Regina Tolls Case

The Board's early action in reducing rates in the East was partially offset by the successful outcome of the Regina Board of Trade's application for relief from the regressive effects of the Manitoba Agreement. This had applied within Manitoba only and was of benefit to Winnipeg distributors against those of Eastern Canada and Saskatchewan and Alberta. It produced higher rates per ton-mile to

Regina than to Winnipeg in spite of the much greater distance from the Lakehead. This ran counter to the generally accepted structure of freight rates in which it was usual to taper the rate, producing successively lower rates per ton-mile as distance increased. In what came to be known as the Regina Tolls Case, the Board found no difficulty in ruling this to be a case of undue discrimination.[9] An appeal against the judgement by Canadian Pacific was rejected by the Supreme Court in the following year, but in its answer to the question regarding the finding of unjust discrimination, the court set a course for the Board which did much to prolong and exacerbate the West's struggle for equity in freight rates. The court said:

> The facts therein set out are circumstances and conditions within the meaning of the "Railway Act" to be considered in determining the question of unjust discrimination with respect to both railways; such facts and circumstances are not in law conclusive of the question of unjust discrimination, but the effect, if any, to be given to them is a question of fact to be considered and decided by the Board in its discretion.[10]

The ruling that "facts and circumstances are not in law conclusive" dealt a body blow to the cause for equity. The essence of the case was that rates for the same commodities and distances were published at different levels in railway tariffs and merely to point this out should be sufficient proof to obtain relief. No logical connection was now held to exist between the mere existence of these differences and a finding of unjust discrimination. In effect, the whole rate controversy from the first issuance of the tariffs to the incorporation of "equalization" into the Railway Act in the 1950's (as a result of the Turgeon Royal Commission) was one long wrangle between the general and the particular. Equity could only come at the discretion of the Board and the nature of its gradual progress toward equity seemed like that of a succession of mysterious acts of grace. The arguments from the particular case could always be made adequate to reject the general conclusion, and in moving toward equalization the Board seemed conveniently to forget its argument from the particular in bowing to public pressure.

The consequence of this type of procedure was obvious. The Board was accused by the West of indifference to the problems and of subservience to its own precedents and to the railways. Its credibility was weakened. At the same time the only effective tactics for the West seemed to be constant pressure, solidarity, and continual efforts to appeal over the head of the Board to royal commissions and the government.

It is not surprising that the concentration and persistence of such assumptions and attitudes over the years should jell, first into a definite folklore and finally into an autonomous ideology. By the time the original goal of equalization was reached it was already perceived by many Westerners close to the issue to have become largely irrelevant. But by that time an underlying belief had been firmly established and was at hand for politicians to exploit at will. Thus, even after the substance had dissolved away, the ritual of driving out freight rate discrimination continued to be observed, much in the same manner as the customs of Hallowe'en have survived the lost beliefs in spirits and demons.

The Western Rates Case

In retrospect, the events leading up to the hearings and conclusions of the Western Rates Case emerge as embodying the quintessence of the freight rate issue in Canada.[11] The opening procedural moves, the positions taken by the various participants, the mulling over of the issue by the Board, and the nature of the conclusions set a general pattern that the later controversies only embellished and built upon. Absent were only the issues of statutory grain rates and horizontal price increases, which did not arise until the late-World War I and post-war inflation, still some three or four years away. The case was the first big confrontation between the West and the railways before the Board. It also might be proper to say it was the first big confrontation between the West and the Board, since in the mind of the West, their differing views on equity and unjust discrimination inevitably tended to group the Board with the railways and the Eastern establishment. Perhaps the most vivid way of presenting the events of the Western Rates Case would be to outline the successive events, including the judgement itself, in chronological order, followed by a commentary bringing out the significance of each at the time and as a portent of future attitudes.

November 14, 1911: The Winnipeg Board of Trade passed the following resolution at a general meeting and forwarded it to the Minister of Railways and Canals and to boards of trade in other Western cities.

Whereas the rates charged by the Canadian Pacific Railway Company for the carriage of freight from Winnipeg and throughout the whole western country were originally based on a much higher scale than those charged for a similar service on the same road in the eastern sections of the Dominion, and

Whereas the complaint being made to W.C. Van Horne, the then head of the said railway, he stated that "as the volume of traffic increased the rates of freight would naturally decrease," and

Whereas the rates of freight have not decreased since then notwithstanding continued complaints being made, and the fact that the tonnage to be hauled now taxes the capacity of the Canadian Pacific Railway and the Canadian Northern Railway to the utmost, as shown by congestion in their yards, and

Whereas the burden of excessive freight rates has for many years been a source of great complaint as well as being a grave injustice to the people of the entire western portion of our Dominion, and

Whereas the Railway Commission, whether from want of sufficient jurisdiction, or whatever cause, have failed to deal with the matter,

Therefore be it resolved that in the opinion of this Board, the time has arrived when the Government of this Dominion should by legislation lay down the principle that rates allowed to be charged by the railways in the western provinces shall not exceed those charged in Ontario and Quebec for a similar service to a greater extent than necessary to cover any excess there may be in the cost of operation in the west over that in Ontario and Quebec, and it is recommended that this Board take immediate action in respect hereto, and ask the co-operation of western Boards in the presentation of facts to the Government through the Honourable Robert Rogers and other western members of Parliament.[12]

Commentary: The resolution is an excellent summary. Compressed into a few paragraphs is the nature of the West's complaint and what should be done to alleviate it. It mentions the general expectation of the West that freight rates, initially set high on the basis of the low density of traffic, would eventually be brought down as traffic increased. The discontent with the higher rates charged in the West is reflected in a loss of confidence in the Board of Railway Commissioners and a direct appeal over its head to the Government. The Board's discretion should be taken away by a statutory declaration of the principle of equalization of rates between East and West, with one concession to the economists: to let any excess over Eastern rates be justified by higher costs of operation. One is tempted to speculate on whether such an exception might not have been prompted by Winnipeg's fairly consistent objection to the lowering or removal of the Mountain Differential which acted like a barrier holding back Vancouver from the Prairie markets.

November 20, 1911: The Minister of Railways and Canals acknowledges receipt of the resolution, saying he has referred it to the Board.
Commentary: This appears to have been the first time since the formation of the Board that a complaint had been made directly to the Minister, who lost no time in referring it to the Board.

November 24, 1911: The Chief Commissioner replied to the Secretary of the Winnipeg Board of Trade:

> The Honourable the Minister of Railways has forwarded to me a copy of a resolution passed at the general meeting of your Board held on November 12th inst. This is the first complaint that has been made directly to the Board regarding freight rates generally in the West. There is no necessity of calling upon the Government to deal with the matter, nor is there any further legislation required. The powers of the Board are ample to deal with not only specific rates but those generally. The resolution that you have forwarded is of an extremely general character. If you desire the whole subject investigated by this Board, it would greatly facilitate matters if you would have your traffic officials formulate a specific case. Our rules are by no means hard and fast, nor do we confine ourselves to the specific case set forth in the complaint; but it is a difficult matter to take up in the way it is placed in this resolution. Indeed, strictly speaking, the resolution is not a complaint to this Commission at all, but it is a request that the government pass legislation. I shall be glad to have your views upon the foregoing.[13]

Commentary: This reply documents very succinctly the failure of any meeting of minds on the matter of Western freight rates. As we shall see from the Board of Trade's reply, it served as a red flag waved at a bull. In the first place, the complaint was not made "directly" to the Board, but deliberately bypassed it. The blunt statement that it was unnecessary to deal with the Government, that no legislation was required, and that the Board's powers were adequate to deal with the general as well as the specific rate complaints indicates already an alarming degree of bureaucratic incomprehension. Despite the claim to be able to deal with general complaints, the Chief Commissioner was forced to ask that the complaint be channelled through a specific case because it was difficult to take the matter up in any other way! Unwittingly, the Chief Commissioner in his short reply seemed to have furnished all the reasons why the West should bypass the Board.

December 4, 1911: The Winnipeg Board of Trade replied to the Minister answering the points raised by the Chief Commissioner's letter. It claimed that the principle of equal basis for rate levels was fair and equitable and that the Government was properly the party to appeal to for changes in the legislation.

> This Board begs to enclose herewith a copy of the letter received

from the Chairman of the Railway Commission, in which it asks that our traffic officials should formulate a specific case. This is exactly what the Board [of Trade] objects to doing. Their [the Board of Trade] charge is that the whole scale of rates in the Prairie Provinces is in excess of those charged in the East. They attached to their original resolution a copy of the covering distances respectively in East and West, and covering from 100 miles up to 1,050 miles, showing that in each case the charges in the three Prairie Provinces were materially in excess of those in the East.

Finally the Board sought, in the event that "the matter should be relegated to the Commission," that the latter be:

instructed to inquire into the facts regarding the whole scale of charges in the Prairie Provinces and their relation to those in the East . . . and in view of the fact that it is a matter of public policy in which the whole of the people of the West are concerned, they would further ask that counsel resident in this city [Winnipeg] and free from all railway corporation control, be appointed to act with this Board and other public interests in establishing the facts complained of.[14]

Commentary: With this letter, the Board of Trade raised the freight rate issue to one of regional and national importance. The original concept of railway regulation taken largely from the British experience, of a mediating body between unequal parties, was far exceeded. This older model was expected to restore, as nearly as possible, the situation that competition and a free market would have established. The problem now had become one of establishing justice in rates between shippers of different regions, regardless of whether they were commercially isolated from each other. Freight rates became the concern of the ordinary citizen ("the whole people of the West are concerned"). Although always strongly stressed, actual economic importance became less of a motivating force than the obstinate postponement or denial of what the West regarded as simple justice. The denial of full equity in freight rates eventually raised the issue to the status of a symbol of all the inequities the West felt it suffered under Confederation. Accordingly the Board of Trade asked for an explicit directive to the Railway Commission to investigate the general nature of the rate structure, and sought assistance in obtaining counsel to better combat the privileged knowledge of the railway companies.

The Supreme Court judgement of December 6, 1911, in the appeal of the Regina Toll Case made clear the discretionary power of the Board in the matter of unjust discrimination. Then, on January 8,

1912, the Board of Railway Commissioners announced a general investigation of all freight tolls in Western Canada indicating it would reduce any that might be found to be excessive. Once again, however, the Board had evaded espousing any general principle of freight rates. The way was open to make arbitrary reductions here and there without committing itself unconditionally to any general principle of equity. A month later, on February 15, 1912, the Board completed hearings and final arguments on an application of the Vancouver Board of Trade of October 6, 1909, for the removal of the Mountain Differential. This case was now joined with investigation of Prairie rates. In the meantime, evidence of sympathy for the West's position on freight rates was not lacking in Eastern Canada. In 1912, W.F. Maclean, a maverick Conservative member for Toronto, offered a motion in the House of Commons, declaring it to be "against the general interests of Canada to have any territorial variance in the application of tariff charges by the Board of Railway Commissioners."[15] Maclean's advocacy of a principle of equality in railway rates gained support from Western members of the Liberal Opposition but was withdrawn before being put to a vote.

At the beginning of the Western Rates Case, the West had rallied to present a united front in the interests of freight rate equalization. At the head of the Western forces were the boards of trade, led by the very active one in Winnipeg, representing distributors, wholesalers, and manufacturers who dealt directly with the railways and were knowledgeable in freight rate matters. Cities whose boards of trade participated in some manner were: four from Manitoba (Winnipeg, St. Boniface, Brandon, and Portage la Prairie); five from Saskatchewan (Regina, Saskatoon, Moose Jaw, Prince Albert, and North Battleford); four from Alberta (Calgary, Edmonton, Lethbridge, and Medicine Hat); and three from British Columbia (Vancouver, Victoria, and Nelson).

In contrast to the major participation by the boards of trade, the only farmers' organization that took part was the United Farmers of Alberta. The Western farmers at this time were more interested in the building of branch lines and were perhaps wary of interfering with railway income that was so essential to the further extension of lines. Also at this time, export grain rates were still held at the level set under the Manitoba Agreement, which was below the Crow's Nest level, and reduced rates for inbound settlers' supplies were still in effect. (However, this does not mean that farmers were indifferent to the freight rate issue.) In addition, for the first time, all the provincial governments were represented by counsel. "Outsiders" taking part were limited to the Canadian Manufacturers' Association and the Montreal and Toronto Boards of Trade.

The judgement in the Western Rates Case remains one of the most important documents in Canadian freight rate history. It contains a thorough review of the relevant sections of the Railway Act and of the Board's jurisprudence. From this it is clear that the Board's practice of dealing with unjust discrimination formed a barrier to the West's attempt to make a case for equity on general principles. However compelling any principles were, there was another factor that restricted the Board's freedom to reshape the rate structure according to regional desires. At that time Canadian Pacific was the only railway operating in all regions of the country. The Canadian Northern remained essentially a Western railway, making a costly attempt to expand into Eastern Canada. Similarly, the Grand Trunk was primarily an Eastern railway, in spite of its equally costly involvement in the Grand Trunk Pacific. Thus, the Board was not free to adjust rates between East and West as in the actual equalization adjustments of the 1950's with the expectation that the companies would recapture in one region what they had lost in another. Nor is it likely that the West would have been satisfied with the solution of having Eastern rates brought up to Western levels. Apart from the doubtful effectiveness of any such attempt, the West's position was that its own rates were exorbitant in themselves and reductions were in order.

Not surprisingly, the Board also heard a new method of rate-making expounded that was claimed would solve the problem. J.P. Muller, an accountant appointed by the federal government to assist the boards of trade, presented a theory "that rates in the West should be made on the basis of cost with the addition of a percentage to be fixed by the Board for the purpose of carrying proper overhead of capital charges."[16] This suggestion, which got bogged down in cross examination, clearly demonstrated there was no simple method of tying all railway rates to costs and ending up with a rate structure in any way compatible with the demand situation. The multitude of exceptions that would be required seemed to throw rate-making decisions right back to the informed or intuitive judgements of railway traffic officers. Apart from the enormous amount of time and expense required to formulate it in the first place, if such a system could have been proclaimed, it would likely have been as ill-adapted for moving traffic as the standard class rates then required by the Railway Act. A new and radical system of rate-making, naturally based on "costs," had little to do with the underlying grievances of the West either then or sixty years later when Alberta and Manitoba presented new systems to the Western Economic Opportunities Conference upon being pressured for concrete proposals.

The Board's solution showed a fair degree of wisdom. Five different rate scales were reduced to three – the Prairie scale, resulting from the extension of the Manitoba scale to the other two Prairie Provinces; the Pacific scale, applying in British Columbia, which was reduced below its previous level of double to one and one half times the Prairie level; and the B.C. Lakes scale which was close to the Prairie rate level. The Board seems to have been motivated almost entirely by considerations of equity after having considered and found wanting the various economic arguments for and against changing the relative rate levels. Density of traffic within Manitoba was rejected as an argument for a rate level difference because much of this density was created by traffic originating from or destined to stations in Alberta and Saskatchewan. While admitting higher costs of operation within Pacific territory, but rejecting any "smearing" of these costs over the entire West, the Board, without leaving any trace of its reasoning processes within the judgement, in effect did "smear" some of these costs over the Prairies by reducing the Pacific scale.

This is of great significance in the freight rate issue. Economic arguments could indeed be used, but they were uncertain alibis since any particular economic premise adopted had the uncomfortable faculty of applying in areas and in ways that undermined any united regional appeal for justice. Economic arguments also tended to become bogged down in the no-man's-land between rates and costs. As a result, such arguments were left to function as ad hoc mercenaries: they were used when advantageous to do so and dismissed in favour of constitutional rights and broad principles of equity whenever they became embarrassing. Yet economic evidence had to be the tinder to start the fire since under the Board's procedures, "unjust discrimination" had to be narrowly and objectively defined. It was difficult, if not impossible, to establish a general grievance based on equity unless the Board decided to be governed by considerations of equity. Even at this early date, the transition from problem to ideology can be seen as inevitable. The sense of grievance mounts, greatly exceeding the causal possibilities of freight rates alone, and is continually frustrated by the rules of the game which claim a rationality and reasonableness of their own. At the same time, the West had learned its lesson in tactics – to pressure the Board to use its discretionary powers in the interests of equity either directly or by going over its head to the federal government. The next thirty-five years are a story of the Board trying to reach a definitive method and at the same time trying to preserve some of its credibility in those very regions that had made freight rates their favourite vehicle of protest.

Ironically, while the Board was striving to give some recognition to Western demands for equity by authorizing reductions in Western rates, the government-appointed management of the Intercolonial

Railway in the Maritimes was carrying out an equalization program of its own. Bringing rates on the Intercolonial up by a series of steps to the levels of rates in Ontario and Quebec provoked a much different reaction when the Maritimers finally realized what was happening. The structure of the complaint here was shrewdly appraised by Henry F. Angus when, as a professor of economics at the University of British Columbia, he was appointed to the Turgeon Royal Commission on Transportation in 1949. His private comment, after listening to the arguments raised from coast to coast at the regional hearings of the Commission, is a useful text with which to begin:

> People are quick to attribute (a lawyer might say *astute* to attribute) adverse economic conditions to "man-made" policies, or to the absence of appropriate remedial action. As many of the representations received by the Commission show, those who ask for relief prefer to base their case on the sacrifices imposed upon them by national policies, rather than to speak in terms of geographical and other disadvantages. The reason is obvious. The disadvantages are, in a sense, the work of God, the policies the work of men. Man alone can be called upon to repair the damage he has done. A grievance, a sense of injustice, a feeling of resentment is on the whole pleasurable and provides the basis for a claim which is entirely consistent with self-respect. No awkward feelings of gratitude need arise if the grievance is removed and justice is done. Indeed, if claims are generously stated, it is clear that justice will never be made, but the basic case of the grievance will be left intact for further use.[17]

With the outbreak of the First World War the freight rate issue was immediately shoved to the background, but the arguments and the attitudes had taken the form that was to characterize them for the next sixty-five years. The issue would survive in its doctrinal purity, and would withstand radical changes in the economy and in transportation. It had become an issue that could survive considerable periods of dormancy only to spring instantly back to life at the properly given signal.

CHAPTER 3
The Twenties: Setting the Pattern of Freight Rate Protest

For the Prairie Provinces, the equalization of rates, brought about largely by the Western Rates Case, had the effect of reducing friction among the main cities over the distribution trade. British Columbia's problems were somewhat different since its objective was still the removal of the Mountain Differential, to which the Prairies were either indifferent or strongly opposed. Equalization within the Prairies caused a small but significant shift in the direction of freight rate protests. The pre-war rate disputes, although bearing a regional stamp, nevertheless were concerned primarily with local disputes on rates that were of direct interest to the shippers and not merely a source of regional theoretical grievance. These disputes involved the shippers themselves and their representatives, the various boards of trade and shipper organizations, and were about a form of discrimination that the Board could rule to be unjust since it involved competing shippers and rival cities. It was not too far-fetched to demonstrate actual detriment.

The Board, however, consistently refused to recognize differences in rates within different regions as *prima facie* evidence of unjust discrimination and left only very vague reasons for the many gradual steps it eventually took toward equalization on a national scale. In retrospect, one can see that the Prairies and the Board were setting themselves on a collision course as the freight rate issue became identified more closely with regional protests and comparisons. The Board was never able to see its way clear to order a complete equalization of the rate structure, despite a long series of proddings by the Cabinet. The Prairie protagonists viewed rate differences as the essence of unjust discrimination. Eventually the contradiction in the plot could only be removed by the intervention of another *deus ex machina* in the form of the Turgeon Royal Commission on Transportation in 1949.

All this is not to say that the West's view of itself as a victim of monopolists – financial and industrial as well as rail – was not already deeply imprinted in the social consciousness. It is rather to point out that at this time, at the end of the First World War, the freight rate issue was still one among several, and that public opinion had not yet brought extreme pressure to bear on the structure of railway regulation and policy. During the following decade this was all to change. Public awareness of the issue hardened into dogma: an ideology developed with all the attention directed to general rate increases, the continuing regional differences in rate levels, and the fight to restore the Crow's Nest Pass rates. This leads to the thread of continuity in the history that follows: *In the early twenties the freight rate issue was transformed from a largely economic issue into a regional ideology. At this time the ideology "took off" from the facts on a course of its own. It thus shielded itself from any impact of newer facts and events that might have justified other interpretations.* The "factual" justification of the ideology became the facts as they were at the period of the take-off, supported by a very simplified economic theory that isolated freight rates from all other factors in the economy. This does not mean that the ideology lacked any substantive value, but rather that that value continuously declined as circumstances changed and the ideology remained fixed until in the seventies we finally reached the wholly vacuous stage.

There were several circumstances that favoured such a transformation during the years between 1918 and 1927, of which the following might be noted. (1) The general rate increases of 1918-27, coming on top of rate differentials that had already been widely publicized during the Western Rates Case, appeared to strike at the whole population of the region and not just particular shippers. The fact that the 1920 increase was limited to 35 per cent in Western Canada, compared to 40 per cent in Eastern Canada, served as a reminder of the unequal bases to which the increases had been applied. A step of such general impact justified the intervention of provincial governments, and the Manitoba and Saskatchewan governments appealed the 1920 increase to the Privy Council. (2) The suspension of the Crow's Nest Pass Agreement, which permitted the Board to apply the general increase to these rates, seemed like a breach of faith to the West, who regarded the Agreement as a "charter" of Western rights and a protection against railway monopoly. That the Agreement calling for fixed rates should be suspended at the very point where its protection would take effect seemed intolerable. (3) The dislocating effects of inflation followed quickly by deflation where particularly severe in a country such as Canada. While farm prices advanced during the inflation they dropped drastically in the subsequent deflation. At the same time, industrial prices, freight rates, and mortgage interest resisted the deflationary pull to a much greater extent, resulting in a worsening of the economic position of the farmer. (4) After the early judgements of the Board in the Eastern Rates Case and the International Rates Case, freight rate issues ceased to be of any public interest or concern in Central Canada. The indifference and satisfaction in this area contrasted strongly with the continuing discontent in other parts of the country.

These factors help to explain the effectiveness of the regional appeal of the issue. The points raised in other areas of regional disparity tended to win arguments by default, the Central Canadian press and public being too bored and uninformed to attempt to reply. Even if many of these points were quietly put aside by Cabinet, there was still a willingness to make concessions to satisfy regional complaints. This reached its peak with the Freight Rates Reduction Act of 1959, when the federal govenment picked up the tab for a railway wage increase rather than permitting a rate increase. On the other major regional issue, the customs tariff, Central Canadian opinion was anything but somnolent. Here it was deeply involved, and actively used its political weight to prevent tariff reductions of the scale sought by the West and the Maritime Provinces. Politicians in these regions gradually came to see that there was a greater opportunity to score points in freight rates than in the tariff issue and accordingly freight rate protests became more vehement as tariff protests became more perfunctory.

The Maritime Provinces were introduced to the regime of the Board of Railway Commissioners when the Intercolonial Railway was absorbed by the new Canadian National System in 1923, and their freight rate revindications accentuated the identification of freight rates with regional disabilities. [The word "revindication" comes from the political group called the revindicationists in Italy in the late 1800's, who sought to annex lands the politicians thought should be part of Italy. Eds.] The effect was to contribute to the building up of a set of regional attitudes on the subject which attacked the allegedly favourable position of the Central Provinces.

The combination of these factors alerted provincial politicians to the possibilities of the rate issue as a vote-catcher. As the issue became primarily a regional matter, it served to unify regional opinion. Any leader who dared to remain lukewarm or hostile to the issue faced the possibility of being quickly outmanoeuvred by the opposition. Up to the present day, few premiers have hesitated to burn incense at the shrine of the freight rate issue. Besides being a very popular issue, it was also almost entirely risk free. The railways were a federal responsibility, and the two major systems were located in Montreal, a block or so from Saint James Street, then the symbol of Central Canadian financial and economic power. Not the least among the reasons for the persistence and increasing virulence of the issue has been its assiduous cultivation by provincial politicians who simply could not bring themselves to discard an issue having so much resonance within the provincial electorate.

With the interest of the provincial premiers came the lawyers and the freight rate experts who, beginning in 1920, made it their business to keep the issue in fighting trim. With a general mandate to press for freight rate concessions or to resist rate increases – in the interests of the people – the lawyers found the fullest scope for ingenuity and rhetoric. The freight rate experts flushed the necessary evidence from the far corners of the freight tariffs, putting the spotlight on obscure rates, many of which may hardly ever have been used to carry a pound of freight, thus adding to the fund of common knowledge and folklore. The point to remember is that even legitimate complaints in this atmosphere might be subject to gross exaggeration, since they were valued as evidence in support of general demands for sweeping changes. Merely the existence of seeming anomalies in rates was sufficient to build up the case and convince the public that vital issues were at stake. The relevance of these anomalies mattered little, and not the least of the factors reinforcing the issue was the "opposition": the railways, the Board, and the federal government, who became three of the most effective bogies ever used to frighten Western Canadian children.

Manitoba and Saskatchewan Intervene in Rate Increases

The first general increase in freight rates was authorized by the Board on December 26, 1917. It permitted a 15 per cent increase to become effective on March 15 of the following year. Coming in the critical year of World War I and at a time when the two newer transcontinental rail systems were bankrupt, coupled with a belief that the inflation was only a temporary phenomenon, this increase received little dissent. Even the Board's General Order 212 increasing grain rates by two cents per hundredweight effective June 1, 1918, could be accepted since the proposed increase left the rates still lower than the limit specified in the Crow's Nest Agreement.

The second increase of 25 per cent effective on August 12, 1918, was necessary to match the McAdoo award to United States railway employees. This came closer to sensitive ground, since the War Measures Act had to be called upon to authorize the increase of the grain rates above the Crow's Nest level. When the War Measures Act was withdrawn after the war, the increase in grain rates was preserved by an amendment to Section 325 of the Railway Act that specified that the Board's powers were not affected by any special Act for a period of three years from July 7, 1919. In effect, this set up a countdown to the ultimate confrontation over the Crow's Nest level of grain rates. At the same time, it kept the issue quiet during the intervening period.

With the war concluded but inflation reaching a new peak, the rate increases authorized by the Board's General Order 308 of September 9, 1920, in response to the Chicago award to U.S. railwaymen, finally encountered formal opposition from Manitoba and Saskatchewan. The two provinces jointly engaged H.J. Symington, KC, as counsel to represent their interest at the Board's hearings in August. At the last minute, Saskatchewan appointed its own counsel, D'Arcy Scott, who had formerly been with the Board. The hand of the legal tactician is immediately evident in a communication from Symington to Saskatchewan Premier W.M. Martin:

> The attitude of the Commission seems to be to rush the matter through, whereas the position I intend to take is that the Railways must furnish us with the fullest information and that we be given full opportunity to digest the material and satisfy ourselves what increase if any is necessary.[1]

The prolonging of the proceedings in rate increase applications was later developed to a fine art by provincial counsel, such that the opening stages of the hearings tended to become stereotyped as the openings in a chess game.

The increases authorized by the Board were the largest of any single increase before or since. From September 13, 1920, to the end of the year, rates were to go up by 35 per cent in Western Canada and by 40 per cent in Eastern Canada, and after January 1, 1921, they were to be cut back to 30 per cent and 35 per cent respectively. The two governments immediately appealed to the Privy Council, which rejected the appeal (P.C. 2434, October 6, 1920). The provinces then went back to the Board to urge that the interim surcharge be suspended and the rates be dropped by 15 percentage points in January. The Board rejected these requests in a judgement on December 10, 1920. It is perhaps not surprising that the first contested rate increase case affords an example of the nature and effects of political intervention in these matters, given the context of the Canadian economic and political situation. Three of these "principles" are given and then will be illustrated from available records.

First, attention is directed to the area of maximum public interest or response, notwithstanding the actual matter at issue. While the case before the Board involved an application by the railways for increased rates because of heavy increases in costs, the thrust of the provincial argument was the existence of regional disparities. Premier Martin of Saskatchewan expressed his philosophy thus:

Whatever increase in rates is allowed, however, should be as small as possible, consistent with the absolute need of the railway system, and insofar as the West is concerned we should insist on the removal of the discrimination which exists between the rates in the East and the rates in the West.[2]

The Privy Council was sufficiently impressed by the force of the provincial arguments against rate differentials to direct the Board to conduct an inquiry on the subject in language that all but ordered the Board to equalize rates between East and West "with the least possible delay" and "to the utmost extent possible":

Very strong representations were made at the argument on appeal to the effect that the order continued and indeed intensified an unjust discrimination in rates, it being claimed that higher freight rates prevail generally in Western Canada, that is west of Fort William, ... the committee is strongly impressed with the very desirability of bringing about with the least possible delay equalization of Eastern and Western rates.

The Committee of the Privy Council therefore further recommends that as conditions have probably changed materially in recent years tending more and more to make equalization practicable, an inquiry by the Board be directed to be held at the earliest date with a view to the establishment of rates meeting to the utmost extent possible the above requirements as to equalization."[3]

A second principle of political intervention is that the East-West confrontation is stressed as much as possible. This was reflected in a letter from Premier Martin to a rural correspondent on October 7, 1920, the day after the dismissal of the appeal and the simultaneous order to the Board to conduct an investigation on equalization.

I do not know what the results of the appeal will be but I do not anticipate very much from it and I have come to the conclusion that the proper course for us to pursue in the Province is to have information prepared showing clearly the discrimination between Eastern and Western rates and asking for the removal of the discrimination.[4]

Much less interest was shown on the Prairies for British Columbia's attempts to have the Mountain Differential removed. Winnipeg, Calgary, and Edmonton were strongly opposed, arguing that so long as costs were higher, the rates should be higher. Saskatchewan, with smaller cities and less distribution trade, was not as involved here, and

Martin even replied vaguely but affirmatively to a request from British Columbia to support its removal.[5] This application drew from the counsel for the Winnipeg Board of Trade, Isaac Pitblado, the comment that this was merely an organized effort to expand business in the coast province and would tend to destroy business interests in Winnipeg.[6]

Third, there seems to have been general agreement that the issue should be limited to the freight rate discriminations without going into the broader issues involved, which might only confuse matters and reduce or remove the importance of freight rates. When, in preparation for the Board's inquiry, Symington suggested to Martin that the province might ask for a readjustment of rates involving lower railway wages, Martin's political interest led him to reject it and to remind Symington of the issue having top priority: "The question of wages however, should not enter so much into the main question which will be before the Board, namely, that of discrimination in rates between the East and the West."[7]

With the board ordered to undertake a new investigation of freight rates beginning from the Western Rates Case, all the Western Provinces responded, but in different manners. British Columbia took the lead, having the largest *terra irredenta* and with a premier and counsel who each had a strong personal interest in the subject. [The *irredentists* were another Italian political party of the 1800's advocating a return to Italy of all Italian-speaking areas. Eds.] Alberta remained hesitant, largely because of the inexperience of the new United Farmers of Alberta Government, but as time progressed it was coaxed and pushed by British Columbia. Saskatchewan also did not take a strong initiative and was concerned mainly with possible extension of branch lines, an area where interests seemed counter to rate concessions.[8] Manitoba also had less interest at this time in the East-West differentials, reacting strongly to British Columbia's aggressive demands for the removal of the Mountain Differential. The Winnipeg Board of Trade ran a counter campaign to British Columbia, each endeavoring to enlist the other two provinces on its side.

The Farmers' Interest in Freight Rates

It would be well to examine the main interests of the grain farmers, the largest economic group in the Prairies during this period. While the grain producer had been identified for many years as the strongest supporter for the continuation of the grain rates set by statute in 1925, his interest in other aspects of the freight rate structure had been more general in nature. He tended to support fully the early agitation of the distributors for equalization, but more from his status as a citizen of the West than because of any pressing economic interest. Freight rates on commodities such as farm implements were of interest, but not nearly as important as the customs duties on these and similar items. It would be fair to say that the farmer's aspirations, outside of the Crow's Nest rates, were aimed more directly at free trade than at freight rate equalization, although he could be aroused to support it.

The farmers' grievances tended to accumulate in periods of deflation. While the income and price relationships existing prior to an inflationary period cannot be said to have constituted an equilibrium, they nevertheless tended to be regarded as periods of stability, if only because they served as an intuitive base for measurement of the degree of change brought about by inflation. The difference in the regional economies from that of the Central Provinces, which became significant in inflationary cycles, was their dependence on the fluctuating prices of agricultural and other natural resource products. While they might rise along with other prices they were much more subject to steep declines. Industrial prices, however, through control of output, went through a much narrower curve. Rigidities in prices of industrial goods and services such as mortgage interest, power, and freight aggravated the difficulties of primary producers in deflationary periods. (Figure 2 captures the salient features of the war and post-war inflation and deflation from the point of view of this study.)

The order of priority in the farmers' demands is to be seen in the various formal representations to the federal government and in the platforms of farm organizations. On December 16, 1910, the Canadian Council of Agriculture presented a series of resolutions to the government in what came to be known as the "Siege of Ottawa," in which were treated, in descending order of emphasis: the traffic, the Hudson's Bay Railway, terminal elevators, the Bank Act, cooperative legislation, the chilled meat industry, and finally, the railway. The first point was that the Railway Act should be amended to require the railways to bear a fair share of the responsibility for killing livestock. There follows, prefaced by an "also," as if in afterthought, three resolutions of a general nature that suggest Populist influence and the layman's mistrust of the mysteries of railway rate-making:

1. That the principle of fixing the tariffs in accordance with the competition of other roads or the density of traffic or volume of business be disallowed.

2. That a true physical valuation be taken of all railways operating in Canada, this valuation to be used as the basis of fixing the rates, and the information be available to the public.

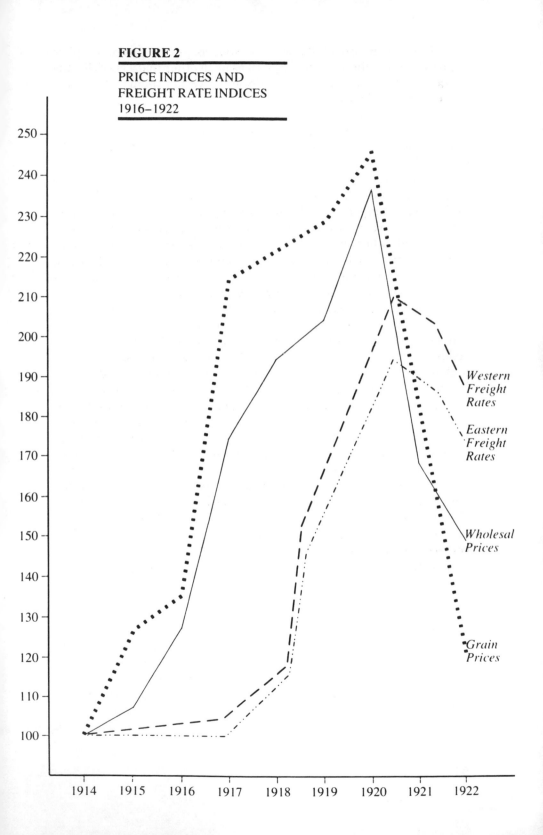

FIGURE 2

PRICE INDICES AND
FREIGHT RATE INDICES
1916–1922

Western Freight Rates

Eastern Freight Rates

Wholesal Prices

Grain Prices

3. That the Board of Railway Commissioners be given complete jurisdiction in these matters as well as in all other matters of dispute between the railway and the people, and to enable them to do this the law be more clearly defined.[9]

When we turn to the "Farmer's Platform" drafted by the Canadian Council of Agriculture in December, 1916, and supported by the principal Prairie farmer organizations, we find once again that the customs tariff dominates. The only reference to transportation is a single point advocating "the nationalization of all railway, telegraph and express companies."[10] In an updating of the same document in 1921, even more space is expended on tariff policy, taxation, returned soldiers, and "other democratic reforms." A brief mention of transportation is hidden in a subsection entitled "Land Settlement." It advocated "public ownership and control of railways, water and aerial transportation, telephone, telegraph and express companies and projects in the development of natural power and of the coal mining industry.[11]

At that time the advocacy of railway nationalization was not purely statement of a socialist ideal but a matter of practical policy. The federal government had several bankrupt railway systems on its hands and had not yet made up its mind how to deal with them. Resentment by farmers of Canadian Pacific and railway monopoly made the advocacy of nationalization a natural consequence; but the farmers had another more pressing interest in transportation – the extension of branch lines. Since capital investment by either the CPR or the government would be required there was perhaps some hesitancy to talk very much about rate discrimination of the sort that only hurt when one opened railways' tariff books. C.A. Dunning, then a minister in the Saskatchewan government, reported this mood in a letter to Premier Martin:

> Judging from the visitors I have had during the Grain Growers Convention, it is of the utmost importance that the Government and the Canadian National Railway say something definite as soon as possible about the mileage they intend to build. That question is almost as important as a general declaration of railway policy.[12]

When it is borne in mind that the Crow's Nest issue had been shelved until July, 1922, the freight rate agitation that arose in Western Canada with the rate increases and the inflation-deflation cycle can be traced, not to the farmers, but to the provincial governments wanting to appear to take some positive action in disturbing times, and to boards of trade to press for new gains or to defend old advantages. The

54

publicity and education role of provincial politicians and their lawyers and experts developed a regional issue that soon took a stronger hold on public imagination than the tariff issue. In freight rate matters these newcomers to Western politics – the United Farmers of Alberta and the Progressive Party members in Parliament – were at first innocents. But, pushed by the knowledgeable parties in Vancouver and Winnipeg and by the need to come to grips with the Crow's Nest issue, they quickly learned and found it rewarding to take a firm stance on freight rates against the railways, the Board, and the federal government. A further sustaining factor was the political situation of the day. The Liberal government of Mackenzie King lacked a majority and depended upon the support of the Progressives. King's determination to woo the West and bring the Progressives back into the Liberal Party meant a much greater sensitivity to Western demands. One is reminded of the situation in the early seventies when a Liberal government once again had to pay particular attention to Western complaints, among which freight rates still ranked high.[13]

British Columbia Takes the Lead

In the immediate post-war period British Columbia seemed to have the largest balance of unsatisfied claims in freight rates of all the Western Provinces. The outstanding grievance was the higher scale of rates charged in the Mountain Territory – one and a half times that of Prairie Territory – a rate scale known as the Mountain Differential. The province had never been reconciled to this state of affairs and continued to urge constitutional, economic, and equity reasons for equalization with the Prairies. With the return of peacetime conditions, a striking change in British Columbia's economic and geographical situation took place. The Panama Canal opened new trade routes for Vancouver and the West Coast seemed to offer unlimited opportunities for growth. Traffic and rates between Vancouver and the Prairies, which had been largely of academic interest, now became a live issue as the port of Vancouver anticipated a bright future as a grain-exporting port and as a distribution point for the Prairies. The freight rate structure had previously been adjusted to the traffic then moving, so that lumber and other bulk materials from British Columbia had already been relieved of the burden of the Mountain Differential in long-distance shipments. A new adjustment followed the opening of a direct water route between the Atlantic and Pacific Coasts with the railways being forced to publish low water competitive rates on traffic in both directions. This in turn created a new situation, much to the distaste of Alberta, in that rates to intermediate points such as Calgary and Edmonton remained at their old level, often well above the competitive rates between Central Canada and Vancouver. It was this situation that led Alberta to claim that it was "at the apex of the rate structure."

Such concessions were made voluntarily by the railways under the pressure of competition with water carriers and U.S. railways. A different situation existed in the freight rates on grain for export. The railways in no way intended to offer the low Crow's Nest rates that applied to the Lakehead. In addition, there was a "chicken and egg" problem in Vancouver as to whether export rates should first be lowered to encourage the building of elevator capacity or whether the facilities should be provided first. The British Columbians were not directly involved in the dispute over the restoration of the Crow's Nest rates since their interests were confined to obtaining parity with the Lakehead regardless of the actual level of rates that might apply. From the British Columbia point of view it was simply a matter of updating that part of the rate structure which was subject to government policy. In this regard, B.C. could count on the support of Alberta because the West Coast appeared to be the logical route for grain produced in the Western half of the Prairies. British Columbia thus had a strong *prima facie* case for relief from its freight rate problems, and the problems were easily grasped by the public and benefited from a strong campaign waged by the Vancouver Board of Trade and the local press. Perhaps even more important in its "greatest hour of need," B.C. happened to be served by a premier and a counsel whose personal interest and energy transformed just another economic and political issue into a crusade for regional justice.

"Honest John" Oliver was Liberal premier of British Columbia from 1917 to 1927. In dress and manner he carefully cultivated the role of a small-time rural politician, or as Russell Walker put it, he demanded recognition as a "man of the people."[14] At the same time he was a dogged pursuer of ideal goals with the shrewdness and resourcefulness to stay afloat in heavy political seas. At the beginning of 1921, when he engaged G.G. (Gerry) McGeer, a Vancouver lawyer and former member of the legislature, to conduct the provincial case before the Board of Railway Commissioners, a team was created that set the tone for all subsequent freight rate agitation in Canada. McGeer was a highly intelligent and articulate lawyer, full of ingenuity and new ideas. He was also a good publicist who understood the ways of rallying popular support behind a cause. It is probably due to McGeer's pioneering efforts that freight rates have become so consciously a part of the West's cultural heritage. He has had many emulators over the last fifty years, and his public postures, although re-enacted by others, have retained much of their effectiveness despite the disappearance of their factual support.

56

Oliver, from the earliest days of his participation in provincial politics, was impressed with the political possibilities of the freight rate issue. In addition he was a bit of a railway buff. One of his ambitions was to ride a train into Prince George. The building of the Pacific Great Eastern Railway by the province interested him greatly although it enormously complicated his struggle for political survival. Oliver's own account of his first raising of the rate issue, in a letter to J.A. Campbell, reveals with great clarity the motives stimulated by the issue and the dimensions of the future battleground.

I would say that when in 1916 Sir Richard McBride [Conservative premier of B.C.] was making his big fight for better terms, I contended that he had not chosen the strongest grounds from which to carry on his agitation, that instead of relying on the excess amount of customs duties being paid by British Columbia, his strongest case was on the ground of the excessive transportation rates charged by the Canadian Pacific Railway Company. To bring this matter to a focus, on April 15, 1907, [sic] I moved, seconded by Mr. Henderson, the following resolution:
'Whereas by section 11 of the Terms of Union the Government of the Dominion undertook to secure the construction of a line of railway to connect the seaboard of British Columbia with the railway system of Canada;
'And whereas large areas of public lands belonging to the Province of British Columbia have been conveyed to the Dominion Government in furtherance of the said railway;
'And whereas the benefits to be derived from the construction of the said railway was one of the inducements which led to the Union of British Columbia with the other Provinces of Canada, as well as for the conveyance to the Dominion Government of the public lands of the Province as aforesaid;
'And whereas the railway above referred to is national in its character, and as such has received a very large measure of assistance of public moneys and lands;
'And whereas it was not contemplated at the time of the Union of British Columbia with the other Provinces of Canada that there should be any discrimination in freight and passenger rates between one locality and other localities, or between one Province and any other Province;
'And whereas numerous complaints have from time to time been made by various Boards of Trade in British Columbia to the effect that existing freight rates discriminate against cities in British Columbia;
'And whereas the Board of Railway Commissioners have ordered

a reduction of passenger rates to three cents per mile upon all railways between Calgary and the Atlantic;

'And whereas the passenger rates charged upon railways in British Columbia is in excess of three cents per mile;

'And whereas such excess is a discrimination detrimental to the best interests of British Columbia, as it tends to prevent development and the influx of population;

'Therefore, be it Resolved, that an humble Address be presented to His Honour the Lieutenant-Governor praying that he will cause a full representation of the facts be made to the government of the Dominion, and the the Board of Railway Commissioners, to the end that British Columbia may be placed in as favourable condition in respect to freight and passenger rates as are other portions of the Dominion.'

This resolution was accepted by the Government and passed unanimously by the Legislature.[15]

Here we already see the freight rate issue unifying warring factions in a provincial legislature against the federal government. We recognize also some of the main arguments that were to receive so much elaboration in later years: the constitutional issue, the controversial needs of Canadian Pacific, and the principle of equity.

The constitutional issue, which figures so prominently in Oliver's resolution, was always regarded by him as British Columbia's strongest argument in favour of equitable rates – some fifteen years before it had been applied to freight rates in the Maritimes. When British Columbia, following up on the resolution, took a case to the Board, the result was a complete failure with an ironical twist. The Board held that Canadian Pacific was at liberty to make different tools under different circumstances, adding that the only party that could complain to the courts about the CPR's alleged non-fulfillment of the contract was the other contracting party, the federal government.[16] Oliver, writing in 1924, blamed this setback on the provincial counsel at the time: "To put it mildly, he made a 'muff' of the situation."[17] However, Oliver and McGeer between them were unable to do better.

Oliver lost his seat in the election of 1909 and did not return until 1916 when he became Minister of Agriculture and Railways in the new Liberal government, becoming Premier in the following year on the death of Premier Brewster. British Columbia did not join Manitoba and Saskatchewan in their appeal against the last post-war increase in freight rates, but when the Cabinet, in dismissing the appeal, called upon the Board to investigate the possibility of rate equalization, the Vancouver Board of Trade began to prepare a case for submission.

This group approached Oliver in December, 1920, for a grant of $10,000 to enable them to employ counsel at the hearings in Ottawa. The result of the meeting was that Oliver convinced them – likely without much difficulty – that the province was the only body that could successfully pursue the case. McGeer was hired and for the next few years the Board and the Cabinet were kept busy with applications and appeals from the two.

The story becomes very confused, since in addition to working toward the removal of the Mountain Differential, British Columbia kept shifting its position with respect to the Crow's Nest rates. We shall endeavour to unscramble the story both to indicate the degree of activity in freight rates that occurred during these few years, and to stress the impact of Oliver's activities. As a provincial premier, he appeared on different occasions before the Board and the Cabinet, keeping both himself and the freight rate issue in the national spotlight.

On the Crow's Nest rate issue, Oliver was opposed to the restoration of the original agreement since it had no reference to a similar level of rates on grain to Vancouver. It also involved ceilings on a number of commodities in the general category of settlers' needs and effects movings from Central Canada to the Prairies, whereas rates from the Prairies to Vancouver were high due to the Mountain Differential. Thus at the beginning there was a conflict of interest between B.C. and the Prairie Provinces, the latter wishing to have the original agreement restored. Only after this had been achieved with respect to grain in July, 1922, was Alberta, and to a lesser extent Saskatchewan, ready to support British Columbia in having the same rates apply westbound to Vancouver. Oliver was bitter about the failure of the Progressive Party to support his position before the Select Parliamentary Committee. Commenting in this letter to Campbell:

Before the Parliamentary Committee ... I pointed out that if grain rates were reduced eastward and no reduction westward, there could be no grain movement westward to the Pacific Coast. The Progressive Party, who are now solidly behind B.C. in respect of the Western movement of grain, absolutely ignored our position at that time and I contend that they could have had a westward rate on grain equal to the eastward rate had they so demanded in Parliament at the same time.[18]

Early in the summer of 1922, however, British Columbia was able to register two important victories in the freight rate issue. On June 30, the Board issued Order 366 – its decision on the equalization investigation undertaken under P.C. 2434. It kept the Mountain Differential,

59

but reduced it using the constructive mileage within Pacific Territory of one and a quarter miles for each actual mile at the Prairie scale of rates instead of one and a half miles, the province having admitted that costs were still higher than on the Prairies. The Board's reasons for reducing the differential were brief and vague as can be seen from the paragraph justifying the reduction:

Following the reasoning of the *Western Rates Case*, a revision in the mountain scale as provided for in the Pacific standard is justifiable. On careful consideration, the reduction hereinafter provided for should be made; the Board does not feel justified in going any further.

It seems obvious that the Board was caught in a self-created dilemma, having officially recognized general differences in costs as justification for differing levels of rates. Thus the persuasive arguments based upon equity plus the heavy political pressure were still not sufficient to carry the day so long as some differences in costs were recognized. The Board's wavering attitude encouraged Oliver and McGeer in the belief that just one more push would be enough to topple it altogether. The fight to remove the remaining differential was assiduously pressed for another ten years, but without further success during that time.

The second victory followed shortly after Parliament amended the Railway Act to confirm the Select Committee's recommendation that the Crow's Nest rates on grain alone be restored, but suspended the provisions referring to westbound commodities for another two years. The Board's decision to reduce the Mountain Differential had done little for the westbound movement of grain, and the restoration of the eastbound rates was estimated to cost the railways seven million dollars annually in lost revenue. Clearly neither the government nor the Board felt able to order further concessions, but there was a strong desire to soften the blow to British Columbia. J.A. Argo, in describing what happened next, merely states that, "effective August 1, 1922, rates [on grain to Vancouver] were voluntarily reduced 20% to reflect the reductions made in rates to Port Arthur and Fort William effective July 6, 1922."[19] The Board's account suggests that it was a matter discussed between the railways and itself on its own initiative:

The Board realized that there would be complaints against the size of the spread between eastbound and westbound movements of grain, if there were no reduction made in the export rates on grain to Vancouver, and so informed the representatives of both the Canadian Pacific and Canadian National Railway Companies. As a result of these conferences, the railway companies voluntarily made a general reduction in export rates between Prairie points and Pacific Coast points of 20%.[20]

Oliver's account in his letter to Campbell sheds some more light on what actually happened: "Both Mr. McGeer and myself kept up the correspondence with the Government at Ottawa and they used their influence with the railway corporations, with the result that a reduction of 6 cents 100 lbs. was given on grain moving westward from Calgary and Edmonton."[21]

Despite McGeer's efforts to rally support in the other provinces, the credit for the result must go to British Columbia's own efforts. The reply of Premier Dunning of Saskatchewan to McGeer's bid for support on the westbound grain rates indicated the same lukewarm attitude with which Premier Martin had responded to McGeer's request for support on the Mountain Differential issue: "As you know, Saskatchewan is not at the present time vitally interested in this phase of the question, but I can assure you that we shall follow with a great deal of interest your progress in regard to this matter."[22] For Oliver and McGeer this had only been a battle, but by no means the end of the war. British Columbia had fought almost alone, the other Western provinces being too preoccupied with the eastbound rates and too hostile to any further reduction in British Columbia's general rate structure to go along with any united front. The obvious ally in attacking freight rate discrimination was Alberta, but the newly-elected United Farmers of Alberta administration was still cautiously feeling its way among the intricacies of the national political scene, as was the large Progressive representation in Parliament. The Crow's Nest issue was comparatively clear, but the issues involving the Mountain Differential and grain rates to Vancouver were more controversial. In this field initiatives were still being taken by the Boards of Trade, particularly in Winnipeg, Calgary, and Edmonton, since the Prairie governments had not yet engaged their own freight rate advisers. When Oliver began putting pressure on Premier Greenfield to have Alberta take a stand in the investigation of equalization, it would appear that the Alberta government engaged its own freight traffic officer, A.W. Chard, largely to have someone able to interpret what Oliver and McGeer were talking about.[23] Chard attended the Board's hearings in Ottawa in February of 1922, where Greenfield wired him to take no part in the discussion of the British Columbia case but to gather all information possible.[24]

In the later part of that year the British Columbia government decided to appeal to Privy Council the Board's General Order 366, which had kept the Mountain Differential, and began exerting pressure on Greenfield to have Alberta associate itself with British Columbia in the appeal. McGeer wrote to the Alberta Premier on the subject on November 13; Oliver on November 25. A telegram from McGeer and a plea from R.J. Cromie, publisher of *The Vancouver Sun*, were sent on December 5. Oliver sent a telegram on December 6 asking why there had been no reply to his letter. Greenfield parried these threats in a letter to Oliver on December 11, asking him to stop in Edmonton en route to Ottawa to appear before the Privy Council. Finally, after another telegram from McGeer on January 15, 1923, Greenfield wired back on January 22, "you are authorized to state that the Alberta Government is joining the Government of B.C. in appeal."[25]

Oliver appeared before the Governor-in-Council at an *ex parte* hearing on February 3 to present a statement on British Columbia's constitutional case for equality in freight rates, a subject long dear to his heart. He followed this with an eight-page letter to Premier John Bracken of Manitoba outlining the "constitutional case," with a copy to Premier Dunning endeavoring to counteract the strongly antagonistic position of Isaac Pitblado who had recently been retained as counsel for the Manitoba government.[26] The appeal was heard on August 9.

Already Greenfield's decision to align Alberta behind British Columbia was causing him some embarrassment because both the Edmonton and Calgary Boards of Trade were strenuously opposed to any support being given to the removal of the Mountain Differential. By now, Alberta cities were up in arms over the transcontinental competitive rates, which seemed to confer tremendous benefits (ratewise at least) on British Columbia, leaving Alberta at the apex of the rate structure. In view of these circumstances, assisting British Columbia to gain further rate concessions was the last thing they wanted the Alberta government to do. When Greenfield wired Chard for an explanation, Chard replied on February 9 with a lengthy wire giving the requested justifications. When the Edmonton Board of Trade read the contents of Chard's telegram it immediately passed a resolution offering a point-by-point refutation. It commented that "unfortunately, Mr. Chard appears to be completely dominated by the representatives of British Columbia." It recommended an immediate application to the railways to have the low transcontinental rates apply to Edmonton and Calgary.[27]

Greenfield, it seems, was able to mollify Edmonton over the next few weeks, but the Transportation Committee of the Calgary Board of Trade remained hostile. Greenfield wired this news to McGeer on March 27, suggesting that a public meeting between Oliver and himself might create the impression that they had a good case "demanding exceptional measures in rebuttal." McGeer quickly picked up this offer and replied by wire the same day saying that "it would be good business for you and Premier Oliver to speak at Calgary on inter-provincial trade and its value. Such propaganda would be effective not only locally but in the East."[28] In his letter to Chard, McGeer took up the task of providing the basic training for the green Alberta troops. His views here are of great significance, for he is seen widening the issue and broadening the appeal which, within a very short time, have the underpinnings of an ideology of freight rates. After McGeer, those who fought in the freight rate battles were not simply asking for the removal of certain anomalies in the rate structure, but were to see themselves as crusaders in a grand cause. Even on rather trivial issues public opinion could be mobilized instantly through the reiteration of slogans that had become impressed in folk memory.

With reference to Premier Oliver and Premier Greenfield speaking at Calgary, I am satisfied that this is a good practical propaganda work. The Eastern papers have been carrying considerable material against British Columbia and Alberta's contentions. The activities of Winnipeg and Calgary are actuated by the railway companies or by those who are very easily convinced by the railway companies that our contentions are incorrect.

You must remember that our appeal to Ottawa is an appeal to a political body, and that the weight of public opinion is a matter of more than secondary importance. The threat will be made that if rates go down in Alberta and British Columbia they must be raised elsewhere. The justice of British Columbia's claim is evidenced to some extent by the consistent demand of the whole community. The fact that Alberta and British Columbia are joining hands is, to my way of thinking, one of the most important things in our appeal that has happened since the application commenced. Premier Oliver and Premier Greenfield speaking together in Calgary would, I believe, result in a very widely distributed publicity in the east, and it would be a matter of great political significance and an event of more or less historical value. Two Prime Ministers speaking together and waging, with the public support of two great Provinces, a contest which means greater development of the trade and commerce of Western Canada. It is an awakening in the West, and every Eastern newspaper will view it as such, and it will be an opportunity for us to get a great deal of information to the public of Winnipeg and to the public of the Prairies and to the public of the East which is bound to have a reasonable effect in offsetting the propaganda of the railways.

McGeer thought it would be necessary for Chard to spend two weeks or a month working with him in Vancouver and proposed a meeting between the Vancouver, Edmonton, and Calgary Boards of Trade in order to have both provinces "absolutely united at Ottawa." To this end Premier Greenfield should go to Ottawa and make a statement to the Privy Council outlining the effect of discrimination on Alberta. "We can prepare this statement for him and he will be able to present it without serious inconvenience to himself in the matter of preparation."[29]

For all McGeer's enthusiasm and careful preparation, the appeal itself was something of an anticlimax. The Cabinet, and most certainly the Prime Minister, had no desire to take over the Board's responsibilities, which would probably have left them permanently in Cabinet hands. The westbound grain rates and the Mountain Differential were referred back to the Board in two separate Orders-in-Council. P.C. 2007 of October 2, 1923, noted that the rates on grain to Vancouver had not been dealt with in the Board's judgement, and therefore were now referred to the Board "for immediate determination and such effective action as it may deem necessary." The Board acted promptly, issuing a judgement on October 10 that required a 10 per cent reduction in westbound grain rates. This figure was determined by a complicated comparison with ton-mile rates on eastbound movements in Western and Eastern Canada but left the rates higher than the Crow's Nest level on eastbound grain.

The Mountain Differential issue was sent back to the Board by P.C. 2166 of October 24, 1923, indicating that the Board should take the necessary action, if transportation conditions change, so as to render practicable a newer approach to equality of rates between Prairie and Pacific Territory. This was quite a different tone from that used with the westbound grain rates and the Board felt under no pressure to take further action. A year later, the Chief Commissioner of the Board, H.A. McKeown, advised Premier Oliver that conditions had not so changed as to immediately justify the elimination of the differential.[30]

Oliver was particularly disappointed with the result in the Mountain Differential appeal. He told J.H. King, Minister of Public Works and British Columbia member in Cabinet: "The strong feature of our appeal and the one on which we most relied, namely our rights under the Terms of Union, appears to have been completely ignored – no mention of it is made in the Order."[31] This appears to have ended British Columbia's use of the constitutional argument in connection with freight rates in any serious fashion. McGeer's later approaches put their trust more in statistics, inconsistencies in the application of costs to rates, and general considerations of equity.

This setback, however, did not dispel interest in freight rates, and in the months that followed we see a new strategy that was to govern provincial interest and intervention off and on over the next fifty years. McGeer by now had raised freight rates to become his main interest, and had transformed the subject from a business negotiation between shippers and carriers to a popular crusade for provincial and regional justice. The broadening of the appeal had the inevitable result of widening the demands, and instilling the conviction that freight rate discriminations were a serious threat to prosperity and development, and therefore of direct interest to every citizen in the province. He thus enrolled not only those who had claimed to suffer directly from a grievance, but also those who liked to have a cause that could be raised above the level of narrow business self-interest. Like any stream that occupies the bottom of the valley, it picked up volume by being joined by many smaller streams of protest and discontent. It was only a matter of a short time before freight rates had become, so to speak, *the* regional ideology. McGeer's tactics were designed to keep the issue alive and active, at least until the existing freight rate discriminations had been removed, and also to intervene wherever there seemed to be a likelihood of them being increased.

Fortunately, a new issue arose. The express companies applied for an increase in rates on fresh fruits and McGeer leaped into action, asking Oliver's approval to go to Ottawa to intervene on behalf of the province. Oliver may not have been unwilling, but apparently he failed in two meetings of the Cabinet on January 4, 1924, to convince his colleagues. The following day he advised McGeer of the reasons for the refusal. The Cabinet was becoming sensitive about the money being spent on freight rates since the amount of fees had been soundly criticized by the Opposition. As Oliver's letter reveals, they thought of other reasons as well:

> The executive cannot believe it to be possible that any rate increases will be sanctioned by the Board of Railway Commissioners, especially in view of the fact that the other three Western Provinces are opposing the application. There is also a strong feeling in the Executive that British Columbia has borne the burden of the fight on freight rates, by means of which both Saskatchewan and Alberta, particularly the latter, have largely benefited, and that they have not shown any great desire to carry a fair proportion of the cost.
>
> The Executive also feel that B.C. is entitled to a reduction in express rates and that owing to having to face an investigation by a Royal Commission, they do not want a rate case on their hands in addition. They also think that they are entitled to make an application for a reduction of express rates at any time and would prefer to

do so at a later period. I have to advise you, therefore, that it is not the intention of the Government to be represented by counsel at Ottawa upon the hearing of the present application."[32]

McGeer was not prepared to give up so easily, and it may be assumed that he continued to put pressure on Oliver. The latter finally told him on February 21 that he was not going to send counsel to Ottawa for the Express Rate Case. McGeer replied the following day in a letter that clearly brings out his intense involvement in the issue and the persuasive force of his arguments. It was not to be the last time that he was to offer to serve without fees.

I beg to acknowledge receipt of yours of 21st inst., in which you state that you are not going to send counsel to Ottawa on the Express Rates Case.

Frankly, I think that this is a mistake in view of the fact that we have secured a very decided spirit of unity in Western Canada on the equalization of freight rates issue. I think the action of the Government of British Columbia in not appearing in the Express Rate issue would be construed as indicating that British Columbia was dropping out of the fight.

Further, I think the Board of Railway Commissioners will be very materially affected by the action of this Province in the Judgement that they will have to write pursuant to the Privy Council Order referring the whole freight rate issue back to that body. I greatly feel that a policy of indifference to the Express Rate Issue will set back the Province of British Columbia in its fight for adjustment of freight rates many years, and will have the effect of undoing very much of the splendid work that was already done....

... in view of the criticism that you have been submitted to, and for the reason that I sincerely believe in the interests of the Province and Western Canada generally that this Province should be actually represented at the Express Rate Enquiry, and for the purpose of cooperating with you in carrying out what I believe are your real desires on this issue, I am prepared to go to Ottawa and represent the Government on the Express Rate Enquiry without fees. I think, however, that it would only be fair that my actual out of pocket expenses should be covered, but if you feel that you cannot expend any further moneys whatsoever, I think the funds necessary for the payment of my expenses could be raised locally in Vancouver and if not, I will pay them myself.

I trust you will believe me when I say that I think that it would be a great mistake to allow the Express Rate Case to go on in Ottawa without representation on the part of British Columbia whose work and whose activities during the last three years made equalization of freight rates one of the livest public issues that has ever been discussed in the Dominion of Canada, on an internal measure, and which has, to my way of thinking, brought about actual conditions that strongly indicate the dawning of a new era of unparalleled prosperity, not only to British Columbia, but to the whole of Western Canada."[33]

The story thereafter quickly reached a climax and a happy ending. On February 26, Oliver gave his consent, coupled with a warning to McGeer not to say anything offensive to the express companies. McGeer was back the next day with a parting compliment to Oliver: "Few men have done so much for the West as you have and if you are successful in your efforts there will be no greater boon ever extended to the prosperity of this country."[34] On the policy that the best defence is attack, McGeer immediately filed an application for the equalization of express rates to counter the companies' application for a general increase. At the hearing itself, he also insisted on filing an application for a reduction on grain rates to Vancouver. The Chief Commissioner, F.B. Carvell, while observing that "this had been settled two years ago," nevertheless accepted the application.[35] The express rates issue then promptly disappeared from sight, there being no record of it in the Board's published judgements.

The General Freight Rate Investigation

The General Freight Rate Investigation conducted by the Board of Railway Commissioners over the period 1925 to 1927 has not received the attention it deserves, especially from recent transportation economists. Its importance – or better, its lack of importance – has been measured rather narrowly in terms of the merits of the specific rate issues involved. The minimal response of the Board has been interpreted as an index of its significance. Essentially, the investigation has been forgotten. But to overlook this critical period in the history of the freight rate issue is to lose the piece essential for solving the whole puzzle. Otherwise it becomes impossible to understand an attitude that grew up in one environment and survived essentially unchanged long after that environment had disappeared. The investigation represents a focal point in the history of the issue, dividing with some sharpness what went before and what came after. Up until then, the issue had been treated largely as substantive, although the course of events from the end of the war until 1927 clearly showed that to exaggerate the substance of the issue required the injection of a sizeable ideological component. Yet the arguments were basically about the economics of freight rates and the general assumptions about the making of rates were shared, at least nominally, by the Board, the railways, the provinces, boards of trade, and individual shippers. After the Board had issued its judgement, some of the contested points produced fainter and fainter echoes for a few years; but in general the issue entered a period of dormancy which lasted, apart from a few fitful stirrings, for twenty years. The railways' application for a 30 per cent increase in freight rates in October, 1946, brought it back to life, no longer as a substantive issue but as an ideology.

The investigation came as the climax of a number of developments that raised freight rates to the first rank among national issues. Successive attempts to defuse the issue by a piecemeal handling of the separate controversies seemed only to build it up toward the grand climax. The basis for public attention to freight rates was the dislocating effect of the rapid cycle of inflation and deflation following the First World War, a cycle which had been heaviest in the Prairie and Maritime Provinces. This made necessary general increases in rates, which in turn stirred up another hornet's nest in overriding the maximum levels of the rates under the Crow's Nest Agreement. The rate increases also drew attention again to the differences in regional rate levels which had been an issue in the Western Rates Case less than five years earlier. A logical connection between regional difficulties and the levels of freight rates was easy to draw. As politicians had already discovered, it served even better than the tariff as a means by which the regional public could define and focus their discontent. It provided what appeared to be a logical and concrete cause for the dissatisfaction and pointed to obvious and easily understood remedies.

While such attitudes had always been latent in the Prairies these factors could hardly have served by themselves to produce the actual climax. They were aided immeasurably by a very favourable conjunction in the political heavens. With clearly defined objective goals and strong personal motivations, the team of Premier John Oliver and lawyer Gerry McGeer had been waging a permanent campaign to gain for Vancouver and British Columbia freight rates equal to those applicable to the Prairies and the Fort William gateway. Applications were made to the Board at every opportunity. Where these were unsuccessful, appeals to the Supreme Court and the Cabinet were instantly launched. When the latter, as it usually did, rejected the appeal, it usually left the door ajar for another round by issuing a new directive to the Board to examine whether conditions now justified a different answer.

In ordinary circumstances, the Cabinet might have acted more decisively to stamp out the grass fire before it spread out of control. This was impossible, however, in light of the unprecedented delicate balance of forces in Parliament that gave the Western Provinces a political clout they never before had. With the Liberal government dependent on the support of the Progressive Party, the majority of whose members were from Prairie constituencies, Prime Minister Mackenzie King saw the future of both the Government and the Liberal Party dependent upon either absorbing or neutralizing the Western protest vote. When the Maritime Provinces complained that they had been left out of consideration, they were able to recover on the rebound by successfully urging that they were due some offsetting compensation in the area of freight rates (the story of which will be told in the following chapters). Under this constant harassment, driven into a corner by the Supreme Court judgement that created an impossible situation in the Crow's Nest Pass issue, and with an election approaching, the Government realized that it would have to smother the freight rate issue with some decisive action or face certain annihilation. Its position was truly stated a year later by the Saskatchewan Attorney General, Col. J.A. Cross, in an opening address to the Board at the regional hearings in Regina in connection with the General Investigation:

> But I think it can fairly be said that the Government of Canada – not only the Government of the day but past Governments – have been very anxious to get settled, if at all possible, the question of freight rates, and to avoid the more or less constant applications to them in conjunction with the matter....[36]

The Government's answer to this problem was the issuance of Order-in-Council No. 886 of June 5, 1925, which certainly ranks as one of the most important documents in the history of the freight rate issue. It contains notice of the final disposition of the issue of the Crow's Nest rates—to make the rates on grain and flour under the original agreement a statutory maximum, but to remove rates on other commodities from the protection of the Agreement.

> The Committee [Privy Council] are further of the opinion that as the production and export of grain and flour forms one of the chief assets of the Dominion, and in order to encourage the further development of the great grain growing provinces of the West, on which development of the future of Canada in a large measure depends, it is desirable that the maximum cost of the transportation of these products should be determined and known, and therefore are of the opinion that the maximum established for rates on grain

and flour, as at present in force under the Crow's Nest Pass Agreement, should not be exceeded.

The Committee are further of the opinion that, before such investigation is undertaken, it is essential to ensure that the provisions of the Railway Act in reference to tariffs and tolls, and the jurisdiction of the Board thereunder, be unfettered by any limitation other than the provisions as to grain and flour hereinbefore mentioned.[37]

Legislation was introduced and quickly passed later in the same month to give effect to this decision.[38] While intended to be a permanent solution, this legislation, in effect, has created a permanent problem in which social and political attitudes have become inextricably mixed and brought into conflict with transportation economics.

All the other issues were simply handed over to the Board for a "thorough and complete" investigation. As it did in P.C. 2434 in 1920, Privy Council again stated that "the policy of equalization of freight rates should be recognized to the fullest possible extent as being the only means of dealing equitably with all parts of Canada." It also mentioned three specific areas to be taken into account. First, there were the claims of the Maritime Provinces. In effect, these were transferred to the forum of the Duncan Royal Commission on April 7, 1926, when Maritime counsel formally asked leave to withdraw from the General Investigation just prior to the proclamation of the Maritime Freight Rates Act on April 14, 1927. Second, the movement of traffic through Canadian ports was to be considered. This referred to the continuing Maritime dissatisfaction with the fact that a large part of the export grain movement went via United States Atlantic ports. To this was added, by Order-in-Council No. 24 of January 7, 1926, an injunction to deal with the City of Quebec's complaint that the grain had not moved on the direct line of the National Transcontinental even though its completion for that express purpose had taken place ten years earlier. The third factor to be considered was traffic to and from Pacific coast ports whose possibilities had been greatly expanded by the Panama Canal and the growing trade with the Orient.[39]

The latter point presumably covered, among other things, British Columbia's complaint that the failure to give grain export rates to Vancouver at the same level as to Fort William inhibited the flow of grain through that port. This issue had already been before the Board, since at a hearing covering various other matters in Vancouver in November, 1924, the newly appointed Chief Commissioner, H.A. McKeown, and Commissioner Frank Oliver had granted leave to McGeer, acting for the province, to add a petition on the subject to the agenda. Introducing a new application in the course of a hearing on other applications had become a tactic of McGeer's to keep continuous pressure on for all of the provincial demands.

The Board reserved judgement and little more was heard of the matter until August of the following year when Vancouver shipping interests protested against the delay in handing down a judgement. This was two months after the General Investigation had been announced and the remaining Commissioners, in an attempt to forestall any unilateral action on the matter, passed a resolution that the subject be incorporated into the General Investigation. In a countermove on the same day, September 2, 1926, the Commissioners who had heard the Vancouver case issued Order 36769, authorizing the Crow's Nest level of rates on westbound export grain. This public split hardly added to the Board's stature and provoked a storm of protest from Regina to the Atlantic. However, these protests were unsuccessful in having the Order either rescinded, delayed pending appeal, or heard as part of the General Investigation. The Board's General Order 448, which gave effect to the decisions of the General Investigation, merely confirmed Order 36769, but specified that Canadian Pacific could base its rate from Calgary to Vancouver on the longer mileage from Edmonton of Canadian National.

The mystery behind this intriguing episode has never been fully exposed, although many have assumed the intervention of a "higher power" without having any evidence except the putting of two and two together. It does suggest, however, that freight rate objectives had become rather high-valued chips in the intergovernmental poker game, justifying a flexibility in tactics that a mere technical rate problem would never have been capable of inspiring. The effect was that British Columbia entered the General Investigation with one of its major complaints already satisfied, allowing McGeer to concentrate his fire on the Mountain Differential.

The nature of the General Investigation contrasts strongly with similar investigations that preceded and followed it. Coming little more than ten years after the Western Rates Case, it covered a national range of interests, saw a much more intense participation by provincial governments, and inevitably came closer to the problem of reconciling the "philosophy of freight rates" with the demands arising from a variety of grievances, real and fancied. Compared to later investigations by the Board and various royal commissions, freight rates were still considered to be the main issue. While the ideological tone kept breaking in, particularly in McGeer's case, it was offset by a serious commitment to base demands on the "facts." There were laborious efforts to relate the minutiae of freight rates, operating procedures, and costs to the macro-grievances upon which the politicians and

71

public had been clamouring for action. In the end, it proved impossible.

The Board's conclusions were of a rather restricted importance, and were based not on the analysis of such detailed investigations (although there are copious references to them in the judgements) but on a shrewd consensus of what minimum concessions it might be expedient to grant without leaving itself unconditionally committed to any principle of equity based upon comparisons of a purely mathematical nature. The General Investigation found the various provinces each taking care to define its own interests and not hesitating to oppose another on a particular grievance. The day of comradely unanimity had not yet arrived when grievances would be moulded into one or two great generalities, such as horizontal percentage increases and regional development, to which all could subscribe with a clear conscience, but with very cloudy recommendations.

With the Crow's Nest Pass level of rates now applying to export grain through Pacific ports, British Columbia's sole major grievance became the Mountain Differential. Domestic grain rates to the province were still excluded from the Crow's Nest level and this supplied a further talking point. For British Columbia, equalization meant nothing more than the removal of the Mountain Scale, but both Oliver and McGeer looked toward the day when there would be complete equality from coast to coast. Alberta supported British Columbia on the issue of the Mountain Differential, putting in second place the long-standing complaint of the boards of trade that the constructive mileage of the Fort William Terminal Class Rates gave an undue advantage to Winnipeg over cities located further west. This was closely followed by the transcontinental competitive rates, a post-war development that seemed to isolate Alberta "at the apex of the rate structure." Ranking after some grain rate revindications, equalization appeared at the bottom of Alberta's shopping list, thrust there undoubtedly by the realization that it would be illusory to expect both the Mountain Differential and the East-West rate differences to be removed at one stroke.

Progressing eastward the weight of positive demands diminishes and neutral and defensive positions become more prominent. For the most part, Saskatchewan's positions constituted a "me too" to Alberta's, but uttered much more softly and hesitantly. No major grievance existed for Saskatchewan to concentrate on and make its own, except for a number of minor complaints, including some local rate situations which were dwarfed in the national setting of the Investigation. On the transcontinental rates Saskatchewan saw itself as unaffected unless any of them were too low to be compensatory. Similarly, the province wished to remain "neutral" on the Mountain Differential, although it held that, if costs were higher, the differential should remain – a position shared by Canadian Pacific. In the case of Manitoba, defensive stances overshadowed any new rate demands. Manitoba, seconded by the Winnipeg Board of Trade, wanted to maintain any advantages that the Manitoba Agreement of 1901 had given the province in the constructive mileage between Winnipeg and Fort William. It opposed any reduction in the Mountain Differential, with Symington stating in his final argument that the Prairie rates were already too high compared with British Columbia's,[40] and that "Alberta has been and is better treated than any other Prairie province."[41] On the positive side, all that was left for Symington to do was to propose a very modest solution to the equalization issue, namely that the standard class rates should be put on the same basis in East and West (excluding, of course, the Mountain Territory) and that any departures should be authorized by acceptable reasons.[42] It was rather a tame solution to a problem that had been whipped up by exploiting some deeply felt resentment of Prairie people with their general position in the Canadian economy.

Ontario's appearance and active participation in the Investigation will surprise those familiar with the accustomed provincial lineups on the freight rate issue of later years, where Ontario and Quebec remained silently on the sidelines for the most part. In the General Freight Rate Investigation, Ontario, through its counsel J.R.L. Starr, KC, and a succession of witnesses, sought to defend the transcontinental competitive rates so greatly resented by Alberta. These were portrayed as primarily market competitive rates, since water competition was a greatly inferior service to rail. Starr even counterattacked on the equalization issue, making the wholly impermissible step of linking it with the Crow's Nest grain rates:

I submit, with all earnestness, that when they [the Prairie provinces] get the bulk of their traffic carried at a lower rate, they ought to be willing to pay a higher rate on the small amount of their traffic they do pay higher rates on, otherwise it would be unfair to the East.[43]

Quebec interests were represented by the City of Quebec and the Quebec Port Commission, with Louis St. Laurent acting as counsel for the latter. The main argument was that grain rates on the National Transcontinental, now part of the Canadian National System, should be such to enable a substantial all-rail grain movement to reach the port of Quebec. This project had turned out to be a most costly way of demonstrating that a railway can be built but traffic cannot be forced to move over it. The attractions of better service and lower rates using the water route from other Canadian or American ports doomed the line to degenerate to the status of a branch line. The Maritime Provinces participated from the start of the Investigation but transferred their efforts to their own particular enquiry – the Duncan Royal Commission on Maritime Claims, which was progressing concurrently. Near the conclusion of the Investigation, when it seemed that the Maritime Freight Rates Act (MFRA) would shortly be proclaimed, Maritime counsel obtained leave to withdraw from the proceedings.[44] With the MFRA on the statute books, the Maritimes withdrew from the national debate on freight rates as they had done before during the separate existence of the Intercolonial Railway. Only later when they found common cause in the newer issues of horizontal percentage increases and regional development, did they rejoin the Western dissidents.

The railways' position represented a reiteration of the stand they had taken in all the earlier investigations, a careful defence of the status quo by arguments that could not easily be turned against them. They carefully avoided commitment to any particular theory of rate-making. E.P. Flintoft, the CPR counsel, stated that "the rate problems cannot be adjusted on purely theoretical or academic lines."[45] They were able to express agreement in principle with the goal of equalization, but held that equity was not equivalent to equal rates, since rate-making must take into account the phrase in the Railway Act, "under substantially similar circumstances and conditions." Argument could go on without end on the meaning of this phrase. The arguments of some of the provinces against the removal of the Mountain Differential were identical to those of the railways. Their conclusion was that if costs were no longer higher in Pacific Territory then they would be agreeable to the removal of the higher rates. With regard to the differences in rate levels between East and West, Flintoft stated that "Western rates have not been made high to offset any losses in the East, and if the reasons held by the Board in the past to justify the Eastern basis no longer obtain, then the proper method of equalization is to raise the Eastern rates. That is our position."[46]

The terms of discussion insisted upon by the railways were based on previous judgements of the Board and the railways' responsibility to gain sufficient earnings from rates to cover expenses and make what profit they could. This has proved to be a particularly hard defence to crack throughout the history of the freight rate issue. In its most extreme form this argument led to a most rigid defence of the existing situation, since, in theory, it could be used to deny the need for any separate investigation of the rate structure. The existing rates had been approved by the Board, or at least not declared unreasonable, as recently as the Western Rates Case. Those who wanted change were limited to using two approaches: proving that mountain costs were no greater than Prairie costs, or demonstrating that there was no competition in Eastern Canada.

Provincial counsel wavered between acceptance of, or rebellion against, these terms of reference. McGeer tried manfully to meet the cost argument head on, but he also appealed to wider grounds, declaring at one point that P.C. 886, which disposed of the Crow's Nest issue, had inaugurated a new national policy with respect to rates.[47] Symington for Manitoba and Pitblado for the Winnipeg Board of Trade strongly supported the railway position on both costs and equalization, their demands in the latter case being little more than that equalization be granted a token recognition in the little-used standard class rates. While Alberta might be thought to have had the strongest reasons for wanting to break from the traditional justification of rates and rate levels, the provincial counsel, S.B. Woods, KC, declared himself ready and willing to play the game under the old rules:

> This I do know, that under the Railway Act this Board is absolutely unfettered in its discretion as to what it will take into account in fixing just and reasonable rates ... and if this Board fixes a rate ... that rate, *ex facie* is a fair and just and reasonable rate, and it is fallacious to discuss that subject upon the ground that there may be some intrinsic academic justice apart from this Board. The statute makes this Board the complete authority, subject to appeal, upon what is a just, fair and reasonable rate.[48]

This is a surprisingly strong self-denying ordinance. While it seems to justify the Board's acceptance of a principle of equity, it in no way makes it obligatory, leaving little basis for complaint with a decision of the Board. The accepted objective conditions – costs and competition – were sufficiently broad and vague to shelter almost any judgement within reason that the Board might be likely to make.

The historical significance of the General Investigation far overshadows the practical effects of any of its recommendations, which were extremely moderate reaffirmations of the position taken in the Western Rates Case.[49] The Mountain Differential was retained unchanged by a vote of four to two, on the general grounds that costs in the mountains were still higher than elsewhere. Similarly, East-West equalization was rejected on the grounds that competition was still effective in holding down Eastern rates. The earlier controversial judgement in the application of the Crow's Nest Pass rates in westbound export grain was reaffirmed, and the grain rate structure was modified to place Canadian National points in northern Alberta and Saskatchewan on the same basis as other Prairie stations. The distributing class rates were extended to apply to Canadian National points where formerly they had been restricted to points on the Canadian Pacific. With regard to the grain rates on the National Transcontinental to Quebec City, the Board took care to free itself from any charge that it was obstructing the original purpose of the railway by ordering a rate of 18.34 cents per hundredweight from Fort William and Armstrong, the comparable point on the NTR. The rate was given a good pedigree. Commissioner McLean explained that it was "not out of line with the rate from Calgary to Fort William" and "approximately on a level with" the lake-and-rail rate from Fort William to New York via Buffalo, all of which seemed designed to show that the ultimate in reasonable concessions had been made. Notwithstanding this, the rate remained purely a "paper" rate, symbolic of the victory of economics over politics. As compensation, Quebec City was equalized with Montreal for grain rates from Georgian Bay and other Ontario ports.

Despite the meagreness of the results after the investment of so much time and expense by the provincial governments, the General Investigation, together with the Crow's Nest Pass issue and the Duncan Commission, must be credited with laying a firm base for the ideological takeoff of the freight rate issue. The length of the hearings and the number of cities in which they were held (five points in Eastern Canada other than Ottawa, thirteen points in Western Canada, of which eight were in British Columbia, perhaps indicating the province which had been most active in "educating" its people on the subject of freight rates) were all calculated to impress firmly in the public mind the idea that freight rates were in the top rank of national issues, particularly for the regions outside of the Central Provinces. Even more important in the long run was the fact that, while giving wide publicity to what were interpreted as serious regional grievances, the Investigation left still alive and kicking most of the issues that the public could easily comprehend and associate with inequity. The Board played with each of these issues like a cat with a mouse, finally letting it get away so that it could become the object of another hunt. After so much strong resentment had been aroused in issues such as equalization, the Mountain Differential, and the transcontinental competitive rates, no one could doubt that it had been only one campaign in a continuing war. The Board's later specious arguments in favour of maintaining the existing situation were anything but convincing to people who by now had formed a firm conviction that they had been victimized by an arbitrary freight rate structure.

Perhaps the most important factor in keeping the issue alive, if only as a smouldering resentment capable of being blown into flames at any favourable time, was the treatment of the equity question. This was one factor that the public could easily grasp and felt most strongly about. The equity argument seemed to be self-evident and took priority over other considerations. Arguments opposing theoretical equity that tried to refer to the complex nature of railway costs, revenues, and rates were likely to be treated as irrelevancies designed to block the realization of equity. The Board's recital of precedents was regarded as stuffy legalism. The railway's stonewalling in defence of the existing rate structure was thought to be for selfish reasons. The most exasperation and scorn was aroused by the negative arguments used against equity, which seemed to be used as sandbags to plug any hole in the dyke. For example: "There may be discriminations in the rate but it is not unjust discrimination." Or, "There has been nothing to show that this rate is unreasonable in itself." Or, from the railways, "The Board already examined these rates in the Western Rates Case and found that they were not unreasonable." All these considerations were firmly embedded in the record and in the briefs and arguments prepared by provincial counsel and shippers' organizations. It was possible to claim that such arguments had in no way been invalidated by the Board's judgement, and they remained alive in folklore awaiting a new call to arms.

The mid-twenties was a period of major confrontation from which two regional "charters" emerged – the statutory grain rates and the Maritime Freight Rates Act – which were to serve in later years as evidence of the prime importance for all time of the freight rates issue. The twenties also marked the beginning of a major shift in transportation technology and service. The first intercity paved highway was built between Toronto and Hamilton in 1919, and the steady development of the motor truck and highways began to offer mounting competition to the railways. The results are all too well-known to need repeating, but it is important to note that the relationship of the railway to the other sectors of the economy underwent a radical change. Passenger services, less-than-carload traffic, and much of the high-rated general merchandise traffic was lost. Thousands of small businesses became independent of railway services, including many who had previously shown the greatest interest in rate matters and complained the loudest of the effects of the railway monopoly.

The ideology, however, remained firmly attached to the conditions that prevailed at the time of its origination during the great confrontations such as the Western Rates Case and the General Investigation. The memories of those conditions were kept alive in briefs and arguments to the Board, to various royal commissions, and to the federal government over the next fifty years. Remedies that had lost most of their relevance due to the passage of time were still demanded. In the process, transportation policy was to become transformed into a kind of witchcraft: a combination of incantatory spells, propitiatory gifts, and rites of exorcism to banish the evil spirits whose presence was felt everywhere but defied any concrete identification.

Freight Rates After 1927: The Ebb Tide

After several months of failing health, Premier Oliver of British Columbia died on August 20, 1927, just six days before the Board issued General Order 448, which implemented its judgement in the General Investigation. From this date on, interest in the freight rate issue rapidly dropped, despite the efforts of some provinces and counsel to keep it alive. It had been a long, exhausting struggle, and the costs to the provinces had been high, certainly in proportion to the results achieved. Since the General Investigation had had such wide terms of reference, it left little ground for raising new issues of any importance. New applications being out of the question, the only possibility of keeping the game going lay in the making of appeals against General Order 448. This had been an essential part of McGeer's tactics of permanent war. Since 1920 almost every Board judgement affecting British Columbia had been appealed. For McGeer it was simply a case of business as usual, but some months went by before anyone reacted. With the Liberal government in British Columbia facing an election in the spring of 1928, however, McGeer tried to persuade the new Premier, J.A. McLean, to appeal against the Board's failure to remove the Mountain Differential. McLean, who resembled a conscientious deputy minister by temperament and approach, had no interest in the freight rate question nor did he have any of Oliver's charisma or liking for the political game. He did not even accept McGeer's offer to serve without fees rather than "see the abandonment of the cause."[50]

When the Conservatives won the election on April 28, bringing Dr. Simon Fraser Tolmie into the Premier's office, McGeer was even further isolated, for the Conservatives had already made political capital out of the amount of the fees paid to him over the years. Despite the fact that McGeer was sitting in his office with all the knowledge, experience, and data, they could not afford to engage his services without suffering some loss of face. At the same time, if McGeer was going to keep the issue alive, they could not be indifferent to the subject. On June 23, 1928, a letter from A.M. Manson, Minister of Labour and Attorney General, informed McGeer that the four Western provinces had agreed to have Isaac Pitblado act for them. It was explained that the Government had accepted this "in view of the fact that this Province has borne the brunt of the rates fight."[51] This must have seemed like a betrayal of the cause to McGeer since Pitblado had acted for the Winnipeg Board of Trade in the General Investigation, and he and the Manitoba counsel had taken positions that had almost no common ground with those of British Columbia. After some preliminary sparring, McGeer flatly refused to send copies of exhibits in his possession to Pitblado and nothing further seems to have come of this attempted united front.

For the rest of the year McGeer pursued two possible appeals, one to the Supreme Court in the matter of the failure of the Board to make the Crow's Nest rates to Vancouver applicable on domestic as well as export grain, and another to the Governor-in-Council on the Mountain Differential. He failed to interest the Government in letting him make the appeal in his own name, offering once again to serve without fees "rather than see it drop."[52] The Government waited until January 7, 1928, before it appointed Leon J. Ladner, KC, a Conservative Member of Parliament, as its counsel. It was just in time, for McGeer's friends among the farmers' organizations had begun to protest his exclusion while the Winnipeg city solicitor was claiming that McGeer possessed no status to file and appeal. A routine visit of the Board to Vancouver in early January saw McGeer in his usual aggressive form, interrupting proceedings to make application for a blanket rate from points in the British Columbia interior on canned fruits, and setting into the record another attack on the low Eastern rates which "had been paid for by all of Canada due to the building of canals with tax revenue." The railways accused him of trying to reopen the General Investigation. However, the request to the Board for leave to appeal to the Supreme Court over the decision on the domestic grain rates saw a curious succession of events resulting from the provincial government's extreme caution in handling such a highly charged issue. First, McGeer applied in the name of the Fraser Valley farmers for whom he was acting, but stated that his application was made with the consent of the Attorney-General. Ladner followed with a formal application from the Attorney-General at the same time endorsing McGeer's application.

The following months saw a continual jockeying for position between McGeer and Ladner. A Conservative organizer complained to Ladner that McGeer was getting too much publicity, but Ladner had to move circumspectly since McGeer, with his experience and arsenal of documents, might pounce on anything that could be made to look like ineptitude.[53] The province changed its mind and decided to appeal to the Governor-in-Council and disputes arose over the date of the hearing. At this point McGeer seems to have decided to drop negotiations with the province and carry his case to the people, in this case an organization calling itself the United Farmers of British Columbia (UFBC). When Manitoba sought an adjournment of the date of the

hearing before Cabinet, McGeer was able to mount a successful telegram campaign to head it off. A certain crusading zeal becomes apparent in his thanks to the UFBC. He wrote, "with your support a right-
eous cause though out-numbered ten to one prevailed against the host
of error."[54] Letters in response to his campaign came from all quarters,
including some of the most unlikely. The Communist Party of British
Columbia saw freight rates as an instrument of exploitation. Even the
Knights of the Ku Klux Klan of Canada, Grand Realm Council of
British Columbia, felt obliged to put together a few paragraphs on
freight rates in support of McGeer in a letter signed "the Scribe in
charge of the Seal." McGeer's routine letter of acknowledgement was
duly addressed "Dear Scribe in charge of the Seal." McGeer offered
further evidence of his dedication to the cause in a letter to Prime
Minister King on November 29, 1929. In expressing the hopes that he
would not have to serve as counsel a second time at his own expense,
he nevertheless added that "The Honorable John Oliver declared before his death that we were in this fight to the finish and as far as I
am concerned I am going to make the Honorable Mr. Oliver's word
good."[55]

While McGeer's success in keeping the issue alive almost single-
handedly was an indication of the degree to which the concrete issues
had been transformed into a general ideology, the fact was that the
provinces had had enough, and the federal government wanted least
of all to see the issue revived in yet another election. Public feeling
being what it was, burying the issue involved a long, protracted funeral
ceremony during which all sides felt obliged to express doubts, and to
act as if the corpse were not really dead even while bringing it to the
ceremony. The Cabinet heard the British Columbia appeal on January
17, 1930, but did not give a decision. In September, the province
prodded the new Bennett government for a decision but the Cabinet
was preoccupied with an Imperial Conference being held in London.
On January 11, 1931, British Columbia, Alberta, and Saskatchewan
made a new formal request for action, and in the fall of the same year
Ladner had to ask again for a hearing. Similar requests were made in
March and October of the following year, but by now the Duff Royal
Commission on Railways was in progress, affording the federal government a new reason for procrastination. In January, 1933, a new
strategy was revealed when the Saskatchewan government confided
that it wanted to delay the appeal in order to keep the matter open. The
Cabinet finally got up its courage to throw out the appeal on February
25, 1933, and with that the last spark of the freight rate conflagration
of the twenties went out.[56]

This abandonment of the provincial interest for the time being did not stop others from plugging away on their own, particularly if their freedom of action was not restrained by being members of the party in power. On April 17, 1934, Thomas Reid, MP for New Westminster, introduced a resolution in the House calling for greater equality between rates on grain to British Columbia for export and domestic use. The Minister of Railways and Canals, R.J. Manion, deflected the thrust by advising that it should be referred directly to the properly authorized body – the Board of Railway Commissioners. Reid acted accordingly, leading his clients, the Frazer Valley Surrey Farmers' Cooperative Association, to the Board, only to have the Board once again reaffirm the existing situation in a judgement of January 19, 1935.[57] Long before this, however, government and public attention had been diverted to the immeasurably graver problems of the Great Depression. This was obviously an international and world-wide problem so that the distress and complaints did not flow through the usual regional channels of discontent. The few that did were on the matter of the protectionist tariff policy.

McGeer gave up the freight rate crusade but promptly found a new one in monetary policy, which had become a strong focal point of interest. He spoke and wrote widely with his same enthusiasm, exchanging correspondence with Major Douglas, the Social Credit founder, John Maynard Keynes, and Franklin D. Roosevelt, among others. He also entered into an active public life as Mayor of Vancouver, Member of Parliament, and Senator. His freight rate career tended to become forgotten during the eclipse of the issue, but by a stroke of poetic justice it was to end many years later in a final blaze of glory as the issue greeted a new dawn after the Second World War. In the *Ottawa Journal* of June 27, 1947, appeared an editorial entitled "McGeer to the Rescue." It is worth citing:

> Mr. McGeer who is, among other things, mayor of Vancouver and a Senator from British Columbia, is a man of extreme versatility. He proved this again the other day.
>
> The Board of Transport Commissioners was holding sessions in Vancouver, in its hearing of the application of the railways for an increase in freight rates, and the case for British Columbia against the increase was in a bad way because the chief counsel for the province, Mr. C.H. Locke, had just been appointed to the Bench. It was, says the Vancouver *News-Herald*, a field day for the railway lawyers, while B.C. business men looked on from the sidelines in "indignant frustration."
>
> Then into the crisis came Gerald McGeer – let the *News-Herald* tell the dramatic story:

"Into the situation stepped Senator G.G. McGeer, mayor of Vancouver, with two maps and an armful of books. For three hours to the noontime recess and for an hour and a half in the afternoon he talked the British Columbia rate case to the Commissioners without a written note. Freight traffic experts, newspapermen and others who had seen McGeer in the 20's winning his various freight rate battles before other members of the Board agreed that this was probably the most brilliant and effectual performance of 'Gerry's' colorful career. He left maps and most of his reference books behind him as records for the Commission.

"When he walked out of the room McGeer had done two things. He had picked up the floundering British Columbia case and put it back on solid ground. And he had left behind in the official transcript a priceless legacy of fact and argument upon which a later pleading for final removal of the mountain differential could be based."

Only a short time later, McGeer died suddenly. It was within a year of the Board's judgement removing the Mountain Differential. There is a delightfully ironic touch to McGeer's last stand, for it shows him true to his basic strategy of permanent war. The issue before the Board was an application for an increase in freight rates. McGeer, as well as other provincial counsel, took occasion to reiterate the now classic grievances that his province had with the rate structure as it stood, to demand that these should be rectified before any consideration be given to increases. In the freight rate arguments that arose after the Second World War, provincial counsel showed that they had learned much from the master tactician.

CHAPTER 4

The Maritimes: From Confederation to World War I

Anyone who overhears the current debate on the terms and meaning of Confederation with respect to the Maritime Provinces might be pardoned for concluding that it was all a matter of an agreement over freight rates, and that despite what had been concluded in 1867 and all that had been done since, the federal government had never lived up to its original undertaking. The preoccupation with freight rates in the Maritime Provinces is in its way as obsessive as that in the Prairie Provinces, though the two have had entirely different origins and histories. It is fascinating to trace their separate stories and to discover that as the respective ideologies became increasingly detached from the real world, they were able to meet and merge into a common doctrine of revindication against Ottawa. The evidence of this is the spectacle of three Prairie premiers and three Maritime premiers marching shoulder to shoulder to Parliament Hill to demand a "new transportation policy." That they are often accompanied by the premiers of British Columbia and Newfoundland is explained largely by sentiments of regional solidarity and the inclusion of other issues of broader interest. The demands are as vague as the ideology on which they are based and it is left to the federal government to perform the miracle of finding the answer. Perhaps this is because the only possible way of satisfying such vague demands would be to defray the entire costs of transportation by huge subsidies. There is, however, a certain reluctance, even at this late date, about being explicit on this point, particularly by a region experiencing unprecedented prosperity.

In approaching the history of the freight rate issue in the Maritime Provinces we need to be aware that there are two versions for the period from 1865 to 1912. The first describes what actually took place and what public opinion was. The second describes what has been read back into the history of that period by those who tried to anchor the freight rate issue in the terms of Confederation itself, beginning with the Maritime Rights Movement during the final years of the First

World War. We have seen the constitutional argument in connection with freight rates used by Premier Oliver of British Columbia. This argument was not available to the Prairie Provinces since they were created by the Dominion out of lands purchased from the Hudson's Bay Company. They did not negotiate their way into Confederation.

For the Maritimes, the constitutional argument had particular force. From the beginning the Maritimes were a small part of the expanding country, both in area and population, and they became an even smaller segment over the years. Their political weight in Confederation declined in the same measure, despite some holding points in representation in both the Senate and the House of Commons. Under these circumstances, if particular treatment was to be sought, it would be much more effective to trace the right to that treatment to the terms of Confederation by which it would become a constitutional obligation of the federal government. When the Maritime Provinces focused upon freight rates and transportation policy generally as the prime causes of their economic disability, it was natural that these should be found to have their origins in broken Confederation promises, unmindful of the fact that at the time of Confederation and for nearly fifty years after there seemed to have been little consciousness of these things.

When the freight rate history of the Intercolonial Railway was brought to light, largely through the efforts of F.J. Cornell, a traffic adviser employed by the Maritime governments, it seemed obvious that if there had ever been a critical period it began around 1912. At that time the newly elected Borden government, led by a Maritimer, laid its hands on the Intercolonial with the avowed purpose of running it like a business and started to raise rates. By the time of its absorption into the Canadian National system in 1923, rate levels in the Maritimes had been brought to parity with those in the Central Provinces. The recommendations of the Duncan Royal Commission (1926) were aimed at the restoration of the pre-1912 conditions, about which there had been no complaint at the time. Even before this, however, the Maritime Rights Movement had opted wholly for the Confederation argument, and the official interpretation had become, in a phrase that is taken up again and again by political rhetoricians, that Maritime industry has been "strangled by freight rates."[1]

In the early years, there was little trace of these subsequent connotations that have been squeezed out of the constitution. The Fathers of Confederation, like most of their contemporaries in the early growth period of the railways, were mainly concerned that the Intercolonial Railway should be built. The colonies of New Brunswick and Nova Scotia did not have the resources for this task, but with the enlarged credit base of the new Dominion it became practicable to make railways an obligation of the federal government.

Within Ontario and Quebec there seems to have been little economic interest in having an all-weather, all-Canadian route to Atlantic ports to escape dependence on American routes and ports. The British government was strongly in favour of the line for this reason. Apart from some general language to the effect that trade between the two regions would be stimulated by the mere presence of the railway, the level of rates and traffic seem to have been largely unconnected with any Confederation obligation. It is safe to say that they were not regarded as a problem and it occurred to no one to make any stipulations regarding them. The federal government's obligation was to maintain and operate the railway, to which perhaps could be added an implicit obligation to charge a level of rates that would reasonably encourage traffic. Here we must be careful, lest we read into situations of a hundred years ago the public attitude of today toward railway rates and subsidies. This was the period of the full flowering of the laissez-faire philosophy in economics, even though the railways were creating new complications, such as monopoly and capital assistance by governments, that made inroads on the practice of the doctrine. Trade chose its own routes, and apart from the custom tariff, governments neither made nor were called upon to make any direct intervention. Typical of this view was Prime Minister Alexander Mackenzie's statement to Parliament in 1877 that he "had arrived at the conclusion that no government should have anything to do with the governing or controlling of commercial affairs" and that there was "no more reason why a government should work a railway than a cotton mill."[2] There was no concerted challenge to such a view, neither on constitutional nor on any other grounds.

Discussions in the House of Commons on the Intercolonial Railway over the years reflected this consensus. Had it been different, the House would have been the obvious forum in which to raise other opinions, especially if they concerned political or constitutional obligations. The early discontent with Confederation in Nova Scotia, for example, was based mainly on financial matters and had no reference to transportation. Even the secessionist appeal, with which Premier Fielding won the 1886 provincial election, seems to have contained no transportation complaints but to have been a tactical manoeuvre to extract better financial terms from the federal government.[3] In any case, opposition to secession was strongest in Cape Breton and in Guysborough County, where federal support was being sought to complete railway projects. Secessionism and the railway promises are at opposite poles since the former implied forgoing the latter.

From time to time there were indeed complaints about freight rates by Maritime members in the House, but they were scattered and mostly mild in tone. They could not be suspected of being the ancestors of the modern species, nor do they foreshadow any awareness of the "constitutional promises" that have since been injected into the discussion. Thus a Prince Edward Island member stated that his province had few grievances with its railway, asking only a "slight diminution in rates charged for freight and passenger traffic."[4] (What M.P. could ask for less!) Again in the same year the member for Northumberland (N.B.), Jabez Bunting Snowball, stated: "There has been a great deal of complaint lately that the rates of freight are in excess of what they have previously been since the Intercolonial was opened ... another complaint is that goods are carried at through rates for less than rates to intermediate points."[5] There were also complaints of increased rates in 1890 when the Intercolonial adopted the Central Freight Classification.

For the most part, however, Maritime members seemed content to defend the existing level of rates on the Intercolonial against the attacks of Ontario members who affected to be shocked at the low efficiency and the operating deficits of the line.[6] An unfailing reply to these attacks was to point to the canals in Central Canada which had been built at public expense and had been toll-free since 1903. Ottawa did recognize that the Intercolonial was not to be run as a privately-owned railway. Sir Charles Tupper commented in 1888: "In reference to government railways, I do not think we can attempt to make them pay. Our object is not to make a profit out of them, but to promote the trade and business of the country."[7]

In the course of introducing his estimates in the House, it was the custom for many years of the Minister of Railways and Canals to make a general statement and review of the operations of the Intercolonial to afford members the opportunity to ask questions or air their grievances. He was generally able to begin his remarks by noting that the Intercolonial had the lowest rates of any railway in the world.[8] These rates increasingly came under criticism as deficits rose. In 1905, the Minister, H.R. Emmerson, made what sounded like a policy statement:

The Intercolonial has fixed rates. There may come a time when it may be necessary to depart from this policy, but that is not likely to come until Parliament has equipped the Intercolonial as it should be equipped, and it is then still found impossible by a large sum to make ends meet.[9]

The time came much sooner than he had expected. In the following year he was to report that rates had been increased by ten per cent.[10]

While Maritimers were to defend the Intercolonial as something of their own, they would hardly have claimed at any time that it had been

an unqualified success. In fact, there had been several disappoint-
ments. Although lower rates were maintained on westbound traffic, in
1906 three-quarters of the traffic was eastbound.[11] The railway was
bringing manufactured goods from the Central Provinces into the
Maritimes but carrying very little Maritime traffic back. Most serious of
all, and most closely connected with the aspirations of Confederation,
the Intercolonial proved unable to attract traffic to the port of Halifax.
Much the same applied to Saint John after Canadian Pacific completed
a much shorter route in 1888. For this both geography and economics
were responsible. The strength of ocean competition through St.
Lawrence ports had not been foreseen, since too great a competitive
strength had been attributed to the railways.

Furthermore, the Intercolonial was poorly integrated into the continental railway network. It was dependent on the Grand Trunk for
export traffic, yet the latter served not only Montreal and Quebec but
also Portland, Maine. Combination rates mitigated against the Intercolonial route, even to the extent that flour from southwestern Ontario
could be routed more cheaply to Halifax via Boston and schooner.[12]
Concerning Western grain, Ottawa found itself powerless to insist on
an all-Canadian route to an Atlantic port, even had railway and port
capacity been adequate. The railways turned grain over to the lake
carriers at the Lakehead and so lost control of the movement, although
even there, there was no question of interfering with a shipper's right
to choose the route. Most Canadian grain was discharged at Buffalo
and found its way by the Erie Canal or rail to a United States Atlantic
port. What grain went through the Welland and St. Lawrence Canals
would be exported from Montreal. During the years that Western
grain production was increasing, the federal government was too
deeply involved in railway extensions in Western Canada to perfect
either the routes or the rates to the Atlantic. It was not that it did not
try. The National Transcontinental Railway was a very costly attempt
to pay off a number of political debts. Built from Winnipeg to Moncton
through what was then largely unsettled country, it was to connect the
Grand Trunk with its new subsidiary in Western Canada (the Grand
Trunk Pacific), give the Western farmer a direct route to the Atlantic,
secure for the port of Quebec a share of the grain trade, and finally,
with the extension to Moncton – said to be a compromise choice over
Halifax or Saint John – it was to put the Atlantic ports on the main line
for the grain trade. This stupendous effort was not an economic
project in any sense of the word but rather a sort of monument in ties
and rails to the government's faith in transportation as the way of
solving problems and promoting national growth. It probably has
played a part in instilling in the public mind the idea of the prime

importance of transportation to growth and prosperity. When the building of the lines themselves – the Intercolonial, Canadian Pacific, and National Transcontinental – did not bring about the millennium, emphasis shifted to the rates they charged. The railways were a good thing. All that was wrong was that the rates were too high to bring about the expected development. In the West, it was claimed that Canadian Pacific fattened itself on its monopoly position, and in the East, under the newly perfected doctrine, it was claimed that government policy maintained rates on the Intercolonial in disregard of "promises" made at the time of Confederation.

Another factor delayed the awareness of Maritimers to the political value of the freight rates issue. Being operated by the government, the Intercolonial was not put under the jurisdiction of the new Board of Railway Commissioners in 1903. Thus the Maritimes watched, as distant and uninterested spectators, the first major round of cases involving the rate structure in other parts of the country – the Vancouver and Coast Cities Case; the Regina Toll Case; the Eastern Rates Case; and the Western Rates Case. As long as rates on the Intercolonial were the "lowest in the world," the main problem was building up traffic through Maritime ports. Part of this was the extension of the Intercolonial to Montreal where it could interchange with other railways in addition to the Grand Trunk. Internal feuding, as we saw in Western Canada, also blunted the issue in the Maritime Provinces. Here it was the rivalry between the ports of Halifax and Saint John. Canadian Pacific's short route to Saint John threatened to undermine the whole basis of the Intercolonial's operations, and agitation arose to extend it westward to Montreal and to maintain the low rates in the face of the new competition. For many years Halifax campaigned for rate equality with Saint John on export and import traffic, finally succeeding over the protests of Saint John.

A gradual consolidation of regional opinion on transportation policy was ultimately initiated by changes with respect to the Intercolonial when the Borden administration took over in 1911. The Conservatives were then the business and protectionist party, having a power base in Ontario and being much weaker in the outlying regions. Running the government and government undertakings as a business seemed to be a self-evident proposition. There were comparatively few government-managed operations in those days, and their performances tended to stand out as glaring exceptions. The Intercolonial Railway was an obvious target for the reformers. Apart from what was then the scandal of the annual deficits, its detractors in Parliament had long charged that it was riddled with political patronage and simply operated in an inefficient manner. In the past, Maritime MP's had had no serious difficulties turning aside such criticisms.

But a new twist in 1912 aroused their forebodings as to the purpose of the new administration. The Intercolonial reported a small surplus, due in part to an increase in freight rates. For more than forty years it had been operated on a loosely defined premise of a national purpose. Since this principle had rarely been challenged there had been little need for the Maritime Provinces to order their thoughts on the subject in any more explicit fashion. Discussions in Parliament on the Intercolonial were almost entirely concerned with practical matters and led to no regional confrontation on fundamental assumptions. But this new challenge could not be sidestepped. In no way could Maritime opinion accept the proposition that the Intercolonial should be run just as any other business. Thus, Maritimers found themselves outlining a regional philosophy in Confederation which, as it moved to wider issues, gave birth to the Maritime Rights Movement. Here we have located the source of the very high priority given to the freight rate issue in the Maritime Provinces. Since the only economic clause in the British North America Act referred to the Intercolonial, and since it was an issue affecting the Intercolonial that forced a self-examination on the part of the Maritimers, the Maritime problem became identified with a railway problem. Because constitutional arguments seemed to be the most effective weapon for a small area to use to gain its ends, and the constitution mentioned obligations connected with a railway, Maritimers felt obliged for many years to prove that all they wanted from Confederation would be achieved through freight rates. And this was something they felt had been promised to them, if only implicitly, in the Act and the prior discussions. While events in 1912 precipitated the self-examination, for the effectiveness of the argument it was necessary for it to be backdated to utilize the negotiations prior to Confederation to support the thesis. If Maritimers had not raised the issue between 1867 and 1912 it could only have been because they had been asleep at the switch and had abandoned the assertion of their rights.

The Minister's announcement in the House of the surplus on the Intercolonial produced an immediate reaction from E.M. Macdonald, for many years member for Pictou.

> The Intercolonial Railway has no business to have a surplus. Every dollar that is reported as a surplus on the Intercolonial Railway means so much money taken out of the pockets of the people of the Maritime Provinces and for no good....
>
> If a Minister of Railways has a surplus on the Intercolonial, it is not to his credit but to his discredit, for the reason that he has discrimi-

nated against the people of the Maritime Provinces in making them pay more than they had necessity to pay.[13]

Already the future stance of the Maritime Provinces can be seen taking form. There is no indication that the Fathers of Confederation were opposed to the Intercolonial being a profitable venture or at least making ends meet. While rates were kept low, in line with the national purpose of the railway, there had been little challenge to the principle that the railway should show as favourable a financial position as possible. Macdonald's statement indicates the shifting of the ground from defence of the deficits as regrettable, but unavoidable, to a claim that the deficits on the Intercolonial were a right of the Maritime Provinces. During the next ten years the participants in the Maritime Rights Movement were able to produce a formal justification of this position, tracing it back to the intentions of those who had accepted the British North America Act. In doing so, they embodied claims so sweeping in nature that they would have been impossible to attribute to the minds of politicians acting in the economic climate of the 1860's. Once the inhibitions regarding deficits and subsidies were removed, the new position took form rapidly. A.H. Smith, the third member of the Drayton-Acworth Commission, which in 1917 considered the problem of the two bankrupt transcontinental railways and various government-owned lines, noted in his minority report the presence of this new Maritime attitude toward the Intercolonial: "Evidently its rates are too low or its expenses are too high, but the use of this line, at the rates enforced, is regarded in some quarters as a right of the people of the Maritime Provinces."[14] Ten years later the Duncan Commission recorded its surprise in finding the same attitudes widespread in the area.[15]

Despite early rumblings of discontent, the government went ahead with its plan of making the Intercolonial a paying proposition. In 1913, a former Canadian Pacific official, F.P. Gutelius, was appointed general manager and was given the full support of the Minister to place the road upon a business basis. Freight rates were raised and the Board of Management was replaced by Gutelius as sole commissioner. The rates took effect on June 2, 1913. In August a deputation from the Maritimes saw the Minister to protest. In response, some rate concessions were made.[16]

The outbreak of the First World War in 1914 brought about a truce in these matters, but even before the end of the war a new cycle of events began that culminated in building up the freight rates issue as *the* grievance in the Maritime Provinces. While freight rates never ceased to be important from the earliest days in Western Canada, the new Maritime attitudes, which now came to resemble the much earlier Western ones, were developed within a period of scarcely more than ten years. The peak of the development was reached in the Crow's Nest Pass statutory rates and General Freight Rate Investigation for Western Canada and in the Duncan Royal Commission and the Maritime Freight Rates Act for the Maritimes. All that occurred between 1925 and 1927. What has followed since then has been ideology.

CHAPTER 5

Establishing the Freight Rate Issue in the Maritimes, 1919-1927

The new business-oriented policy on the Intercolonial was, as we have seen, construed as a threat to whatever benefits the Maritime Provinces had ever gained from Confederation. In the years following, the general rate increases had been applied in Maritime Territory as well as in the rest of Canada, and were seen as a renewed threat to the special independent status of the Intercolonial. The financial collapse of the Canadian Northern and Grand Trunk Railways had brought on the Drayton-Acworth Royal Commission, which pointed toward a consolidation of the various lines under government ownership with a single management. This rationalization became a reality in 1921, reducing the Intercolonial to the status of a small division of the national system.[1] Thus, the Intercolonial lines became subject to the jurisdiction of the Board of Railway Commissioners whose powers under the Railway Act included no reference to special regional considerations or constitutional "promises."

The war economy had made a big difference in the Maritime Provinces. Halifax had become the busiest port in the country and industrial production had reached new heights, demonstrating what might have been the case had policy in peacetime been given a similar direction. The aftermath of war was a disaster for the area. The war-stimulated port traffic and industrial production dropped catastrophically in the post-war inflation period and idle factories and coal mines gave rise to serious unemployment. Unlike other parts of the country, the Maritime economy had little power to rebound to "normal" conditions and threatened to sink back into the sluggish pace of the pre-war years. It was easy to conclude that freight rates, which had gone up and stayed up, were the prime villains responsible for the "strangling" of Maritime industry.

Maritime opinion was in no mood to bear silent witness to this relapse. The wartime changes had awakened a mood of self-examination and comparison. Wartime political exhortations amounting to a Canadian equivalent of Lloyd George's promise to make Britain "a land fit for heroes to live in," created an expectation of better days and a feeling that the federal government had a responsibility to bring it about. The first gun to be fired could be said to be a speech in the Nova Scotia legislature in 1917 by J.C. Tory, Minister of Finance, in which he demanded that the federal government reduce freight rates on goods exported from or shipped to the Maritime Provinces in fulfilment of the undertakings given in connection with the Intercolonial Railway. This makes it clear that attention was directed to the freight rate issue because of what was happening or threatening to happen to the Intercolonial.

It took a few years for the grievances to focus on the freight rate problem since other aspects were still being given attention. The Maritime premiers took an active part in the Interprovincial Conference held in Ottawa in 1918, when possible compensation to offset the federal concessions of lands in the Western Provinces was discussed. In the same year, J.B.M. Baxter, Conservative Attorney-General of New Brunswick, came out strongly for Maritime Union in a speech to the Moncton Canadian Club. He said such a union would result in less expensive government and increased influence in national affairs.

When we look at the particular position of the Maritime Provinces in Confederation, and the then accepted limits to government intervention in the economy as well as issues in railway transportation at that time, it would appear almost inevitable that the post-war Maritime grievances and revindications should be channelled into freight rates. The strongest arguments would have to be traced back to those sections in the British North America Act that referred to transportation.

The Maritime Provinces had their own direct concerns over freight rates – the wartime horizontal percentage increases had applied to the Intercolonial. They were also observing closely the freight rate agitation being conducted by the West. While they disapproved of the actual aims of the Western Provinces, seeing the Crow's Nest rates as a burden of which they would have to bear a share,[2] they could hardly fail to note the political effectiveness of the freight rate issue, not only in gathering local support and in giving hard-pressed provincial governments a distraction from local problems to offer the electorate,[3] but also in winning actual concessions from the federal government. Chronologically, the Intercolonial issue and the general freight rate increases came first, and concentration on these yielded a theory of "Maritime Rights," tracing back to Confederation the origins of the contemporary economic plight of the Maritime Provinces. Later economic difficulties, port problems, and the disappearance of the Intercolonial into the Canadian National only served to reinforce the original position which had quickly become political orthodoxy. It was taken up by the boards of trade, newspapers, and politicians, and today, more than fifty years later, it continues to serve as a credo of the Maritime position, claiming a continuous existence since Confederation. Those who today accept it as unquestioned fact are unaware that it arose as an ad hoc response to the situation in the decade following the First World War.

Our immediate problem is to discover how a dissatisfaction with a depressed economy, such as the Maritime Provinces experienced in the early twenties, should have become channelled almost into a single cause and a single remedy – freight rates. We have seen many instances of current problems in transportation, and fears for the loss of certain transportation advantages, but the problem certainly involves many more factors, some of which are unquestionably fundamental to any explanation of regional differences. While it would not be accurate to state that the Maritime Provinces, in taking stock of their economic situation, put all their eggs in the one basket, insofar as popular acceptance and understanding of the matter is concerned, the freight rate argument contains the quintessence of the protest against the disabilities that Confederation is said to have imposed upon them.

A consolidation of views quickly took place. In 1919 the Maritime Board of Trade was revived, which meant that Halifax and Saint John had buried their rivalries in order to present a united front along with the provinces on the main issue of the day. On June 1, 1921, the *Canadian Annual Review* reported that "a large delegation from the Maritime Provinces, the first since 1867 in which the three provinces had been united, waited upon the government at Ottawa. It urged that the Intercolonial Railway should be put back on the basis established at Confederation and be put under the control of the Department of Railways."[4] In the same year, the Nova Scotia legislature passed the following resolution on transportation:

> Faithful observance of the terms and conditions of the compact of Confederation and a generous national spirit require that the convenience, accommodation and welfare of the people and of the industrial interest of the Maritime Provinces be steadily kept in view as the primary purpose to be achieved in the administration of the Intercolonial Railway.[5]

Seeing the phrase "compact of Confederation," we may be confident in having detected the presence behind the scenes of the great theoretician of the Maritime Rights Movement – A.P. "Sandy" Patterson of New Brunswick. Patterson was active in the Liberal Party in New Brunswick for many years and was interested and involved in the

Maritime Rights discussions in the early stages. When the Boards of Trade formed the Maritime Rights Transportation Committee, Patterson became its first president. Although not a lawyer by training he had plunged deeply into the issues and circumstances of Confederation and the British North America Act. One may suppose that he was originally led in this direction by a concern, shared by many Maritimers, over the apparent loss of the unique status of the Intercolonial in Confederation.

The course of development of Patterson's theory and its wide acceptance in the Maritime Provinces becomes more understandable if we try to reproduce the workings of his mind. Thus we must look at his conception of the threat (the loss of the status of the Intercolonial), the most effective method of meeting this threat (linking it to constitutional obligations), the nature of the demonstration (Section 66 of the London Agreement which he referred to as the "Confederation Treaty"), and the inferences to be drawn from it for federal policy (that the Maritime Provinces were entitled to rates on the Intercolonial that would enable them to market their products in the rest of Canada). This places his program in its contemporary context. It was essentially a case for immediate action, and in that regard was geared to what was politically and economically practical. Patterson's argument provided a basis for Maritime claims, and must be given some credit for the practical concessions won, notably the Maritime Freight Rate Act, without its ever having been accepted in the rest of the country. Its logical impact was much less than its emotional impact. Like a battle cry, the Patterson argument rallied Maritime spokesmen, giving them dignity and self-confidence while making their demands. Significantly, Patterson's broader views on the constitution, which seem to have been originally a by-product of his prime concern with freight rates, aroused very little response in any quarter. In my view, however, they seem to go more deeply into the whole problem of regional discontent and are therefore of much more lasting interest than the ad hoc case he was able to put together in the matter of freight rates.[6] It was the latter that evoked a most enthusiastic response from his fellow Maritimers and provided the main structure for the Maritime version of the freight rates ideology, which, like its Western parallel, took essential form in the early twenties.

Patterson's argument about the status of the Intercolonial Railway under Confederation was based in the history of the successive drafts of what became Section 145 of the British North America Act. We will confine our attention there, hoping to avoid becoming entangled in the many complex and controversial issues that have surrounded the Confederation negotiations and the Act itself.

Section 145 of the Act reads as follows:

Inasmuch as the Province of Canada, Nova Scotia and New Brunswick have joined in a declaration that the construction of the Intercolonial Railway is essential to the consolidation of the Union of British North America and to the assent thereto of Nova Scotia and New Brunswick, and have consequently agreed that provision should be made for its construction by the Government of Canada. Therefore, in order to give effect to that Agreement, it shall be the duty of the Government and Parliament of Canada to provide for the commencement within six months after the Union, of a railway connecting the River St. Lawrence and the City of Halifax in Nova Scotia, and for the construction thereof without intermission and the completion thereof with all practicable speed.[7]

At the Quebec Conference in 1864, two resolutions were passed referring to transportation and communications:

No. 68 – The General Government shall secure without delay the completion of the Intercolonial Railway from Rivière-du-Loup through New Brunswick to Truro in Nova Scotia.
    No. 69 – The communications with the North-Western Territory, and the improvements required for the development of the trade of the great West with the Seaboard, are regarded by this conference as subjects of the highest importance to the Federated Provinces and shall be prosecuted at the earliest possible period that the state to finances will permit.[8]

At the London Conference, held just prior to the drafting of the Bill for introduction in the British Parliament, these resolutions were re-numbered and changed as follows:

No. 65 – The construction of the Intercolonial Railway being essential to the consolidation of the Union of British North America, and to the assent of the Maritime Provinces thereto, it is agreed that provision be made for its immediate construction by the General Government, and that the Imperial Guarantee of £3,000,000 sterling pledged for this work be applied thereto, so soon as necessary authority has been obtained from the Imperial Parliament.[9]

No. 66 is the same as old No. 69 with the exception that the words "Federated Provinces" have been replaced by the word "Confederation."

On Sir John A.Macdonald's advice the results of the London Conference were not published since that would re-open the disputes and jeopardize the passage of the Bill, a point Patterson was able to demonstrate by quoting a letter from Macdonald to Sir S.L. Tilley, the First Minister of the New Brunswick government:

> It appears to us to be important that the Bill should not be finally settled until just before the meeting of the British Parliament. The measure must be carried *per saltum* (by leap or jump); and no echo of it must reverberate through the British Provinces until it becomes law.
>
> If the delegation had been complete in England, and they had prepared the measure in August last, it would have been impossible to keep its provisions secret until next January.
>
> There will be few important clauses in the measure that will not offend some interest or individual, and its publication would excite new and fierce agitation on this side of the Atlantic. Even Canada, which has hitherto been nearly a unit on the subject of Confederation would be stirred to its depths if any material alterations were made.
>
> The Act once passed and beyond remedy, the people would soon learn to be reconciled to it.[10]

Of the original two resolutions regarding transportation and trade only a simple section was included in the Act, which on careful reading will be seen to refer only to the "construction" of a railway by the Government of Canada as being essential to the Union. Good reasons can be given for this wording. The British Parliament, after its experience with the colonies which became the United States, had, in principle, avoided legislating on any matters deemed to be the internal affairs of a self-governing colony. Macdonald had argued that the construction of the railway was not a part of the Constitution, but yielded to the outcry against its proposed exclusion from the Act, and Section 145 was made acceptable to British parliamentary principles by its lengthy preamble stressing that the construction was the will of the governments concerned and not something being imposed upon them by the Imperial Parliament. Macdonald's original position had been accepted by Governor Gordon of New Brunswick, as shown in an interesting dispatch from Gordon to the Colonial Secretary:

> Mr. J.A. Macdonald, a leading member of the Canadian Government, is reported to have used what appears to me very sensible language in connection with this subject, to the effect that the con-

struction of the Railway was certainly not part of the Constitution (a proposition that is self evident) and that, consequently, *with many other details agreed to by the Conference*, it would not be embodied in the Imperial Act, but that it was one of the conditions on which the Union was based and must therefore be carried into effect at the earliest possible period by the Legislature of the Federated Provinces.[11]

The phrase emphasized in Gordon's letter refers to the critical point in Patterson's argument, namely that the Act itself did not embody all the undertakings given at the time of Confederation. If he could successfully take this last hurdle he was in the clear and could safely infer not only what was actually contained in the resolutions of the earlier conferences, but from after-dinner speeches, appeals to the common sense, and intentions of the participants, supplementing their foresight with his own hindsight. In this respect we find him using arguments directly parallel to those Premier Oliver of British Columbia was using before the Cabinet and the Board of Railway Commissioners. His basic inference on the position of the Intercolonial might be summed up in the following passage:

> And it must be equally clear that, never for a moment, would Nova Scotia and New Brunswick have accepted the I.C.R. [Intercolonial] as the *quid pro quo* for their Confederation sacrifices had they not been definitely promised that is would be operated as a National Work which would eliminate their geographical handicap in relation to commerce with the rest of Canada. The I.C.R. was the one outstanding advantage that the Maritimes were to receive from Confederation. It was offered to offset, in some measure, all the other results of Confederation which augured so disadvantageously for them. Further, it was plain that unless the Railway were operated so as to eliminate Maritime geographical disadvantages within the Union, it could not enable them to trade with the rest of Canada.[12]

It is a fascinating, ingenious, and closely reasoned argument, at least until it gets by that last hurdle which allows him free rein to include as much as he likes in the federal obligations proceeding from Confederation. Patterson, however, could not afford to congratulate himself on the precision of his argument since, from the point of view he espoused, it had to appear as something that was wholly obvious and self-evident. And obvious and self-evident it has since appeared to many Maritimers who have been persuaded by it that promises, even if only implicit, were made to them; promises which, even today, if taken literally, stagger the imagination of anyone having to find a way to effectively implement them. We must turn next to examine the probable nature of the understandings openly or tacitly arrived at in the immediate pre-Confederation period.

Among other things, Patterson's argument involved reading the thoughts of the participants in the Confederation negotiations, or even reading thoughts into their minds, but naturally this created little impression when related to the courts or to the Rowell-Sirois Commission on Dominion-Provincial Relations in 1937. The Commission's staff gave the New Brunswick case a thorough examination and rejected it.[13] (At that time, Patterson was Minister of Education and Minister for Federal Affairs in the New Brunswick government, a position tailored to his own interests and projects.) To go behind the language of the statute is always a perilous step, much like opening a gate for hungry stock to get to waving fields of grain. Once past that gate, Patterson had tried to appropriate all possible benefits in sight. Taken even at its face value, the language of London Resolution 66 was far too general to support the extravagant claims that Patterson tried to tie to it. The Commission even pointed out that Resolution 66 had been of Upper Canadian origin to reconcile Upper Canadians to the construction of the Intercolonial.[14]

To operate the Intercolonial so as to "eliminate" Maritime geographical disadvantages and to enable Maritime natural and industrial products to be marketed anywhere in the rest of the country, which today remains more of a slogan than a program, could hardly have entered the minds of those who were engaged in business or politics in 1867. If taken literally, the enormity of such a claim would greatly damage its credibility. This may explain why it had remained a safety valve for regional discontent with no serious attempt having been made to seek its implementation except in very general ways such as rate freezes, reductions covered by subsidy, modifications of horizontal percentage increases, and so on. To my knowledge, it has not been seriously proposed that to enable a Maritime manufacturer to compete in Toronto with a Toronto manufacturer, the "terms" of Confederation require the railway freight rate to be nil. If one shrinks from drawing this logical conclusion, the ground of the argument has been changed and the problem is no longer a choice between black and white, but a matter of degree, in which other relevant considerations must be taken into account.[15] Otherwise, freight rates would be required to compensate for all other unfavourable factors that might exist in the situation, whether there are diseconomies of small-scale production, productivity, managerial capability and efficiency, pricing and marketing policies, distribution, research, brand-name advertising, or the smallness of the local market. Facile solutions to regional problems such as these have not been suppressed. They have never existed.

And yet, the Rowell-Sirois Commission's refutation of Patterson's arguments leaves something to be desired. For one thing, decisive as the Commission's argument may appear to be, it has hardly budged Patterson's theory one bit from the firm place it has come to occupy in Maritime belief. Politicians, newspapers, business association spokesmen, and the average Maritimer in parlour or tavern discussion will appeal, as a matter of course, to the "promises" of Confederation. This alone would indicate that there are some even more strongly based implicit arguments underpinning the freight rate arguments. The Commission's discussion seems to overlook Patterson's point that, under British practice, the legislation contained, apart from the carefully constructed language of Section 145, nothing that might be regarded as matters of internal policy. Yet there undoubtedly were some understandings regarding the Intercolonial that distinguished it from other railways. But these were products of the economic thinking of the times, so much so that they were accepted almost without question or protest and were regarded as fulfilment of the Confederation obligation. Thus, the Intercolonial was forgiven interest on its capital debt and was not required to charge rates that would ensure an annual surplus. As we have seen, as late as 1905, the rates on the Intercolonial were described by the Minister of Railways as fixed, and the railway did its best under the circumstances, making some rates extremely low in order to move important traffic, notably coal. Only when this state of affairs appeared to have been disturbed by the rate increases beginning in 1912 was Maritime attention directed back to the basis of the Intercolonial's operation. One result of this was the formulation of Patterson's theory.

Patterson's biggest problem was to account for those first fifty years of Confederation during which Maritime opinion betrayed almost no knowledge of the Confederation positions that he had so strongly attributed to them. Were they lost in a Rip Van Winkle-like sleep, or was Patterson imperiously rewriting history? Patterson's difficulties here are obvious, and he talks here and there in his writings about Maritimers having been patient while awaiting the fulfilment of the promises, and having tried "quietly and courteously to point out that they were not receiving a square deal."[16] On the other hand, he conceded that:

Macdonald did not forget the pledges given to the Maritimes, and it is but fair to say that while he and others responsible for Confederation remained in power, the Federal Government did in some degree, at least, fulfill its Maritime obligations; but subsequent efforts of the Federal Government to implement Confederation pledges have been frustrated by Central Canadian interests.[17]

This seems to point directly to the years around 1912 as those of the great awakening and Patterson would appear to have unwittingly slipped back into describing history the way things actually happened.

The conclusions can be tentatively summarized at this point. Over a long period Maritimers' protests against Confederation were based on unsatisfactory federal-provincial relations rather than transportation or freight rates in any explicit way; first, because there had been nothing beyond the construction of the Intercolonial specified in the British North America Act; and second, because they, like all others in the Western world during that period, accepted the verdicts of economics as something beyond the sphere of government intervention.

The slow growth or stagnant state of Maritime ports was a constant source of dissatisfaction but no drastic government interference with the free flow of commodity trade was ever seriously proposed. Regional dissatisfaction, when it built up from numerous causes in the early twenties, was thus lacking a forceful point of attack. The Maritimes were more faithful to free enterprise than the Western Provinces, who shocked business opinion by their socialistic demands for a permanent Wheat Board, but left open the question of what to do about the backwardness of the Maritime economy. There was understandable reluctance to attribute their difficulties either to the will of God, to the verdict of geography, or to some deficiencies on their own part. There was also the hard fact that Maritime influence, both political and economic, was small and declining relative to the rest of the country. Yet the solution to the problem could not be found within the Maritimes themselves but was linked to their association with the other provinces in Confederation. The tariff policy was increasingly seen as a dead end, in terms of the reductions that would be acceptable to Canadian manufacturing interests concentrated in the Central Provinces and the minimal efficacy that any such concessions would have in relieving the economic plight of the area.

Left in this situation, the Maritime Rights Movement, having run out of ammunition both in theory and in practical proposals, would have expired, becoming no more than a few random shots by scattered individuals. It is not necessary to claim that Patterson was either the sole originator or proponent of the views described here, but like a popular tune, his composition caught on almost immediately and everyone was humming it. Going back to the constitution and the debates that preceded it provided the leverage felt to be necessary to influence national policy. Such an approach also laid the main responsibility on the federal government. For the next fifty years this strategy linked Maritime regional grievances and demands to freight rates, regardless of the complexities of the regional problem and despite the rather obvious inadequacy of freight rate measures to satisfy the enormous demands and expectations placed upon them. If Patterson's theory provided the justification, a subsequent detailed analysis of the freight rate structure suggested the concrete measures that federal policy might take. That the theory went back to 1867 while the practical effects could only be traced as far back as 1912 did not seem a serious inconsistency; although Patterson's theory might lose all the pitched battles, as far as Maritime opinion was concerned it had won the war.

We must return to the mainstream of events in 1925 to follow the fate of Patterson's argument in the national field. By this time it could be said that Maritime opinion had become sufficiently aroused and united to attract the attention of the federal political parties, who were increasingly of the view that something must be done for the Maritime Provinces. Under these circumstances it was inevitable that there would be a search for the necessary and sufficient justifications for treating the Maritimes as a special economic problem. Prime Minister Arthur Meighen, in his unsuccessful campaign for re-election late in 1921, endorsed the movement of Canadian trade through Canadian ports and the decentralization of the Intercolonial. However, these ideas in themselves involved no specific commitments to satisfy the demands of the Maritimes that were building up on the basis of rights previously denied them. The problem for Meighen and the Maritime Conservatives in federal politics was to reconcile a strong commitment to tariff protection with a policy that would satisfy Maritime needs.[18] This was particularly important to J.B.M. Baxter, Minister of Customs in the final year of the Meighen administration, an active supporter of "Maritime Rights" and later to become Premier of New Brunswick from 1925 to 1930. His problem was that facing any regional politician under the monolithic Canadian system of government – having to support the national party without abandoning regional goals of the greatest importance to his electorate. Baxter believed protectionism to be the only basis of national prosperity and of defence against absorption by the United States. His solution involved a more down-to-earth approach than the constitutional stances of Patterson. To Baxter, Maritime Rights was not a criticism of national policy or of Confederation, but a plan to integrate the region into the national economy.[19]

All roads, however, seemed to lead back to freight rates as the basis of the solution, whether they originated in constitutional rights or in national economic self-interest. Meighen's uncompromising attachment to tariff protection, even though it was an anathema to Western and Maritime opinion, was now to be made acceptable by calling upon freight rate policy to offset any undue advantage accruing to any region. Meighen regarded the value and justification of the tariff policy as self-evident. Between his defeat in 1921 and the expected election in the summer of 1925, Meighen worked out an approach calculated to give him the best of both worlds. In a resolution he presented to Parliament on June 1, 1925, he coupled a ringing defence of a protectionist tariff policy with the outline of a compensatory freight rate policy that curiously anticipated the provisions of the Maritime Freight Rate Act of 1927 and the Bridge Subsidy of 1952. The final clause read:

That to enable the products of the Western and Maritime provinces to reach more readily the markets so developed [by the tariff] the special transportation burdens borne by these provinces should be shared by the whole Dominion either by contribution to long haul freight costs or by assistance in some other form.

In speaking to the resolution, Meighen was more explicit:

The Maritime provinces are separated from the mass of our population by a very considerable stretch of territory along which little or no business is done. The western provinces are likewise separated from the same central provinces of Canada. These are two wide chasms fixed by nature, against which Canada has had to struggle through the whole course of her history.... I think it is an inevitable conclusion that the burden of transport chiefly comes upon those further removed from the centres of population. It would in my judgment be good national policy for the whole Dominion to bear a share of that transport cost.... There is no reason why the whole Dominion, not just the shippers along the lines of our roads ... should not carry whatever percentage seems fair of the cost of bridging these two great chasms between the extremities of our land.[20]

The idea of compensation had an immediate appeal to politicians for it enabled them to derive from a rather nebulous issue clear demands and tangible results. It constituted the reduction of the Maritime Rights issue to the compact stature of a practical and politically popular issue. Baxter was wholly in accord with Meighen's reasoning, summing up a speech on the tariff issue in the House of Commons, "... in other words, give us compensation by the solving of our transportation problem."[21]

The fate of the Intercolonial – the raising of its rates, its incorporation into the Canadian National system, and its coming under the jurisdiction of the Board of Railway Commissioners – was what triggered the sudden concern with the subject of freight rates. But there was an ambiguity in the argument centring on the precise meaning of running the railway "as a business operation." Members of Parliament from other parts of the country had no special position on any "national purpose" that might be attributed to the Intercolonial. In favouring its absorption into the national system, they seemed more interested in its no longer being run as a "political railway." This referred to the acknowledged fact that political patronage had been operative on a wide scale, with local members being able to find jobs for constituents similar to what was then the case in many government departments. Maritime members were loath to see this change in status. They defended the previous situation by adopting the arguments of Patterson and others that the Intercolonial should be used to eliminate the geographical disadvantages of the Maritime Provinces, making the first president of the Consolidated Canadian National Railways, Sir Henry Thornton, the main target of their ire.

Within the Maritimes, boards of trade and provincial governments held many joint meetings and put forward the "new line" based on Patterson's arguments. His influence shows up in different quarters, not only in the many briefs that were being prepared and submitted but also in the stand taken by the provincial governments. When Premier Armstrong of Nova Scotia proposed to Premier Veniot of New Brunswick that the provinces should join forces to hire a competent freight rate expert, the New Brunswick Premier replied, cautioning against "too much haste in the appointment of such an expert for fear that in doing so our actions might be misinterpreted as being willing to forgo our claims as constitutional rights, so far as the old Intercolonial Railway is concerned."[22] This would indicate concern lest the relatively modest adjustments, equivalent to those later recommended by the Duncan Commission in 1926, might be regarded as full measure for the Maritimes' freight rate disabilities under Confederation (as the Duncan Commission so stated), thus cutting off the open-ended demands that Patterson had inferred from his very broad interpretation of Section 66 of the London Agreement.

With so many converging streams of protest, the tide of Maritime Rights rapidly swelled to a flood. In 1923, W.A. Black, running on a Maritime Rights platform, was victorious in a by-election in the federal riding of Halifax, and in the same year H.W. Corning, leader of the

Conservative opposition in the Nova Scotia legislature, introduced a resolution calling for a referendum on secession from Confederation. Corning's resolution was defeated by the Government, which substituted its own resolution containing a broad catalogue of grievances in addition to freight rates on April 29, 1925.[23]

With the traditional intensity of political feeling prevailing in the Maritimes, the Maritime Rights issue fell naturally as a perquisite of the Opposition party in Ottawa, the Conservatives. Although Liberal Premiers Veniot and Armstrong tried to place themselves at the head of a "non-partisan" protest movement, they were both defeated in their next election campaigns by men who, as might be expected, were strong Maritime Rights supporters – Baxter in New Brunswick and Rhodes in Nova Scotia. The failure of Prime Minister Mackenzie King to make any conciliatory gesture or action on the freight rate issue at this time left the Maritime Liberals to plug the second-best issue, the tariff, as a source of Maritime discontent. In the post-mortems on the Black by-election victory, the only dissenter from the popular interpretation was a Liberal member who blamed it all on the tariff!

The momentum was maintained through 1925, which might displace 1926 as the *annus mirabilis* for the freight rate issue in the Maritime Provinces. Events crowded one after another, building up to the climax on January 8, 1926, when the hard-pressed Liberal government – no longer even the largest party in Parliament – announced in the Speech from the Throne its intention to appoint a royal commission to investigate Maritime claims. The progress thereafter was all downhill to the proclamation of the Maritime Freight Rates Act on April 14, 1927. A chronology of the more important events as they involved the Maritime Provinces will simplify the complicated succession of events in 1925.

February 26, 1925: A delegation of over one hundred, sponsored by the Saint John and Halifax Boards of Trade, met with Cabinet Ministers and Members of Parliament on Maritime problems, notably the use of the Atlantic ports.[24]

April 29, 1925: Resolutions in the Nova Scotia House of Assembly called upon the Cabinet to prepare a "statement of particulars" on the prejudicial effects of Confederation on Nova Scotia.[25]

June 5, 1925: P.C. 886 was issued ordering the Board of Railway Commissioners to conduct a general investigation into railway freight rates having due regard to, among other things, "the claims asserted on behalf of the Maritime Provinces that they are entitled to the restoration of the rate basis which they enjoyed prior to 1919, [and] ... the encouragement of the movement of traffic through Canadian ports."[26]

June 27, 1925: Royal Assent was given to an amendment to the

Railway Act establishing the Crow's Nest Pass levels of grain rates.

July 15-16, 1925: A Maritime Economic Conference, arranged by the Maritime Board of Trade, was held at Moncton to discuss policies to be advocated in a program bringing the Maritime case to the attention of other parts of Canada. Subcommittees were formed to prepare reports for a second conference in Charlottetown. A committee also was formed to ask the Maritime governments to engage a traffic expert to present the case in the Board of Railway Commissioners' General Investigation. Following the Moncton conference, the Maritime Rights Transportation Committee was formed with A.P. Patterson as its first president. F.C. Cornell, formerly secretary of the Canadian National Millers' Association, was appointed its first traffic expert.[27]

September 2, 1925: Chief Commissioner McKeown and Commissioner Oliver issued their controversial judgement requiring the railways to extend the Crow's Nest level of grain rates to grain moving to Pacific ports for export. Maritime opinion was unanimously opposed to this judgement. Nova Scotia and New Brunswick, together with the Boards of Trade of Halifax and Saint John, joined others to ask that the order be rescinded and the matter referred to the General Freight Rate Investigation. It was regarded as a threat both to the possible eastbound grain traffic to Atlantic ports, and to the possibility of obtaining lower freight rates for the Maritimes because of the loss of revenue to the railways.[28]

September 4, 1925: Parliament was dissolved and an election called for October 29.

September 29, 1925: The application to rescind the Order extending the Crow's Nest level of rates was heard and rejected. Premier Baxter and the Nova Scotia Minister of Natural Resources and Provincial Development represented the Maritime interests before the Board.[29]

October 29, 1925: The Liberal government was reduced to a minority, but announced its intention of continuing in office to meet Parliament.

November 4-5, 1925: The Charlottetown conference agreed on eight resolutions to be laid before the Dominion Conference of Boards of Trade and Chambers of Commerce at Winnipeg later in the month. The freight rate resolution read: "The Maritimes should be conceded a revision in freight and express rates to modify the disabilities under which they labour in marketing their goods in other parts of Canada."[30]

November 16-18, 1925: Maritime views were well-received at the Winnipeg conference, which adopted unanimously a resolution urging the Dominion government "to immediately take such steps as may be necessary and justifiable by the circumstances as will remedy the economic disabilities which prevent the Maritime Provinces from realizing those advantages which, under Confederation and the subsequent development of the Dominion of Canada, should have accrued to them."[31]

Some of the points these events brought out might be noted. First, freight rate grievances in the different regions were still sufficiently specific to prevent the formation of an interregional common front such as developed after the Second World War when grievances had become wholly generalized. Second, the success of regional claims, both in the East and West, was facilitated by the unusual instability in the federal political situation. This instability gave bargaining power to areas and causes that would not have been as important to stronger governments. Third, Maritime interests had not yet become wholly identified with freight rate policy, the latter being the subject of only one of eight resolutions. However, the results of the Duncan Royal Commission were almost entirely connected with freight rates, both in public memory and in fact, and served to shift future emphasis in this direction, even though the Commission had rejected Patterson's interpretation of the transportation terms of Confederation.

The combined activity and agitation during 1925 undoubtedly got the Maritime cause under way. With the resolution of the Crow's Nest Pass grain rates problem it was a foregone conclusion that the Maritimes' turn would come next. In speaking on second reading of the bill establishing the Maritime Freight Rates Act (in 1927), R.B. Hancow (Conservative, York-Sunbury, N.B.) made the point "that this legislation brought down today is the direct result of the action of the people of those provinces in 1925."[32] The result was that during 1926, the Maritime Provinces had not one but two courts to which to address their complaints and demands: the General Investigation and the Royal Commission. In the midst of the presentation of the Maritime case to the Board's hearing in Moncton on April 6-8, the government issued Order-in-Council P.C. 505 setting up the Royal Commission on Maritime Claims with Sir Andrew Rae Duncan as its chairman.[33]

This Commission's task was made easier than the technical difficulties of its assignment would lead one to suspect. The leaders of the two major parties were convinced that some compensation was due to the Maritime Provinces, if not to offset the statutory protection given in the previous year to the Crow's Nest grain rates, then to offset the effects of the tariff or to recompense for other disadvantages suffered by reason of Confederation. We have aready noted Meighen's ideas on the subject. A comparable opinion on the Liberal side is furnished in a letter of the Hon. W.R. Motherwell, Minister of Agriculture and leading government spokesman in the Prairie Provinces, to the Minister of Railways and Canals. After discussing the Western rate situation (the letter is dated May 8, 1925, prior to the final decision on the Crow's Nest rates), Motherwell continues:

> I am further of the opinion that the Maritimes should be given some consideration, having regard to the compact that these provinces entered into at Confederation. The character of these considerations, of course, should rest with the Maritime Provinces to suggest, and if their demands are too heavy on the railways for these burden-bearers (from their standpoint) to carry, then the balance of Canada, particularly the middle East and the middle West, may have to give up some additional advantage regarding freight rates that they now enjoy, provided an acceptable *quid pro quo* can be discovered, such as (for the West) the speeding up of the Hudson Bay Railway and the establishment in the straits of additional radio stations, light houses and other modern aids to navigation.[34]

It seems plain that the politicians had reached the horse-trading stage in the discussion of freight rate disabilities and compensation. The Maritimes had opposed the Crow's Nest rates being affirmed by statute, and in due course the Progressives in the West were to stand in opposition to the Maritime Freight Rates Act, each for the same reason that they represented an unjustified advantage being given to one region that the rest of the country would have to pay for. The course of letting the Maritimes decide what compensation should be was impossible to follow since they were wary to commit themselves to more than very sweeping general statements of what they felt entitled to because of alleged Confederation promises. Taken literally, there was no possibility of the theoretical demands being conceded and it was better strategy to wait for the Royal Commission or the federal government to make the first move, which could be accepted and used as a stepping stone to the next stage of the campaign.

The problem, however, was solved by the very able and thorough presentation of the newly-engaged rate expert, F.C. Cornell, in the brief of the Province of Nova Scotia to the Duncan Commission. Cornell's work on the rate structure, its history and anomalies, paralleled the work that was being done in Western Canada on the same subject, and for the first time provided the Maritimes with a searching, concrete analysis of the subject. While actual rate structure analysis was secondary in importance according to Patterson and the Confederation theorists, Cornell's work took the story of grievances no farther back than 1912. But in so doing, it documented the actual events and changes that had given rise to the Maritime Rights movement in the first place, and demonstrated the deterioration of the once-favourable rate situation on the Intercolonial, providing support for arguments against its inclusion in the Canadian National Railways.[35] Most important of all, in showing that from a level of 80 per cent of the Central Region rate prior to 1912, Maritime rates had, within the next decade, been brought to parity with those of Central Canada, the brief provided the Duncan Commission with the necessary "handle" to dispose of its problem.

Politicians such as Meighen had already pointed the way, and public opinion in the Maritimes had become acutely conscious of the erosion of the favourable rate position. What more logical proposal could there be than that the old rate relationship should be restored and that it be made possible by payment of the resulting revenue deficiency of the railways by the federal government in the form of a subsidy? However, in the climate of economic thinking in the twenties, the granting of a rate subsidy looked to be even more difficult to get than a divorce. Parliament had still not absorbed the shock of the annual deficits of the Canadian National system,[36] and, despite the railways' claims of losses, had required them to meet present and future deficits on the Crow's Nest Pass rates out of their own resources rather than concede a rate subsidy. Yet, with the statistical evidence so clear and the possibility of discovering a more convenient measure almost nil, the Commission seems to have had little difficulty making up its mind.

We feel that the increase arising from the changes that have taken place in freight rates since 1912 – over and above the general increase that has taken place in other parts of the National system – is as fair a measure as can be made of the special considerations, and accordingly should be transferred from the Maritimes to the Dominion so that the original intention may be observed.[37]

The Commission's problem was not how to open the Pandora's box of subsidies but how to get it closed again to forestall the very human inference of "the bigger the better." There was good reason for the Commission's concern on this point for the Confederation promises were already tending to be measured not by some specific requirement that was alleged to have been conceded or assumed to have been so at the time, but by the actual differences in the levels of economic development and prosperity between the Maritime Provinces and the rest of Canada. So long as this difference existed, there would exist for some a plausible basis for a claim. The Commission sensed this in the evidence it received:

Much of the evidence we heard in the Maritimes left the impression on our minds that witnesses thought the railways should be operated to the advantage of the trade irrespective of the financial results to the railway. In other words, what a railway administration might concede, in the exercise of its judgement on what was good business or might ultimately be good business for itself, seemed to us to be demanded as a right by the trader so that his own business might be profitably developed whether the operations of the railway were remunerative or not ... we cannot conceive of a national system being efficiently administered on such a principle as that....

We must add that we were surprised to find, in the course of our investigation, business people who were in some cases prepared to press for a reduction in railway rates without regard to whether it formed a large or small proportion of the total cost of their commodity, or whether other items entering into their costs were more capable of bearing the reduction, or even as to whether their trading results required it.[38]

These misgivings enable one to understand the careful insistence of the Commission on what function the subsidy should serve. It had already rejected the argument based on Patterson's interpretation of Confederation and some of its corollaries. It pointed out that neither freight rates nor Confederation nor the federal government since Confederation were by themselves the cause of the current economic conditions in the Maritime Provinces. The Commission made its position very clear:

The principle upon which we are proceeding, namely that *all arguments in connection with Maritime rates, in so far as they rest upon national, imperial and strategic conditions*, attaching to the Intercolonial Railway, can be broadly assessed on the basis of the reduction which we recommend.

We think that this broad measuring, *once and for all*, of these considerations has such decided advantages that it should not be qualified or delayed by minor criticisms. It *separates completely* considerations of national public policy from considerations of railway policy proper.[39]

With the passage of the Maritime Freight Rates Act, which attempted to tie rate concessions to the facts of history, the freight rate issue passed into pure ideology, since the *terra irredentia* now became the vast and boundless area pointed out by Confederation theorists such as Patterson. The Maritime Freight Rates Act, instead of disposing of the issue once and for all, became a mere signpost along the road to greater concessions. It was at once regarded, as were the Crow's Nest rates in the West, as a regional "charter" – not the satisfaction of the claims, but the recognition of the right to press further claims.

Once the formula for dealing with Maritime freight rate grievances had been agreed upon, progress was swift. The Duncan Commission had been established on April 7, 1926. Its report was submitted on September 23 of the same year and released to the public on December 10. The Canadian National-Eastern Rates Bill,[40] by which name it went through Parliament, passed second reading and the Committee of the Whole on one day, April 4, 1927, and was proclaimed a week later. Opposition was confined to Progressive and Labour Members from the Western Provinces, some of whose best debaters, Robert Gardiner (Acadia), John Evans (Rosetown), G.G. Coote (Macleod), J.S. Woodsworth, and A.A. Heaps (both from Winnipeg), criticized it as preferential treatment for one section of the country, being careful to draw a distinction between it and the Crow's Nest legislation. On the question of the longer route taken by the Intercolonial, they were able to point to the evidence of Frank Watson, traffic expert for Canadian National at the General Investigation, to the effect that the rates between the Maritimes and the Central Provinces had never been based on actual mileage but had been based on a series of rate groups or blocks, all of which represented a reduction of 200 miles or more when set against the mileage scales.[41]

Minds were made up, however, particularly since the legislation could be regarded as the last spike locking up the freight rate issue that had been so worrisome to politicians during the previous ten years. A lengthy preamble to the Act adopted much of the phraseology of the Duncan Report, as if to stress a straightforward acceptance of the Duncan Commission's conclusion that the departures from the intent of Confederation began only around 1912 and were now fully compensated for by the measures recommended. There was sufficient ambiguity in the wording, however, to keep Patterson's theory alive:

> Whereas the Royal Commission on Maritime claims ... has in its opinion, confirmed the representations submitted to the Commission on behalf of the Maritime Provinces, namely, that the Intercolonial Railway was designed, among other things, ... to afford to Maritime merchants, traders, and manufacturers the larger markets of the whole Canadian people instead of the restricted market of the Maritimes themselves....

Once the new law was in effect, Patterson had no difficulty in assimilating the Duncan Commission's recommendations and the Act into the wider campaign for the fulfilment of the "Confederation compact" in transportation. By 1930 he was claiming that:

> The recommendations of the Duncan Commission with respect to our freight rate structure or transportation policy have not been implemented, with the exception of one recommendation – namely, 20% reduction in certain freight rates, to relieve the people of the Maritime Provinces of an unjust burden which as the Duncan Commission states, "it was never intended that they should bear," and which has been but partially implemented.[42]

The unfulfilled recommendations included the application of the subsidy to overseas export traffic and to traffic terminating in the United States as well as the granting of discretionary powers to the Board of Railway Commissioners to order special rates to assist particular industries who might have some claim to such assistance.

This latter recommendation, put forward by the Commission in sympathetic tones, possibly had the aim of no more than opening a crack in the door to take in exceptional cases. It was rightly seen by the government as a not very long fuse, the lighting of which would have blown the economics out of railroading completely. Patterson, who saw this to be "no doubt, the most important and far-reaching recommendation of the Duncan Commission," claimed, in a novel semantical twist, that on rejecting it, "both great political parties and the Senate have shown sectional favouritism unjust to the Maritime Provinces and not in the national interest." "We can rest assured," he added, "that the Royal Commission, headed by Sir Andrew Rae Duncan, would not make any recommendations that are not in the national interest."[43]

Patterson also thought that if the Board were to be given this additional power, then each province should have a member on the Board nominated by its legislature.[44] This is enough to make it plain that had any such power been given to the Board, the irresistible levelling forces of justice and equity would have quickly transformed its exercise from a rare exception to a general rule, obligating the federal government to indefinite amounts in subsidies to sustain the railways. What defence could be guaranteed to hold against arguments such as: Why his business and not mine? Are not all Maritime industries equally important? Why have most of the subsidies gone to this or to that province? How can the Board show favouritism for one industry or discriminate unjustly against another? Are there not struggling industries in all parts of the country?

Blandly ignoring the Commission's explicit description of its subsidy recommendation as being something "once and for all" and as separating public policy from railway policy, Patterson appropriated it for the purposes of his ongoing campaign:

> The Duncan Commission confirmed our claim for transportation improvements as a federal right and the Federal Parliament in the Maritime Freight Rate Act, in effect, confirms the fact that the Maritime Provinces have the federal right to transportation improvements which will ensure fair trading relations between the Provinces.[45]

In short, the stage was set for the perpetuation of the freight rate ideology by regarding the Maritime Freight Rate Act as merely the first step along an interminable road toward vague and impossible goals. While it is fair to say that few Maritime spokesmen seriously pressed for the literal realization of Patterson's objectives, the continuous presence of unsatisfied goals has kept attention focused closely on freight rate matters. In other words, the church has continued to flourish even though the hopes of the millennium have been quietly relegated to the indefinite future.

In spite of the undiminished eagerness of Patterson, there was in the Maritime Provinces, as in the West, a noticeable let-down after the big push of the twenties. The Maritime Freight Rates Commission, with Cornell as its traffic adviser, continued to function for a time, being involved with studying the implementation of the Maritime Freight Rates Act. When the Depression set in, the provincial governments, financially hard-pressed, cut off the Commission's funds and Cornell was forced to take a job as traffic manager of the Halifax Harbour Commission.[46] The issue was not dead, but sleeping, and, as it happened, only very lightly and fitfully.

CHAPTER 6

Depression and War: Freight Rates to the Background

We have noted a decrease in activity in the freight rates issue following the Crow's Nest legislation, the General Investigation, and the Maritime Freight Rates Act, all of which had been achieved by 1927. Despite even Gerry McGeer's efforts there was little chance of a major reopening of the issues. It is important to note, however, that despite all the thought and effort applied to them, none of the major issues could be said to have been definitely settled and relegated to the history books. At best they had been rendered dormant, but they remained available for use in the future or again could become disturbing factors in their own right. In the latter category was the statutory level of the Crow's Nest rates, which thrust itself out more conspicuously with every increase in price levels. Equalization and similar rate anomalies had not been put away by the Board's negative decisions in the General Investigation, which had merely tied them to empirical conditions such as differences in costs and competitive circumstances, and these might change. The General Investigation had bypassed the arguments based on equity, which had lost none of their cogency or popular appeal. The Maritime Freight Rates Act had the immediate effect of focusing attention on implementation and interpretation, while the wider goals of the Confederation theorists were placed in the background or kept on hand mainly for rhetorical effect. The issues of horizontal percentage increases and regional development that rose to first rank in the later period of the freight rate ideology had not yet come up since there were no general rate increase applications between 1920 and 1946.

With the depression and industrial unemployment a further deemphasis of the freight rate issue occurred, its place in the sun being taken by tariffs and monetary policy. One of the first major acts of the Bennett government in 1930 had been to sharply increase the customs tariffs, in response to the Hartley-Snoot tariff enacted by the United States in the previous year. Tariffs and imperial preferences and their effects on regional economic activity again became a lively subject for discussion. In Nova Scotia, Premier Angus L. Macdonald, an economist by profession, ordered a provincial economic inquiry (the Jones Commission of 1934, of which Harold Innis of the University of Toronto was a member) to examine the effects of the tariff on Nova Scotia.

In the West, monetary questions took priority. McGeer had turned to monetary policy when the freight rate issue petered out, and in the Prairies, Alberta seemed to forget all other concerns when William Aberhart began his campaign in favour of Social Credit. The scale of the economic disaster in the Prairies, by reason of the collapse of prices and markets due to the depression and the production losses due to the drought, obviously called for more fundamental measures than an equalization of freight rates. The decline in wheat prices made even the Crow's Nest rates seem oppressively high, but there was no way that the railways, already faced with highway competition and declining traffic, could be expected to contribute to an easing of the situation, and demands on federal revenues were such that no funds were left for transportation subsidies after paying for the deficits of Canadian National.

In the Maritimes, however, Angus Macdonald was instrumental in the revival of the Maritimes Transportation Commission, whose demise in 1930 had not ceased to be deplored by boards of trade and others. The Commission was reconstituted in 1934, with Rand H. Matheson as executive director, a post he held for more than twenty years, becoming the unchallenged "Mr. Freight Rates" of the Maritimes. Matheson provided a continuity in policy and interest in freight rates, concerning himself with every actual or potential transportation problem or change that came up. Whereas boards of trade or provincial governments could only give intermittent attention to the freight rate issues, Matheson was always on the job, developing and refining the arguments on the traditional issues, and even creating issues of matters that otherwise might have passed unnoticed. With a permanent position, supported by the three provincial governments and governed by a board of directors made up of prominent shippers and businessmen, no one in the Maritimes could doubt the high priority given to Matheson's role. The Commission ensured that freight rate issues were continuously under discussion, and it took on the duty of safeguarding the fundamental transportation rights of the Maritime Provinces as spelled out in the Maritime Freight Rates Act and in Confederation theories.

The biggest issue involving the interpretation of the Maritime Freight Rates Act in the thirties was the relevance of the many new competitive rates issued to meet the first big wave of truck competition in the Central Provinces. The subsidies paid to the railways were deductions from the "normal rates"; with the shipper benefiting from a lower rate by the amount of the deduction. However, if a local rate in Central Canada was to be lowered to meet truck competition, did this require a corresponding reduction in the rate from the Maritimes to maintain the "statutory advantages" assured by the Act? The Maritime Transportation Commission brought a case to the Board of Railway Commissioners in 1935 in connection with rates on potatoes.[1] The Board's judgement handled the subject with the same subtlety it usually employed in turning aside complaints. It conceded that "the purpose and object of the Maritime Freight Rates Act does not apply to competitive traffic established outside of 'select territory'" but held that whether the statutory advantage had been undermined was a question of fact. The Board noted that, since almost all Ontario potatoes were then being marketed by truck, cancellation of the Ontario rate would be of no benefit to Maritime shippers, and thus evaded the question of whether the maintenance of the rate and the establishment of a correspondingly lower rate from the Maritimes would be of benefit. It can be assumed that the latter had been desired by the Maritime Transportation Commission, not the cancellation of the rate. The Supreme Court affirmed the Board's decision in a judgement issued in 1937.[2]

A familiar ring in these judgements should not escape notice. They might be described as sandbagging operations – keeping the statute within reasonable bounds, or in its "normal" channels, preventing it from spreading itself far and wide by the irresistible and irresponsible force of logic. Although neither the Board nor the Supreme Court cited it in their judgements, this is the doctrine of the Regina Tolls Case of 1906, first applied to the equalization issue and now applied to the Maritime Freight Rates Act. In the former case it had been argued that equity required equal rates, in the latter case it was argued that statutory advantages should be defined as requiring a certain mathematical relationship in all cases. Chief Commissioner Guthrie noted in his judgement:

> Counsel for the applicants submitted, among other things, that it was merely necessary for the applicants to produce these competitive tariffs showing the reduction in rates in Ontario and Quebec to establish their contention. In my opinion, it is necessary to go farther than this and prove some actual or probable destruction of Maritime trade, or some prejudicial effect thereupon, either heretofore sustained or likely to ensue as a result of these competitive tariffs.[3]

The Board thus escaped having to take on the unending task of keeping rates and subsidies consonant with the quickly changing picture of competitive rates in Central Canada, let alone having to ascertain unpublished for-hire or unknown private trucking costs or rates. The logic of the statute could not be permitted to be stretched that far. The Board and the Supreme Court made their case without having to play a final trump card. The preamble of the Act had its own escape clause: "... insofar as it is reasonably possible so to do without disturbing unduly the general rate structure in Canada ...." There being no further court of appeal, the Maritime Transportation Commission and the provincial governments could only draw to the attention of later royal commissions the "erosion" of the advantages secured by the Maritime Freight Rates Act and endeavour to obtain some form of compensation.

The Rowell-Sirois Royal Commission

A new and perhaps somewhat unexpected forum for renewing the freight rate issue presented itself in the Royal Commission on Dominion Provincial Relations in 1936.[4] The Commission, whose raison d'être was to enquire into the problems of federal and provincial finances and the sharing of taxation power, which had been severely strained by the Great Depression, took a broad view of its duties and regarded "railway questions which impinge on Dominion-Provincial relations as coming within our terms of reference."[5] The result was that the Commission, while it strove to keep clear of the detail of rate complaints, found itself conducting a form of general rate investigation on the side, thus filling the gap between the General Freight Rates Investigation of the 1920's and the Turgeon Royal Commission in 1949.

The nature of the provincial representations ten years after the General Investigation and the Maritime Freight Rates Act reveals the progress of the ideology. A time for talking about freight rates had come around again, and the writers of the briefs had to do their best to justify the expectations of the public, who by now were firmly convinced that in freight rates lay both the cause and the relief of the disabilities they felt themselves to be suffering. The Maritimes had something new to raise since the Maritime Freight Rates Act had not been in existence at the time of the previous investigation. The Maritime Transportation Commission, Nova Scotia, and New Brunswick all referred in their briefs to the erosion of the advantages of the Act due to competitive conditions within Central Canada. The Commission refused to become entangled in the intricacies of the situation, observing that more than one mode of transport and divided jurisdictions were involved. The Commission also declined to support

117

the recommendations of the Duncan Commission and the Maritime Transportation Commission that the powers of the Board be enlarged to enable it to assist the development of industry and trade. This, it was felt, would give undesirable managerial power to the Board; the government then would "clearly be involved in responsibility for the financial consequences to the railways."[6]

The Rowell-Sirois Commission's real importance to the freight rate issue was the very thorough examination it made of the Maritime claims that had been linked to the understandings said to have been reached at the time of Confederation. One chapter of the report was given over to an analysis of the arguments that unconditional guarantees in the matter of freight rates could be implied both as to the carriage of Maritime traffic to Central Canadian markets, and to the movement of grain and other exports through the ports of Halifax and Saint John.[7] The Province of New Brunswick presented the most complete case for the Maritime claims, since it had been prepared under the direction of Patterson himself, then the Minister of Education and Federal Affairs. It is not necessary to repeat the Commission's discussions and analyses; a mere extraction of the conclusions is significant for the purpose at hand. On the import of Resolution 66 of the London Conference, the Commission stated:

> We are thus unable to accept the contention of New Brunswick that Resolution 66 of the London Conference constituted in any sense a contract or agreement with the Maritime Provinces; or that the term "improvements" used therein implied the means of forcing trade through Maritime ports as New Brunswick contends; or that the term "seaboard" means only the seacoast of the Maritime Provinces. But we have examined the submissions of New Brunswick carefully and, we trust, with detachment, in the hope that a complete review may not merely show why we were unable to recommend that this claim be allowed, but may also serve to remove a sense of grievance which has been long standing.[8]

On the purpose of the Intercolonial Railway, after noting with approval the Duncan Commission's findings that the rate reduction later embodied in the Maritime Freight Rates Act would meet the obligations of Confederation and that it would be a retrograde step to withdraw the Intercolonial from the Canadian National system, the Commission asserted that "we think that the criticism of the New Brunswick brief to the effect that the Intercolonial Railway is now run as a 'commercial operation which is entirely contrary to the scheme of Confederation' is not well founded."[9] On the matter of the ports of

118

Halifax and Saint John, the Commission concluded: "we have not found that any contractual, or quasi-contractual rights of the Maritime Provinces in the matter of Dominion transportation policy have been violated. Nor can the Dominion be fairly accused of having ignored the legitimate claims of the Maritime Provinces to the use of their ports for the external trade of the Dominion."[10]

After the defeat of this major effort to substantiate his claims, Patterson seems to have suffered a decline in political fortunes. He lost his seat in the provincial election of 1939 and left the government. A year later the portfolio of Federal Affairs was abolished.[11] Still, neither the Maritime Transportation Commission nor the provincial governments ever seemed to have formally abandoned Patterson's basic positions, which remain largely unquestioned articles of faith for the great majority of Maritimers, however vague the knowledge of their specific content. Just as the average church member will claim to believe, but be unable to expound the doctrine of the Trinity, so the average Maritimer certainly believes, but he is not necessarily either a freight rate expert or a constitutional expert. The substance of the claims continued to be put forward in more vague and generalized terms, as if appealing to a matter of common knowledge. A witness for the Maritime Transportation Commission later told the Turgeon Commission in 1949 that "The national background in connection with our Intercolonial Railway was to afford persons and industries to get into the market of Central Canada. This is the basic principle."[12]

The submissions of the other provinces to the Rowell-Sirois Commission – and in at least one case the absence of any submission from a province – are of greatest interest to us since we entered into the purely ideological stage of the freight rate issue after 1927. The public's interest had been greatly aroused but the substance of the complaints, so far from growing *pari passu*, were diminishing even from the already rather small empirical base from which they had started. Unfortunately, before one could plausibly shout "I'm hurting all over!" one had to start by identifying some concrete symptoms, however small. In the years from 1927 to the present, and indeed for many years before that, the task of the lawyers and rate experts has been to establish this basis for the more sweeping statements and allegations, which the public has become conditioned to believe the freight rate issue is all about.

The performance by the provinces in 1937 is an intriguing one. Ontario, then under the rather boisterous leadership of Premier "Mitch" Hepburn, delivered an attack on the level of the Crow's Nest rates, which it claimed gave to the Western Provinces "unusually favourable treatment."[13] Ontario did not, however, make any specific suggestion for a reduction in the rates elsewhere. The Commission noted this shortcoming, and deflected the thrust of Ontario's argument by stating that an examination of the profitability or otherwise of the grain rates would be a contribution of value, but one for which it had no evidence to make a finding.

Manitoba made a lengthy submission to the Commission but apparently made no reference to freight rates, which in itself is of some significance. After its early bargaining with the Canadian Northern Railway, Manitoba had little to demand for itself and consequently was mainly on the defensive in freight rate cases against the demands of the other Western Provinces. Thus, in the General Investigation, Symington had inveighed strongly against both the railways and freight rates, but his sharpest arguments were directed against Alberta and British Columbia. His positive proposals boiled down to a rather half-hearted advocacy of equalization. The same stance applied to the Winnipeg Board of Trade. But the appeal of the freight rate ideology was as strong to Manitobans as to other Westerners, so that the government, except in this one instance, always felt obliged to at least join the chorus. This task became somewhat easier in later years when the emphasis shifted to the more general issues of horizontal percentage increases and regional development.

In the case of Saskatchewan we have a province that has had only slightly more to complain about than Manitoba and somewhat less to complain about than Alberta, but the complaints have had to be loud enough to be heard over the satisfactions of the Crow's Nest rates. On this occasion Saskatchewan had to turn, in the Commission's own words, to a restatement of a long-standing complaint of the Prairies, the equalization issue. This lost much of its punch with the Commission's insistence on bringing the grain rates into the total picture. Saskatchewan also supported the enlargement of the Board's powers to permit it to make developmental rates, as had been recommended by the Duncan Commission.

Because of Premier Aberhart's rancour against the federal government for its disallowance of Social Credit legislation, Alberta ignored the Rowell-Sirois Commission but did prepare a brief of its position, which was sent to almost everybody else. Under the circumstances, however, the freight rate issue was not neglected; rather, it was brought before the Commission in the briefs of the Edmonton Chamber of Commerce, the Municipal Districts of Alberta, the United Farmers of Alberta, and the Alberta CCF clubs. The equalization issue was mentioned but the main emphasis seems to have been on the transcontinental competitive rates that accentuated Alberta's position "as the apex of Canada's freight rate structure." The Commission made no comment on the merits of the case, noting that the Board of

Transport Commissioners alone had the authority to hear the argument and render judgement.

British Columbia took the opportunity to again raise the issue of the domestic grain rates to the Pacific coast that had not been given the benefit of the Crow's Nest rates. This issue had been left smouldering since the General Investigation and had only recently been dismissed by the Cabinet and again by the Board. A reference to the effects of the Mountain Differential was again made, this time contrasting the inequitable situation whereby bulk goods and natural products shipped eastbound enjoyed commodity rates from which the Mountain Differential had been removed, whereas manufactured goods were brought from Eastern Canada at high rates. The transcontinental competitive rates, however, do not seem to have been mentioned in this section of the British Columbia brief.

As a result of its acceptance of the relevance of freight rates to its terms of reference, the Commission found that it had heard a vast amount of evidence on which it had neither authority nor competence to make any recommendations. For the experts and the brief-writers it had been a kind of fire drill, serving to keep them fit and ready for the time when the real fire should again break out. The Commission again reviewed the Board's judgements that had been used to meet the same freight rate issues on earlier occasions. It noted in particular the Board's avoidance of general formulae and its insistence on treating discrimination as a matter to be evaluated on the merits of individual cases. But it failed to note that this procedure had served to reject arguments based on equity considerations and thus had kept in existence insignificant differences that served as a continuing source of irritation. And this irritation over equity was in large part responsible for the arousal of the general public's ideological attitudes on the freight rate issue. Under these circumstances, the Commission made no specific recommendations but contented itself with a suggestion calculated to satisfy all complainants for the moment:

> ... having regard to the length of time that has elapsed since the last general inquiry, the change in conditions due to the increased range and effectiveness of alternative means of transportation and the increasing signs of a revival of regional questioning as to the justice of the existing freight rate structure, that the present might be an opportune time to have a review of the railway freight rate structure on a Dominion-wide scale.[14]

In one respect, however, the Rowell-Sirois Commission did win the universal gratitude of contemporary and future generations of transportation historians and economists, when it published as appendices to its Report the study "Railway Freight Rates in Canada," edited by R.A.C. Henry, which contains J.A. Argo's "Historical Review of Canadian Railway Freight Rate Structure, 1876 to 1938," and W.A. Mackintosh's study, "The Economic Background of Dominion-Provincial Relations," which dealt with freight rate equalization and grain rates. No royal commission devoted exclusively to transportation has made as solid a contribution to the available knowledge on an issue that still remains confused and obscure.

An Abortive Arson Attempt in 1941

From records preserved in the British Columbia Attorney-General's papers, it is possible to reconstruct the outline of a minor but fascinating episode in the history of the freight rate ideology which will fill the gap that lasted until the final year of the Second World War. It is a case that might be called "freight rate arson" – an attempt to kindle a fire that would arouse a whole population by rubbing a few dry freight rates together. The public saw in the smoke that it produced (there are rarely any actual flames) a threat to the economic future of the city, province, or region concerned. The event is not unique, for the fire hazard had been high in many parts of Canada for a long time, but it is instructive in that it reveals in 1941 the persistence of the ritual pattern of rate protests that had developed in the "take-off" period of the ideology during the twenties. As we shall see later, the pattern has persisted in some areas right down to the present day.

The matter involved a proposal of the railways, announced early in January, 1941, to increase some transcontinental competitive rates effective February 1 of the same year on the grounds that since the wartime scarcity of shipping had removed the source of the competition, there was no longer any justification for holding down the rates. They were to revert more closely to the normal level of rates. Even with the increases proposed – 20 to 25 per cent – the rates would still have been much lower than the corresponding rates to intermediate points such as Alberta, which had been protesting the level of these rates since they first went into effect after the First World War.[15]

The first spark to ignite the campaign was a telegram dispatched on January 7 to Premier T.D. Pattulo, then in Ottawa attending a Dominion-Provincial conference, by "thirty Vancouver manufacturing concerns," mostly in the iron and steel-using industries, because the increases were to be applied mainly to these commodities. The only spontaneous act of the whole episode must have been the initial gut reaction of the manufacturers when they realized that their costs were going to be increased by one agency, the railway, in a single step.

Spontaneity, however, like a spark, dies almost as soon as it appears unless there is someone on hand with tinder to nurse it into a flame. Even the composition of a telegram is too difficult a job for thirty manufacturers to do jointly. We must look for the individual or individuals or the pre-existing organization that would have been capable of sustaining the feeling of protest, much as policemen are said to survey a potentially difficult crowd to pinpoint the leaders without whom the crowd would degenerate into a passive mass of humanity.

From the available records it would seem that the source of inspiration was R.D. Cameron. He seems to have played a leading role in the founding, subsequent to the announcement of the increase, of an organization calling itself the British Columbia Freight Rates League, which used the address and stationery (with the name typed over) of the Granville Island Branch of the Canadian Manufacturers' Association. The purpose of the League seems to have been to egg on the provincial government into the freight rate battle. Cameron explained to Attorney-General Gordon Wismer in a letter of February 10, 1941: "We have constituted ourselves a fact finding body for the purpose of securing all the information, and the giving of all assistance we possibly can to you and your department."

The January telegram to the Premier gave no less than seven reasons why the increase would cause harm in British Columbia: (1) Higher raw material costs would increase costs of production. (2) Industries established because of favourable competitive rates would be jeopardized. (3) The distribution area of British Columbia producers to Prairie and Eastern points would be narrowed. (4) Eastern manufacturers' positions in the British Columbia market would be enhanced. (5) British Columbia would lose out on war contracts. (6) British Columbia's war effort would be seriously curtailed. (7) The railways had sustained no increase in wages or operating costs. The telegram asked the Premier's assistance in obtaining a six-month postponement of the increase. In an editorial comment on the telegram on January 8, the Vancouver *News-Herald* added another indispensable ingredient to all the recipes for freight rate protests – the alleged high sensitivity of industry to even small changes in costs. The paper declared that "the margin on which the B.C. factory operates is the lowest in Canada.... Even a slight increase in costs jeopardizes the existence of many a B.C. industry." In an editorial on the following day, *The Vancouver Sun* added another tendentious comment: "... so our Canadian transcontinental railway lines show all the familiar signs of a return to the policy of charging all the traffic will bear."

The Freight Rates League appointed as its counsel in the matter R.O. Campney, who immediately obtained the assurance of Gerry McGeer that he would be willing to act for the province in cooperation with him. For this the League expressed its thanks to the Attorney-General and reported having held a "very successful mass meeting which appointed a strong committee representing all sides of industrial life." This committee held its first meeting on January 17, 1941, and was "all set for whatever action necessary." Since the rates were to take effect on the first of February, there was a frenzied peak of activity at the end of January, with the *Sun* reporting in a headline a "flood of telegrams" being sent to the federal Cabinet. Within the text of the story itself, it became only "dozens of telegrams," of which were mentioned only the ones of the Vancouver Board of Trade, the British Columbia Freight Rates League, the Granville Island Branch of the Canadian Manufacturers' Association, and "other organizations." The paper also reported that "in addition many industrialists sent individual messages."

In Ottawa, Attorney-General Wismer, who was also attending the Dominion-Provincial conference, saw C.D. Howe, Minister of Munitions and Supply, and other members of Cabinet and also sent a letter to the Prime Minister. Wismer told Howe that his war production program in British Columbia would suffer, and raised the question of whether the increases would be contrary to the government's attempts to restrict wartime profits. To the Prime Minister, Wismer reported a "feeling ... very pronounced in British Columbia" that the action at that time "will be very injurious to national unity." He also hinted darkly to the Prime Minister that "there is a definite feeling that the threatened increase in rates may be the work of Eastern interests." To the press, he said "I am convinced that behind this move is the influence of certain Eastern manufacturing interests which would gain if British Columbia industries were injured and unable to produce war materials at competitive prices." The only plausible suspicion that seems to have been overlooked was that the increase was a plot of Premier Aberhart of Alberta, sitting at the apex of the freight rate structure.

On the same day, January 30, the Board of Transport Commissioners ruled on Campney's request for suspension of the increase, holding that a *prima facie* case for suspension had not been made. In his judgement, Chief Commissioner J.A. Cross reviewed and affirmed the Board's previous positions in the matter of competitive rates to the effect that "Tolls reduced by a railway company to meet competition may, at the discretion of the rail carriers, be brought up more closely to the normal level when the competition becomes less effective."[16] More last-minute activity seems to have occurred before the deadline, but all was in vain. Howe was said to have appealed to both railway presidents and Wismer to have made a similarly unsuccessful appeal to the Chief Commissioner of the Board. Prime Minister King was said to have put the matter before Cabinet which was "sympathetic but had no jurisdiction at present."[17]

Back in Vancouver in February, the participants were taking counsel on their next move. The press reported that "the government is expected to embark almost immediately on a major campaign to forestall increasing freight rates and possibly bring about a reduction in existing rates in order to save the industry of this province from imminent disaster." Attorney-General Wismer expressed his willingness to act, and intimated government support and called upon McGeer to return to the battle on behalf of the industry of the province. He also said, in his opinion, the case would be taken directly to the Privy Council for final relief. The Freight Rates League was pleased with the government's response and passed a motion asking the province to take over the fight against higher freight rates. Unknown to them at the time, this motion contained the seeds of quick dissolution of the whole project.

McGeer, bringing his experience to bear upon the problem, pointed out very clearly to Campney and Wismer that individual complaints must be made, offering evidence of unjust discrimination or undue preference or unreasonableness of specific rates.[18] He felt it would be very difficult to have a case put forward with the province as chief complainant. From this point, misunderstandings began to crop up. The members of the League thought the matter had been successfully turned over to the province and were pained to get a letter from Wismer inferring that the League had changed its policy and was not pressing for a hearing before the Board. But the province was convinced that the initiative for a special hearing on the rates must come from the League. When this message finally got through to the League, interest and support of its members quickly evaporated. It was one thing to sit in the stands cheering the downfield progress of the provincial team under the brilliant quarterbacking of McGeer, but it was quite another matter to get into uniform and go out on the field itself, even if only for one play. Finally S.J. Hammitt, chairman of the League, wrote to Wismer on May 1, 1941:

> The investigations of our League have demonstrated to our satisfaction that there is not enough support among the individual members to justify carrying our cause to the extent of a Hearing before the Board of Transport Commissioners. We do not feel justified in asking that the Provincial Government proceed further with the case and therefore ask that the matter be dropped.

The League quickly faded away, it being reported in September as having adjourned *sine die*. In the post-mortem summing up in the provincial offices it was noted that out of forty members contacted for participation in the case, only three were prepared to sign the application to proceed with the hearing, to prepare a brief, and to fight the case. The province felt that it had been left holding the bag. After having loudly sounded the alarm and having tried to persuade in turn the railways, the Board, the Cabinet, and the Prime Minister to intercede on behalf of the victims, it was disconcerting to have the latter fold up their tents and silently steal away. It was like suddenly removing the orchestral accompaniment to a singer at the climax of the aria, leaving him declaiming in the void. It was unofficially suggested to the League that it was important that it meet again and prepare some sort of statement or "apologia" for its existence and for its decision in fairness to the province and "to avoid confusion by misleading press announcements." In political circles there may also have been some chagrin at the loss of the freight rate issue that had served Premier Oliver so well in similar circumstances to help fight a difficult upcoming provincial election.

So the issue passed, calm returned, and all went on living happily. But the reader may be unsatisfied to have the story end here. He may want to ask, like a curious grandchild: "But, Grandpa, then what happened? What happened to all those industries threatened with imminent disaster? And did they ever find and punish those bad Eastern interests that were the cause of it all?" The answer to such questions has to be, the reader may now be aware, that from the earliest times of the freight rate issue, there has been an inordinate use of theoretical arguments and an abstracting of freight rates from the complexities of modern economic processes. The result has been that freight rate issues have often consisted of excessively large amounts of shadow-boxing or of tilting at windmills. So, in our example, the industrialists were concerned with any increase in costs, and were quite prepared to raise loud objections so long as this might induce public opinion and governments to make protests that might hold off or mitigate these cost increases.

All the arguments used when public bodies such as governments, trade associations, and the like are involved, however, are mainly theoretical and general, as such bodies do not want to get lost in details and business itself shies away from any closely reasoned public analysis of its own affairs. But the latter procedure acts quickly to remove all the inflation and hyperbole that has been forced into the issue. It is a summons to return to the actual context and the actual facts and to check the insidious sliding of arguments from the conditional to the indicative mood. It is no wonder, then, that businessmen, such as those in the British Columbia Freight Rates League, should make haste to say that they were not meaning to complain all *that* much, when asked to be specific about their complaints. Over the years, the general public has only seen the externals of the issues and has had little opportunity or desire to take a more balanced view. When the fires die out the complaints are promptly forgotten together with the reasons for their sudden demise. All that is remembered of it when the next fire breaks out is what a beautiful blaze the last one made while it lasted.

With the recounting of this forgotten episode, we reach a short break in the story because of the overwhelming claims on resources, activities, and interests in the fighting of the Second World War. In view of the depth to which the freight issue had established itself in the public mind, it is not surprising that, with the end of the war, it would quickly rebound to its former place of importance in public policy.

PART II
History of the Freight Rate Issue:
The Joining of the Final Struggle

As the end of the Second World War came into sight with the successful Allied invasion of Europe, attention turned with mingled relief and apprehension to the impending problems of transferring the labour and resources that had been devoted to the war effort back to peacetime production. The bitter experiences during the years following the First World War had not been forgotten and few were optimistic of the country being able to avoid a repetition of the earlier inflation, deflation, and unemployment. The West and the Maritimes were particularly apprehensive; they had borne the brunt of the downswings of the economic cycle in the past and had vivid memories of both the post-war difficulties and the Depression.

In transportation the situation was in striking contrast to the earlier experience. Instead of a financial and operating collapse of a large part of the railway network, both major railways had given a first-class performance during the Second World War. A vast increase in traffic had been successfully handled with no serious problems. Utilization of the reserve capacity of the system and control of wages and prices had enabled the railways to show excellent financial results without the benefit of any general rate increase.

It is in the light of this situation, coupled with the great uncertainties about the immediate future, that we must consider the freight rate issue as it revived with the decline of wartime controls. The issue had not been built up to a major confrontation since the big events of the twenties. On the other hand, it had never been permitted to drop out of mind entirely. The most publicized inequities which had not been removed by the Board of Transport Commissioners' decision in the General Freight Rate Investigation – the Mountain Differential, the East-West rate level differences in class and commodity rates, and the contrast between the low transcontinental competitive rates and the rates to intermediate points – produced enough fuel to keep the kettle simmering. With the degree of conditioning that the public mind had undergone, it was not difficult to bring things to a boil almost instantly by a reminder of the past wrongs that had been permitted to remain. In becoming more ideologically and less economically based, the issue became more volatile, provoking sudden bursts of oratory, angry newspaper editorials, and then months of silence.

The expanding nature of the grievances, as more and more disabilities tended to become chargeable to "freight rate discrimination," outstripped the ability of strictly mathematical equity of freight rates to satisfy them, and it was not long before there was talk of higher levels, or a new form of equity which would justify the tipping of the balance of mathematical equity in the other direction. The Maritime Freight Rates Act had created the precedent, but others were to be attracted as the ideology gradually shifted emphasis from rate inequities to regional inequities, where objectives could be tied to concrete standards of measurement only with difficulty, if at all. The events of the postwar period show very clearly this shift in the freight rate ideology from the everyday world of the traffic man and of transportation economics proper, to the ideal world of ultimate objectives in which the former became almost irrelevant. The period from 1945 to 1975 can be divided into five sections, each showing another step in the life history of the ideology.

Period One covers the closing year of the war to the announcement of the establishment of a royal commission on transportation in September, 1948. This is a period featured by the taking up of positions, particularly with respect to rate increases, from which no retreat could be made without giving up the ideology, which, of course, was unacceptable. In this period a logic of circumstances developed which governed the actions of the participants in a compulsive manner and made the ultimate result appear to have been preordained.

Period Two, from 1948 to the implementation of the Turgeon Royal Commission's recommendations in 1951, represents the final triumph of the principle of equity in the freight rate structure with the removal or mitigation of nearly all of the long-standing rate grievances. If the issue was to survive beyond this point, it would have to be based on some wider conception of equity than simple equality of rates. At the same time, concrete freight rate problems would be reduced to something symbolic.

Period Three, from 1951 to the Freight Rates Reduction Act and the setting up of the MacPherson Royal Commission, is the climax of the life history of the ideology. The logical consequences of the rigid positions adopted in Period One were carried to their ultimate absurdity: the freezing of rates and the funding of any future increases by government subsidy. The goal of the ideology was indeed achieved, but the situation was both absurd and intolerable.

Period Four covers the events from the formation of the MacPherson Commission to the proclamation of the National Transportation Act in 1967. A major attempt to exorcize an ideology that had achieved grotesque effects on the transportation system was made during this period. For a brief time, this attempt seemed successful. The difference in MacPherson's approach from Turgeon's shows the degree to which the ideology had outgrown its original host, the transportation system.

Period Five carries the story to the present time and perhaps covers the most peculiar, yet most revealing, period in the long history of the freight rate ideology. I have called it the "Afterlife of the Ideology" since it was conjured up from the dead by Premier Thatcher of Saskatchewan. The revealing nature of the circumstances – the gap between the psychological demands of the ideology and the transportation system – is at last fully exposed. The remaining ties with freight rates drop away, and the ideology is discovered to have been a cloak for some deep-seated regional discontents. These have been different in different parts of the country, but found a common cause after the Second World War in the issue of freight rates, which the public saw as the symbol of its discontent. [This final part of the history unfortunately has not been written.]

CHAPTER 7
The Resumption of the Struggle

The railways filed an application for a 30 per cent general increase in freight rates on October 6, 1946, the first since 1920. It was hardly a surprise. On the other side of no-man's-land, the freight rate ideologists had been indulging in inspirational oratory for more than a year and a half. Warlike preparations, threats, and imprecations all served to build up public opinion into an intransigent mood by instilling the belief that the fate of their region would be harmed irremediably were any increase in rates to occur or any outstanding rate discrimination to remain. Provincial premiers publicly took up strong positions against an increase well in advance of the application, thus committing themselves to a struggle *à outrance*. Newspapers waged loud "campaigns" that were claimed to be "above politics" in the sense that they urged a regional unity of opinion. In effect, this dampened any expression of diverse opinion by implying that it was traitorous to the region.

Under these proddings the public rankled with a sense of injustice for which it naturally blamed the railways and the financiers, manufacturers, and politicians of Eastern Canada. Under such circumstances a freight rate increase became the occasion, not for a sober analysis of the railways' needs and the effects of satisfying those needs, but for letting off steam from simmering regional resentments. Many of these may have been real and not simply induced, but the pole around which they were invited to cluster – freight rates – would have had little power of attraction on its own to draw out such deep-seated discontent. By 1945, the ideological content of the freight rate issue had already been raised well above the 1927 level, as indicated by the persistent recourse to more general grievances, arguments, and demands, and the eagerness that was evident to open the issue once again, if only on a strategy of "preventive war."

By this time rate discriminations were dwindling in significance, even though they could be made to look bad on paper. Less and less traffic was actually paying class rates. However, these rates still formed the basis for most regional rate comparisons. The motor truck, shortly to be freed of wartime restrictions, was about to begin its transportation and distribution revolution, undermining the symmetrical structure of railway rates based on value-of-service pricing. By the time the Turgeon Royal Commission had sized up the situation, equalization had become too insignificant either to fight for or to resist. The contentions between the railways and the provinces on rate discriminations seemed to be drained of substance and all that was left was *amour-propre* or some mythical "Ashes" such as those over which Australian and British cricket teams have traditionally battled. There was little possibility of settling by negotiations after some minor skirmishing; the ideology had escalated to the scale of total war.

What was really in contention was the right to control the making of freight rates. The provinces had refused to accept the Board's decisions, which to them seemed merely to sanctify the status quo, leaving the railways free to adjust the structure in their own interests without regard for the new objectives the provinces were now putting forth – equity, and going beyond equity, regional development. For their part, the railways took every attack on the rate structure as an attack on their rate-making prerogatives and were determined to resist any outside interferences from "political" forces. To them the question of equity was of minor significance since the whole of the "active" portion of the rate structure, even within groups of competitive rates, was permeated by considerations of equity. While they might be faulted for clinging so tenaciously to the inequities embodied in the oldest and least used parts of the rate structure – the class and commodity mileage rates – the attacks appeared to the railways to have ulterior, if not irrational, motives. Under such circumstances, appeasement appeared to be a futile and dangerous gesture. This attitude was later borne out by events, for no sooner had the major rate inequities been removed by legislation incorporating the recommendations of the Turgeon Commission than the focus shifted to more general matters such as horizontal percentage increases and regional development. Imagination supplied bigger complaints and bigger remedies.

That it was a long, drawn-out struggle, extending more than sixty years, not an early and complete capitulation, can be ascribed to the continuous presence of the Canadian Pacific Railway, a private company required to make its living out of railroading. CP was the major counterweight to the ceaseless pressures put on the federal government and the Board. A standard of revenue requirements did exist. While subject to definition and redefinition, it did set a limit to the extent to which rate concessions could be made for "social" or "developmental" reasons. Had all the railways been amalgamated into one government-controlled system after the First World War, there would have been no way in which the system could have been maintained on anything close to a financially viable basis. Even the modest constraints that had kept the Intercolonial Railway's generosity under control would have been swept away in a flood of political oratory. Who would have been left to make any effective protest, if government had been making up the shortfall in revenue? The national railway deficits would have been on a scale proportionate to those of the Prince Edward Island ferries. In time, however, a way was discovered of getting around even the private company obstacle. Rate subsidies could be paid to all carriers, reducing even Canadian Pacific to the role of a simple implementer of government will. For this to happen, however, the idea of a subsidy had to be freed from the strong inhibitions that had hitherto surrounded it. That story must wait its proper sequence to be told.

Some of the events in this prologue to the railways' post-war rate increase applications are of interest and importance for our purposes. They will explain in part why the hearings in the general application and subsequent rate applications could become little more than a futile knocking of heads with an absence of agreement even on minor issues. The cases were prejudged. Inflexible positions were taken up which could not be withdrawn from gracefully, so that the Board's decisions, far from terminating matters and reconciling the parties, became occasions for renewed howls of defiance and a flurry of appeals.

As befits the precedence British Columbia had acquired from its leadership of the freight rate war in the twenties, the opening gun in the new campaign was a random shot fired in Vancouver on Janary 25, 1945. It was a prestigious occasion. At the annual meeting of the Vancouver Board of Trade, H.R. MacMillian, a leading west coast industrialist, gave an address entitled "Factors affecting the future population of British Columbia." He covered many topics, only one of which was the freight rate situation. He charged that the Mountain Differential discriminated unjustly against British Columbia manufacturers, illustrating his point by a comparison of rates to Winnipeg from Vancouver, southern Ontario, and Quebec respectively. He even went so far as to adopt an oft-repeated phrase to the effect that British Columbians were in danger of becoming "hewers of wood and drawers of water" – the former being more apt than he may have intended!

The Vancouver Sun reported his speech fully at that time, but returned to it the following week after having made a survey "among several heads of large firms" that revealed they were in agreement with MacMillian. Whereupon the *Sun* decided the time had come to make another big "push" to get rid of British Columbia's freight rate discriminations. Beginning on February 15, 1945 it ran a series of well-publicized articles appearing almost every other day for a month. These were often supplemented by lead editorials intended to bring "the facts directly from B.C. industry and from the rate books and regulations that encase our markets and our future in a 'railway tariff' straightjacket."[1] Even more interesting than the facts were the headlines and subheads that drew the reader's attention to the articles:

Rail Rates Choking B.C.
A Right of the People
60 Years of Discrimination
How Vancouver Suffers
Mountain Costs a Myth
Eastern Goods Allowed to Flood B.C.
Coast Business Caught in Freight Tariff's Vicious Circles
Our Loss, East's Gain
Breaks all against West
Fear of Railways Must Not Defeat Rate Fight
Small Business, Workers Lose
Railways Take the Cream
B.C. Manufacturers Tire of Serving as Puppets
800 Percent Advantage for East
Vast Production in B.C. Hogtied
Freight Discrimination Hard on B.C. Interior

A department store public opinion poll carried over a local radio station asked the question, "Should the West have freight rates equal to Eastern rates?" Not surprisingly, over 97 per cent voted yes. The surprising part is that there were as many as 3 per cent who would vote no to a question worded in this manner. These could have only been the votes of newly-arrived Easterners who had not yet been fully assimilated into the local population! The *Sun* confidently declared that "Vancouver is now definitely 'freight rate conscious.'"[2]

At the same time, the provincial legislature had also become "freight rate conscious" and there was an obvious scramble to get on the bandwagon. On March 8, 1945, the leader of the CCF opposition, Harold Winch, jumped the gun on the government by offering a resolution demanding the end of rate discrimination against British Columbia, and the *Sun* reported "considerable interest" in its rate campaign on the part of government members in the legislature. The interesting thing about Winch's resolution is that, except for some updating on one or two clauses, it was almost a word-for-word rendition of John

Oliver's famous resolution of 1907 which had been unanimously adopted by the Legislature at that time. Feeling the wheels of the bandwagon slowly starting to turn, the *Sun* redoubled its efforts and started to herd all parties onto it. An editorial on March 10, 1945, proclaimed that "This is Above Politics" in an admonition to the coalition government not to reject the Winch resolution on partisan grounds. But there was no need to fear this. The government only delayed long enough to figure out how it could get the reins out of Winch's hands. This it did on March 27 by offering an amendment that repeated the language of the original resolution with the addition of a clause:

> ... and whereas the provincial government through its departments, has been and is continuing to assemble all facts and information having a bearing upon railway rates that are discriminatory against British Columbia, having in mind the presentation of such information to the Board of Transport Commissioners and to the Dominion Government in an appeal that such discriminations be removed....

The *Sun* modestly accepted the legislature's compliments on its campaign and promised to continue its efforts without remission until the objective was obtained. Meanwhile, support gathered on all sides: from the British Columbia branch of the Canadian Manufacturers' Association, the Vancouver and New Westminster Trades and Labour Council, the Womens' Liberal Association, and the Labour-Progressive (Communist) Party, among others.

With the movement gathering momentum, the *Sun* could afford to turn its attentions to rebuking dissidents and rounding up stragglers. The dissidents were few, since the railways did not rise to the bait and the *Sun* had only to chastise one local trade magazine for its "tiresome and inefficient suggestion" that unfair freight rates be dealt with one by one,[3] and to excommunicate another with the anathema that "the Canadian Pacific Railway Company could hardly have done a better job of selling British Columbia down the river." This sentence was pronounced in an editorial appropriately entitled, "Treachery at Home."[4] The stragglers also were few, but the *Sun* was puzzled by the strange indecision of the most important of them, the Vancouver Board of Trade. The Board had long been in the front ranks in offering leadership and support in all rate battles since the formation of the Board of Railway Commissioners, but now the *Sun* reported that its officers were saying that "it was 'still studying' the matter." "Obviously," mused the *Sun* in its editorial of May 4, 1945, "the explanation could not be that the president of the board is Mr. C.A. Cotterell, assistant general manager, western lines, of the Canadian Pacific Railway Company." The Board, however, brought itself into line by unanimously accepting an appropriate resolution on May 31. It had been preceded by one week by the Vancouver City Council.

British Columbia also took encouragement from the events taking place south of the border. In March of 1945, the State of Georgia successfully took a case to the United States Supreme Court in the matter of the differing rate levels in Southern and "Official" (eastern) Territories that had long been authorized and maintained by the Interstate Commerce Commission. In answer to the court directive, the ICC ruled in May of the same year that the rate levels had been "unreasonable and unduly prejudicial" to the interests of the American South and West and ordered class rates in these areas to be cut by ten per cent in accordance with ICC docket 28300 findings. A parallel in British Columbia's situation with the Mountain Differential seemed obvious where the regulatory body had been reluctant to act on its own initiative to bring about rate equality. In response to a less than enthusiastic comment of the *New York Times* that "the ICC's new ruling ... raises the question of the extent to which geographical political pressures should be allowed to affect the rate-making process," the *Sun* countered with the same question in the opposite direction, saying that "British Columbia is convinced that geographical political pressures are preventing the same thing here."[5]

By coincidence, on the very same day, the *Calgary Albertan* introduced its readers to the freight rate question in a lengthy article with the heading "Freight Rates Throttle the Prairies." The *Albertan* offered a similar theory for the cause:

It is customary to blame the railway companies for these conditions. Actually, however, the main blame probably rests on greedy eastern manufacturing and commercial interests determined that the west shall develop as a sort of colony of Ontario and Quebec, dependent on them for manufactured goods, and without substantial industries of its own. Discriminatory freight rates have been their most powerful weapon for this purpose.[6]

On July 5, 1945, the *Winnipeg Free Press* said that it had learned from "authoritative sources at Ottawa" that the two major railways were preparing to ask for a steep increase in freight rates. It turned out to be a false or at least premature alarm, but like an air-raid alert it touched off a firing of the defensive batteries that stimulated a real war situation. Within a day the three Prairie governments, through acting premiers in every case, had committed themselves unreservedly to opposing any increase. In Manitoba, the Minister of Agriculture said that "we will certainly not agree to any general increase in tariffs." In Saskatchewan, the Attorney-General announced that the government would fight any move for a general increase and called for a united opposition by the four Western provinces. In Alberta, the Minister of Public Works said that the government would fight any move to increase freight rates and intended to bring pressure to bear to obtain a reduction in existing rates.

Premier Ernest Manning of Alberta had already taken a strong stand in freight rates and the Legislative Assembly had on three previous occasions endorsed a demand for more equitable rates for Alberta. A week prior to the rumour of an increase the Premier had told a delegation of the Alberta Board of Trade that he would do his utmost to have freight rates placed on the agenda of the Dominion-Provincial Conference.[7] When the rumour arose he immediately took an uncompromising stand. In a letter to the Chief Commissioner of the Board of Transport Commissioners, a copy of which he sent to the Prime Minister, he stated:

> Any revision of the Canadian freight rate structure that does not bring about a substantial lowering of the rates as applied against Alberta would still further aggravate a situation that is already serious ... on behalf of the people and the Government of this Province I, therefore, wish to protest most emphatically against the Railway Companies' contention that rates should be still further increased and earnestly urge the Board of Transport Commissioners to refuse favourable consideration to any such suggestion.[8]

It is difficult to imagine any stronger language and reaction had there been a real application for an increase.

In British Columbia, however, Premier Hart reacted cautiously, stating merely that the matter would have to be considered by the Government before any policy would be decided upon. Throughout the West, farm organization spokesmen and boards of trade declared that farmers and consumers would be hit first and hardest. There were few variations on the theoretical possibilities of the theme that were not exploited, in some cases too enthusiastically, as when the *Sun* reported that some organizations saw in the rate increase a *proportionate* increase in the cost of living. The chairman of the transportation committee of the British Columbia Division of the Canadian Manufacturers' Association thought that there was no justification for an increase and that it would be hardest on British Columbia. Being careful to say, "speaking personally," he concluded that if the railways could not operate under the existing rates, and increase would affect the whole Dominion equitably, there could be no reasonable objection because "we must keep the railways going."[9] It was the only reported indication of any readiness to consider the issue on its merits.

A week later Premier Hart announced that the four Western premiers had agreed to meet together to discuss joint action to secure equalization of freight rates. He expressed the view, too optimistically as it turned out, that the differences between the Western Provinces were of "minor importance when considered in relation to the main objective." He had not reckoned with Manitoba's unchanged opposition to the removal of the Mountain Differential. The premiers were reported to be placing the subject of freight rates on the agenda of the Dominion-Provincial Conference, which was to meet in preliminary sessions in early August and then adjourn until the main session in late November. At a meeting of Western premiers at the conclusion of the preliminary sessions, Premier Garson of Manitoba informed his colleagues that, while his province would oppose any proposal of the railways to raise rates, it would not join in any plan for the equalization of rates over all areas.[10]

For the *Sun* this was an act of secession equivalent to the turning of the guns on Fort Sumter. It solemnly redrew the map of Canada and expelled Manitoba from Western Canada. In an editorial entitled "Winnipeg Faces East," the *Sun* declared that: "Western Canada now comprises three provinces, not four. Manitoba read itself out of the family on the weekend when Premier Garson turned his back on the struggle for equalized freight rates." The *Sun* concluded, however, that the real villains were the "Eastern interests" whose machinations came into view at every level:

> Manitoba will string along with the Eastern interests bitterly opposed to letting Vancouver compete on equal terms in the prairie market.... We say – and the present attitude of Toronto proves the point conclusively – that the existing inequity of the Mountain Differential is due very largely to the selfishness of Eastern interests which are determined to maintain their stranglehold on the Canadian economy.

All that could be done now was for the three remaining Western provinces to come closer together without giving up hope for the return of the wayward brother: "The Provincial Government must work fast now to cement a common economic front with Alberta and Saskatchewan. The three provinces together must work upon the conscience of Manitoba, but if necessary, we can go along without Manitoba's help."

After six months, *The Vancouver Sun* now felt it had reached its

141

objective in the campaign: at long last the fight for equalization of freight rates was getting nation-wide attention and would be on the agenda of the Dominion-Provincial Conference. At that conference, the *Sun* said, "British Columbia whose industrial development has been retarded for two generations by discriminatory freight rates favouring the East at our expense, surely has the right to suggest that some at least of this burden be lifted from it."[11] However, the issue dropped almost immediately into the background; after all, this was the time of the atom bomb and the surrender of Japan, and the conference came and went without any public statement on freight rates. The next alarm was to be the real thing, with the railways applying for a 30 per cent increase in 1946.

Here, I propose, in the manner of a Greek chorus, to interrupt the flow of the drama with a brief commentary that hopefully will enable the reader to better understand the outlines of the plot as it develops. The freight rate events of 1945, although occurring at the same time as the stirring events in Europe and Asia that brought the Second World War to a finish, actually occurred in a time of "peace." Railway rates were still frozen by an order of the Wartime Prices and Trade Board. Before arriving at the point where the freight war actually broke out again, it might be well to retrace the logic of circumstances that had been building up. The tighter this became, the more the actors were carried along by its momentum until a point was reached, some fourteen years later, at which it could be said that the situation had gotten completely out of control. All were to become so encased in the logic of their situations as to become completely powerless to break free of it. It was not as if there were no opportunities to back away from the ultimate consequences, but such an action would have meant the abandonment of a major premise of an argument that was still very much alive politically. In other words, it would have meant the giving away of a live issue to the opposition. Moreover, it would have had the connotation of surrendering to the regional oppressors. The only politically feasible solution in these circumstances became that of sitting tight, shouting louder, and hoping that Ottawa might make some tangible concessions that would allow those opposing a rate increase to leave the field claiming victory. But as the stakes escalated this, too, became increasingly difficult without a major breach in the economics of transportation policy. We may spin the web of logic around the issue in the following manner, which also illustrates the structure of the *Sun's* campaign.

(1) The Board had become tied to a series of precedents that allowed it to evade coming to grips with the question of equity (equalization). Any steps it took in that direction were in the nature of *ex gratia*

allowances, detached from its ordinary course of reasoning and the result of strong external pressures, which, if not real, were certainly believed to be so by the public. Thus, the Board could get no credit for the steps it actually took toward equity.

(2) To the West, inequity was the most conspicuous anomaly in the rate structure, not so much because of its substantive importance but because it was an historical survivor that seemed unnecessary and unjust and because it was defended by inconsistently applied and specious reasons. The West felt it was entitled to a basic equity and was under no onus to prove beforehand some actual detriment from the existing state of inequity.

(3) To get action on the equity question required either bringing strong external pressure on the Board, or going beyond the Board to the federal government.

(4) For the provinces to pursue this course of action required a broader complaint than rate comparisons that were unfavourable to a local shipper on either a real or hypothetical basis. The public had to be convinced that its interests in general were involved.

(5) The public's support was most easily mobilized on the basis of a regionally defined grievance. Once the public became aroused on the issue it was necessary on the one hand to focus on a scapegoat or a villain that was alleged to be actively frustrating the course of justice and on the other hand to suppress intra-regional differences.

(6) Manitoba, as the most active and consistent defender of the Mountain Differential, should have been the real villain. But Manitoba was anything but a suitable villain despite the *Sun's* proclamation excluding it from Western Canada. Manitobans were as much Western in their attitudes as any other Westerners, particularly if the freight rate grievances could be built into a general regional grievance, and the *Sun* was right in supposing that the other provinces could "work on its conscience."

(7) This, therefore, meant seeking other scapegoats. The railways and the "Eastern interests" were the logical candidates.

(8) On the one hand, the railways were said to have raised Western rates to compensate for losses on competitive traffic in the East. However, there was never any evidence of such positive action by the railways. The general features of the rate structure remained either unchanged or had been whittled down in favour of the West.

(9) Eastern interests had not shown any lively interest in maintaining the state of inequity either. The Board had pretty well kept the issue alive by its inertia, despite plainly worded directives from time to time in the form of Orders-in-Council. Ontario had intervened in the General Rate Investigation to defend the transcontinental rates and had

taken sideswipes at the "favouritism" of the Crow's Nest rates, but no Eastern interests seemed to have taken the trouble to defend the Mountain Differential. In fact, that hadn't been necessary since British Columbia had made no application for its removal since the General Investigation.

(10) That regional interests finally dwarfed the specific freight rate grievances was seen by the fact that Western solidarity, rather than minimizing local differences in rates, became the goal. At the same time the pressure group was compelled to justify its own estimate of its importance in order to allege grievances and make demands far exceeding the size and importance of the original freight rate equity question. In short, the issue quickly became too big for its britches.

The 30 Per Cent Increase Case

By the time the railways publicly announced on October 10, 1946, that they had applied for a 30 per cent increase in freight rates, the stage had been set for a major confrontation between them and seven of the then nine provinces. The *Sun's* editorial on the following day, entitled "Freight Rate Showdown," captures perfectly the prevailing mood as that of a team that can hardly wait for the opening whistle to charge down the field:

> The Sun is delighted that the Railway Association of Canada has applied for a 30 per cent freight rate increase. This request to the Board of Transport Commissioners will re-open the whole question of rail charges. After being held down for 25 years by iniquitous discrimination, the West will welcome a showdown.
>
> The West has been spoiling for this fight for a long time. Now it is up to every organization with a stake in the West to pitch in and win it. The Government of British Columbia stands at the head of the list. It has the authority of its Legislature granted two years ago, and the promised support of the governments of Alberta and Saskatchewan. The Vancouver Board of Trade, largest of its kind in Canada, is on record by resolution. The B.C. section of the Canadian Manufacturers' Association is in the battle. So is the Vancouver City Council. All of them have their counterparts all over the West.
>
> If the West can't get a square deal this time it never will. It might just as well find out where it stands without any more delay....[12]

Premier Hart had been careful to define his position at all times as being opposed to any increase, *in the absence* of the removal of the Mountain Differential. But the Prairie premiers had committed themselves to oppose an increase unconditionally. More than a year earlier,

Premier Manning had told the Alberta Farmers' Union he had informed both the Board and the Prime Minister that "Alberta would do anything in its power to oppose any upward revision of freight rates."[13] Premier Douglas of Saskatchewan, commenting on the railways' application, said that Saskatchewan would co-operate with Alberta and British Columbia, adding, as if to give the farmers their cue: "There will be the deuce to pay among the farmers of the West when the demands of the railways become generally known."[14] Manitoba's position was given by the Minister of Agriculture, D.L. Campbell: "We couldn't support it. We would have to oppose it in the general interests of agriculture."[15]

With such terms of reference handed to counsel and technical experts, it could be a foregone conclusion that the lawyers would regard themselves as being authorized to throw up every possible procedural and technical roadblock to the progress of the case and that the experts would sift exhaustively the freight tariffs and the railway accounts for every bit of evidence of a questionable nature in order to turn hearings, as much as possible, into a general rate inquiry. At this point we see the ideology dominating the course of events. Over the previous year and a half, the politicians and the public had talked themselves into believing that any increase in freight rates spelled regional disaster. Provincial counsel were like the field commanders of an army that had been refused any authorization to compromise or retreat. Just as such situations produce extravagant or desperate manoeuvres in military strategy, so in the freight rate issue; counsel found themselves compelled to charge headlong into logical traps that under more flexible orders might easily have been sidestepped. They had to strive laboriously to make points, whether on freight rates or railway accounting, points whose sole purpose was that they helped to hold off the eventual increase.[16]

The long, drawn-out nature of the battle in the 30 Per Cent Case compares strikingly with the rather expeditious disposal of the three general increase cases between 1917 and 1920, and reflects the strength of the ideological forces that had been built up gradually over the intervening years. In the 15 Per Cent Case, the application was made on April 21, 1917, the hearings took place during June, and the decision was rendered in December. In the 25 Per Cent Case, there were no hearings at all and an Order-in-Council authorizing the increase was passed within ten days of the application. In the 40 Per Cent Case, the application was made on July 9, 1920, hearings took place during August, and the decision was rendered on September 20.[17]

The 30 Per Cent Case, however, was a pitched battle in which both sides committed all their forces. After a long and crowded course of events, the Board handed down its decision on March 30, 1948, nearly a year and a half from the date of the original application. The subsequent appeal by the provinces to the Cabinet was not disposed of until October 15, 1948, and the final repercussions were not settled until the completion of the following (21 Per Cent) increase case in May, 1950.

The Board had first set January 8, 1947, as the date for the hearings of the 30 per cent application, but in December, at a meeting called at the request of the provinces, it delayed the opening until February 11. At that meeting the provinces had asked for delays from three to six months and raised the question of the Board's conducting hearings in the different provinces. When the hearings began, the Board conceded the granting of regional hearings so that provincial counsel were able to capitalize on local coverage and interest. A long succession of witnesses were introduced who, almost without exception, foretold disaster for themselves were rates to be given any increase at all. The effect of these hearings, combined with the soon-to-follow Mountain Differential Case and the Turgeon Royal Commission, was to indelibly impress in one generation of the regional population the importance of the freight rate issue and its close links with regional interests.

Some of the tactical moves that took place during the hearings show the strain on the ingenuity of counsel to block the way at any cost. No sooner had the first sessions of the hearings opened than the counsel for the Winnipeg Board of Trade, W.P. Fillmore, KC, caught even the provincial counsel by surprise by challenging the Board's jurisdiction to hear an application for a general increase and asked that proceedings be stayed to clarify this point of law. According to Fillmore, the railways must first publish the rates, which the Board could then suspend while it heard, one by one, the specific complaints that might be lodged against them. He concluded that a general increase was a matter for Parliament only. While the speciousness of the complaint was on the order of a barrack-room lawyer's interpretation of the statute, provincial counsel found this a serious point, and when the Board ruled that it had jurisdiction, asked leave to appeal to the Supreme Court before the case should proceed. Four days later Mr. Justice Kerwin heard the appeal in chambers and dismissed it with a minimum of comment: "The matter does not lend itself to extended discussion."[18]

A more substantial point came up as the railways were about to begin their rebuttal of the provinces' financial evidence on September 29, 1947. Isaac Pitblado, having previously acted for the Winnipeg Board of Trade, now was completing a long association with the freight rates issue as chief counsel for Canadian Pacific. He announced that following the Wartime Prices and Trade Board's Order 757 that released freight rates from price controls, the railways proposed to increase competitive rates by 30 per cent at the beginning of November. The provincial counsels' immediate reaction seemed like the operation of a conditional reflex against any kind of rate increase. Notwithstanding the often repeated complaint about the low competitive rates in Central Canada, which supposedly meant the outlying regions would bear the brunt of any general increase, and notwithstanding the arguments that the railways should "fill up the valleys first," including the transcontinental rates, provincial counsel preferred to gamble on another attack, reserving the latter argument as part of their summations and not worrying about the apparent inconsistency. Telling each other that this was one of the most important matters to come before the Board since the case started,[19] provincial counsel claimed that were this increase in competitive rates permitted, the railways would have to withdraw their application for the general increase and present a new one, even though it had been prepared in contemplation of the same increase in competitive rates as in other rates. The Board's decision was a weak compromise – it merely suspended the proposed increase. This denied the provinces their request for a new beginning, which would have ensured further delay. It also denied the railways, who had been waiting a year for the additional revenues, the benefit of the increased rates. This intervention in the realm of competitive rates, hitherto a prerogative of the carriers, provoked sharp dissents from Commissioners Wardrope and Stoneman.[20]

The provinces had built up public opinion on the freight rate issue on the basis of the inequities in the rate structure and had hoped throughout both the regional and main hearings to realize some gains out of the Board's judgement. However, the basic purpose of the case – the need of the railways for more money – could not be set aside. Provincial counsel were forced to take positions on this eventuality, which turned out to be of unusual importance for two reasons. First, the intransigent stance of the provinces left counsel little room to manoeuvre so they were forced to accept the logical and often dangerous consequences of their premises. Second, had the request for a 30 per cent rate increase been an isolated event, the extreme positions taken might quickly have been forgotten and left no binding obligation of future occasions. Unfortunately, it turned out to be only the first of a series of applications the railways were forced to make over the next twelve years. There was no time to forget, and from the almost continuous nature of the argument during the period there was never any suitable occasion for modifying positions in a more realistic direction. A counsel who had strongly urged a certain argument in 1947 was likely to find it still hanging around his neck like an albatross in 1958. To him, of course, it may have looked like the *Légion d'Honneur.*

The fifties became one huge midstream in which it was impossible to change arguments. While the provinces had taken a position opposed to any increase, they were compelled to answer the hypothetical question of what should be done if the Board decided that the railways did require higher rates. The answers of Alberta's counsel, J.J. Frawley, KC, are of interest. He offered three stages of action in such a case, which he repeated in the following increase application hearings.[21] (1) All unduly depressed competitive rates should be raised to levels truly reflecting the competition (despite the fact that the provinces had already forced the Board to suspend such increases when proposed by the railways). (2) "If any deficiency in authorized additional revenue exists" the Ontario-Quebec class rate scales should be brought up to the level of the Prairie scale (despite the comparatively small amount of traffic moving at class rates). (3) For any further increase, (a) a percentage increase should be limited by ceilings on increases applicable to higher rates and longer hauls, and (b) the Board should examine the impact of increases on basic commodities and primary products, and, to the extent warranted limit the increase by setting maximum amounts applicable to these categories.

The key question still could not be avoided, and Saskatchewan counsel, M.A. MacPherson, KC, was the one who had to spell out the full logical consequences of the provincial position: "If a situation develops where the Board finds that there is a need [for increased railway revenue] and there is no other solution for it, then my submission is that it could be best done by a national subsidy."[22]

There could be no question but that the stance of the provinces formulated in 1945 in the absence of any effective counterweight led directly to the rate rollback, freeze, and subsidies in the Freight Rates Reduction Act of 1959. It is beside the point to say that the ultimate result was not originally intended, as it would be wrong, in view of the way in which history is made by the concatenation of a series of highly improbable coincidences, to say that it was inevitable. Yet it did happen and the reason for its happening are not too difficult to uncover. What is puzzling is the apparent lack of curiosity since then about how we got into this rut. This lack of curiosity is perhaps the strongest reason why we are still in it.

The traditional freight rate positions of the other Western Provinces were maintained. A few weeks prior to the issuance of the Board's judgement in the 30 Per Cent Case, British Columbia announced its intention of submitting an application for the removal of the Mountain Differential. Manitoba counsel, Wilson McLean, KC, defended that province's historic rate position, stating that East-West differences, "even if small," should be eliminated, but that since no justification had been found to eliminate the Winnipeg-Fort William constructive mileage, there was insignificant evidence on the Mountain Differential for the matter to be dealt with at that time.[23]

The Board's decision, awarding the railways a 21 per cent increase, was made on March 30, 1948.[24] After some three years during which public opinion was built up to regard any rate increase as disastrous and tantamount to a violation of the constitution and therefore unthinkable, that unthinkable thing had now actually happened. It created a shock wave from which the ripples continued to be discernible for many years. The participants had built up such a role for themselves as dragon-slayers that they had no choice but to go through with it in the most realistic manner possible now that the dragon had actually seized the maiden. In fairness, however, it must be said that few of the participants regarded it as a sham battle. In fact, the intensity of the feelings reflected the high percentage of "true believers" involved. The Board's announcement touched off a crowded series of events in freight rate matters that recalled the hectic days of 1925.[25]

To begin with, it would be worthwhile to sample popular opinion as reflected in the comments of Members of Parliament in the numerous and lengthy debates that took place on freight rates during and immediately after the case. The vehemence of the reaction can be understood in terms of the greatly oversimplified picture of the issue in the mind of the layman. But the simple logic of it was so compelling that speakers were almost inevitably led into the trap of exaggerating the effects of the inequities that they condemned so soundly. They tended to strain the modest and reasonable nature of their demand for equity by getting carried away by a vision of the enormous consequences of "these diabolical things," as Solon Low, the Social Credit leader, once described the discriminations of which he gave the usual examples.[26]

Though now forgotten, April 5, 1948, the day the 21 per cent increase took effect, was a momentous day in the House of Commons. To start proceedings, M.J. Coldwell, the previous CCF leader representing a rural Saskatchewan constituency and highly respected by all members, moved the adjournment of the House to discuss a matter of great urgency - the rate increase. The subject had been raised from time to time so that members had had some opportunity to practise their oratory for the high seriousness of the occasion. Arguments based on appeals for fair play, for simple justice, and for equity lest the whole burden of the increase fall on the Maritimes, the Prairies, and British Columbia inspired a flood of oratory all too rare in the usual humdrum daily rounds of that body. No one could remain unmoved by the passionate sincerity of the appeals. John Diefenbaker remarked on the occurrence of "a most unusual thing."

> There was applause from the government side of the house for many of the arguments [Mr. Coldwell] advanced.... That applause represented an expression of the inward ideas of hon. members across this dominion, who, without regard to any consideration, unselfishly want to see Canada developed as a unit rather than to be balkanized industrially by reason of a differential that denies equality as between British Columbia and Ontario, and that denies equality as between Saskatchewan, Alberta, Manitoba and Quebec, and denies equality as between the Maritimes and Central Canada.... for as long as [this discrimination] continues, this country can never hope to achieve that development she should have, having regard to the resources she possesses.[27]

Pressure on the politicians was high. Major-General G.R. Pearkes, VC, Conservative member for Nanaimo, told a Victoria radio audience on April 11 that the Minister of Transport's statement refusing to interfere with the Board's judgement "was greeted by loud protests from every portion of the House. Seldom has any announcement made by a minister been so poorly received."[28]

Like Diefenbaker, who had noted in the same speech that "discriminatory freight rates have devitalized the potentialities of industrial expansion in the Prairie provinces and the Maritimes,"[29] Coldwell and most of the other participants in the debate were inclined to lay all the blame on "discriminatory freight rates" since these provided obvious standing targets for their moral indignation. The economic effects could not but be expanded to equal the supposed magnitude of the moral infamy. Speaking about freight rates, Coldwell intoned: "I say that they have always been unjust, unreasonable and discriminatory as far as certain parts of the country are concerned, namely, the Maritimes, British Columbia and the Prairie provinces."[30] As for the remedy, he merely asked that "consideration should be given to the equalization of freight rates across the country."

On more than one occasion, Diefenbaker expressed this view that the problems would disappear once the "discriminations" were removed: "When the discrimination is removed there can be no objections to such increases as are necessary to assure a fair and proper return to the railroad companies. No one wants a condition of affairs when deficits will continue."[31] But then, presumably shaking his finger at the Minister of Transport, he added:

150

I suggest to the minister that the responsibility rests with him. He will never have a united federation, he will never build up the type of Canada that we want to see built, where every part of the country is developed according to the resources it possesses, until this unfairness is removed. He will never build the kind of Canada that will assure the destiny that Canada should achieve by having some of the provinces placed in the position where, through the years, they will continue to be "have not" provinces industrially.[32]

G.A. Cruikshank, a government member from Fraser Valley, added his contribution of generalities to the debate, which reveals the underlying motivation – the equating of the issue with a regional cause – that brought so many members to their feet. Some samples from his rather brief remarks will suffice:

... as long as the Maritimes and the West are treated as we now are being treated, we shall never have unity within Canada.... We [British Columbia members] believe that the very future of our province is at stake in this matter.... I want to impress on the government ... that no longer are we going to stand and be sacrificed for the benefit of Ontario and Quebec.... I can assure you, Mr. Speaker, that all parties in British Columbia are unanimous on this question and that we shall fight to the last ditch to see that we get a square deal.[33]

Angus MacInnis, CCF member for Vancouver East, likewise made the whole issue turn on the existence of rate inequities, but in a lower key: "As I understand the position of the people of British Columbia, they are not opposed to an increase in rates as such. They are opposed to the maintenance of an inequitable freight structure."[34]

The degree to which the folklore had been vulgarized in the course of reaching the man in the street is evident in the following remarks of W. Chester S. McLure, Progressive Conservative member for Queen's (PEI):

When this freight rate increase of 21 per cent was announced, with other entanglements, it rocked the Maritime provinces and nearly shook them clear of Canada. It also rocked the Western provinces to the same extent. The central provinces owing to their great wealth and their centralization of great factories, have nothing much to say with regard to it, because both the Maritimes and Western provinces are paying the shot and the central provinces are enjoying the benefits.[35]

The Leader of the Opposition, John Bracken, gave a long and rather prosaic exposition, the most piquant part of which was when he asked himself rhetorically, what are some of the discriminations? The first he mentioned was the Mountain Differential, "which bears so heavily on industries and the consumers of British Columbia."[36] Throughout his long premiership in Manitoba, however, that province had consistently opposed any change in the differential and was preparing to take the same position in the case coming up in the following year.

Another member whose views are of some interest in view of his later involvement is Ross Thatcher, then CCF member for Moose Jaw. Three years earlier, speaking in the budget debate in November, 1945, he had said that higher rates were one of the chief reasons for Saskatchewan's lack of industrial growth and that rates in the West must come down to the level of those in Central Canada if Confederation was to mean true economic equality for Saskatchewan.[37] Speaking on the Coldwell motion, he displayed the same combination as had the other speakers of a reasonable overall approach plus a feeling of regional resentment, which he also attributed solely to the lack of equalization:

> Yet most of us I think agree basically with the railroad men when they say that the cost of railroading has gone up. We know that wages have gone up. We know that materials have gone up. We know that at the same time the rates have stayed pretty well stationary.... I do not argue basically with the contention of the railroad that they must have some extra revenue.
>
> The judgement brought down last week ignores the fact that this heavy and unjust discrimination is already there.... that is our basic grievance. We can see no reason why we in the Prairies, or in British Columbia, or in the Maritimes, should pay rates that are higher than comparable rates in Ontario and Quebec.... As a Canadian who comes from a Western province, I ask for precisely the same treatment as is given to the Canadian who comes from Ontario or Quebec. My constituents ask no more than equality but they will willingly accept no less.[38]

Of course, as a CCF member, Thatcher had to walk the same tightrope as his colleagues who were torn between their identification with both the Prairie farmers and the railway unions, whose wage increases had been an important cause of the railways' application for higher freight rates. In fact, the CCF, like a team of auto racers, was in the course of making temporary repairs to their machine at the pit-stop while the race was in progress. In his speech, Thatcher read a statement "issued only a few moments ago" by A.R. Mosher, president of the Canadian Congress of Labour and the Canadian Brotherhood of Railway Employees and Transport Workers, which supported the rate increase and opposed Coldwell's request to the government for a delay in its application. However, the statement supported the removal of any discriminatory features that existed in the rate structure, and expressed no doubt that differences between the Brotherhood and the CCF would affect their mutual confidence and respect and therefore would be resolved in a satisfactory manner. This apparently left the individual CCF members free to ride off in all directions. Twenty years later, as Liberal Premier of Saskatchewan, Thatcher disinterred the freight rate issue and raised the old familiar battle cries at a federal-provincial conference, performing this feat without having any 1948-vintage freight rate discriminations to rely upon.

We can allow the words of A.L. Smith, Progressive Conservative member for Calgary West, one of the calmer participants, to give consensus to the 1948 debate: "Equalization is the main problem. I think that equalization of freight rates is one of the most urgent matters to be undertaken in this country. If they are equal, who can complain? If they are discriminatory, as they are now, they sow disunity."[39]

Within a week of the announcement of the Board's judgement, the Prime Minister had received telegrams from each of the four Western premiers and the Transportation Commission of the Maritime Board of Trade asking for a thirty-day stay of the increase. The Cabinet rejected the request to intervene by Order-in-Council P.C. 1486 issued on April 7, 1948. At the same time, it issued P.C. 1487, which called upon the Board to conduct a general freight rate investigation. If it hoped by this action to defuse potential explosions in the East and West it was being very optimistic, but even the slightest hope was dashed by a display of incredibly poor judgement.

It was bad enough for the Government to ignore the provinces' lack of confidence in the Board that led to their demand for an investigation of the equity problem by a royal commission, but it was adding insult to injury and an unpardonable exhibition of bureaucratic laziness to make the order little more than a reproduction of P.C. 886, which had set up the General Investigation of 1925, which in turn had had so little influence on the Board despite its explicit recommendation of a policy of equalization. This, and the repetition of the same language from the Railway Act, including the escape clause ("under substantially similar circumstances and conditions"), was sufficient to convince the provinces that the Board would once again simply feel free to decide that there was no unjust discrimination; that the time had not yet come for equalization; and that the greatest possible equalization was already in effect until it could be shown that conditions had changed in a way that the Board was careful never to specify. The provinces were outraged at this clumsiness but it probably only reinforced their original intention to totally ignore the Board's investigation, which remained a dead letter until after the Turgeon Royal Commission's recommendations for equalization had been incorporated into the Railway Act in 1951. At that time, the order for the investigation (P.C. 1487) became regarded as the Board's authority to implement the equalization terms required by the Act.

Prime Minister Mackenzie King, who probably still suffered from nightmares from his harrowing experiences with the Crow's Nest Pass rates and other freight rate issues in the twenties, remained obstinately opposed to any royal commission, especially since he had just committed the Government to an investigation by the Board. Thus, on April 26, 1948, he remained unmoved after a meeting with seven provincial premiers who presented a brief asking again that the increase be suspended and a commission be appointed to look into the rate structure and the existing legislation.[40] The escalation already given to the issue can be gauged by the premiers' recommendation that the rate increase be suspended in its entirety and the Board's order be turned over to the Turgeon Commission for reconsideration. Furthermore, "if in the interim financial need is established to the satisfaction of the Governor-in-Council, then aid should be given to the Railways by way of national subsidy."[41]

The provinces, which seemed determined not to take "disaster" calmly, maintained the pressure by ignoring the Board's successive extensions of the time limit for submitting briefs under its investigation, and kept their options open by obtaining several extensions from the Board of the time within which they could seek leave to appeal to the Supreme Court on the 21 per cent judgement. On April 28, 1948, British Columbia finally made formal application for removal of the Mountain Differential. May and June were relatively quiet but the action picked up again in July. The Maritime Transportation Commission had sent an amplified submission to Cabinet on June 25, and on July 1, the Prime Minister sent a letter to Premier Macdonald of Nova Scotia, replying to the provincial submission of April 26.

This, unlike the hastily assembled platitudes of P.C. 1487, was a much more considered reply, indicating that the Government had a much better grasp of the nature of the problem it was faced with and was concerned to dispel the bad impression that the latter had created, without having to back down to the extent of appointing a royal commission. The Prime Minister was eager to report progress on small matters as well as large. Thus he announced that the railways had now reduced the minimum express rates on eggs from 75 to 50 cents, and that they also, "of their own accord," had cut the increases on coal rates in the Maritimes from 25 to 20 cents per ton. With respect to local and through rates on the Hudson Bay Railway, "it would appear that upon explanation of the government's attitude, the difficulty has since been removed." In an effort to "sell" the Board's investigation to the provinces, he reported that the Board was considering supplementing its investigation with the formation of two new committees, one to make recommendations on "an improved uniform basic rate structure for Canada," and the other to deal with problems of the uniformity of accounts and the segregation of railway assets from other corporate assets. Mackenzie King held out hope that the Board's investigation would be completed "in the next twelve months" and any amendments to the Railway Act could be introduced at the following session of Parliament. A royal commission would only duplicate this effort. He then reiterated the Cabinet's resolve, after having given still further consideration to the matter, not to suspend the Board's Order 70425 allowing the 21 per cent increase. But the most important sentence in the letter, from the point of view of the nature of the freight rate issue, was: "The government believes that it [the Board's investigation] should result not only in a substantially improved freight rate structure but in the elimination of many inequalities whether amounting to unjust discrimination or not."[42] At last, it would seem, that realization was dawning that the frustrating of the principle of equity by opportunist defence of the regional inequalities was a basic cause of the continued festering of the freight rate problem that made it an obvious focal point for local discontent.

As July of 1948 progressed, events expanded into the semblance of a three-ring circus. The main propulsive thrust to the whole machine was supplied by the railway wage negotiations. These were increasingly to involve political intervention for settlement and were necessarily followed by applications for increases in freight rates. Government and railways found themselves trapped between two inflexible taboos – that none should question the railwaymen's right to get all that the ultimate sanctions in bargaining would yield and that under no circumstances would it be acceptable to increase freight rates. On July 14, in an agreement reached after four days of unbroken negotiations and only a half a day before a general railway strike, the railway unions were given an increase of seventeen cents per hour retroactive to March 1. This led Canadian Pacific Vice-President N.R. Crump to make a statement to the press that the railway would need a 15 per cent interim increase, provoking an instant reaction on the part of the provinces, who were still unreconciled to accepting the 21 per cent increase.

On July 20, 1948, the provinces made a formal appeal to Cabinet under Section 52 of the Railway Act against the 21 per cent judgement, submitting in their opening paragraph that, had the Board applied "proper principles," it would have found that Canadian Pacific's position did not justify any increase in freight rates. They also took the occasion to set forth again the reasons why a general freight rate investigation would be unsatisfactory and asked for the appointment of a royal commission. With round one still not concluded, the railways began round two of the freight rate increase battle on July 28 by making application to the Board for a 20 per cent increase, of which 15 per cent was asked for immediately to offset the impact of the new wage award. The pattern that was to become routine in the fifties had already taken form.

Mackenzie King had stoutly resisted the demands for a royal commission on transportation but now the time had come for him to announce his impending retirement from the Prime Minister's office. The Liberal Party held a convention in August to elect a successor and at the same time to review the party platform. A convention is one of those comparatively few occasions in Canadian politics when grassroots opinion of a party in power can, if only for a moment, get a hand on the steering wheel. Just as British Columbia politicians in 1945 had hurriedly taken a stand on the sensitive freight rates issue under the proddings of *The Vancouver Sun*, now the Liberal federal politicians, at least in the Prairies and the Maritimes, with an election likely to be called within a year, were anxious to position themselves properly on the freight rates issue to increase the chances that they would land heads up in the next political toss. Accordingly, the convention adopted unanimously a resolution on transportation policy, noting in the preamble that "transportation has been a major economic problem in Canada; the overhead cost of linking East and West together has been a national concern from the earliest days." The core of the resolution was that the Liberal Party should stand for the appointment of a royal commission to thoroughly review and investigate the whole Canadian transportation rate problem in order to prepare recommendations for an improved uniform basic rate structure.[43] This enabled the Government to gracefully bow to the inevitable and hope that the concession would give some measure of tranquilization to this troublesome issue. The announcement by the Acting Prime Minister, Louis St. Laurent, of the intention to appoint the royal commission was made on September 16, 1948, in time to blunt some of the provincial arguments when the provinces appeared before Cabinet on September 27 to press their case for the suspension of the 21 per cent increase.[44]

In October it was the Progressive Conservative's turn to hold a convention and there was a resolution to "remove freight rate discrimination":

The Progressive Conservative Party supports an investigation of freight rates, particularly in relation to discrimination between the several geographical areas of our Dominion. Our view is that the national policy requires that the several geographic divisions of this country shall share the benefits of and assume the responsibility for a transportation system which will permit every part of this country to enjoy the benefits of our national and industrial resources without discrimination.[45]

With this adding together of so many undefined terms, any resemblance to the existing or any proposed rate structure must remain purely conjectural. It may seem like a surprisingly tame resolution for an opposition party to put forward on freight rates, but it must be recalled that the party had just chosen the Premier of Ontario as its leader and that at that date it was still a party of town mice and not of country mice, as it was soon to become.

The heat was now off the Board to press on with its general investigation and it could get back to the tangled affairs of the increase cases and initiating hearings on the Mountain Differential application. The provinces appeared before the Board on September 21 and were successful in obtaining a postponement of the hearings on the new 20 per cent until January, 1949. The Cabinet announced its decision on the 21 per cent on October 15, 1948, referring the matter back to the Board for a review of its judgement on certain matters in the light of any further evidence, with any adjustment to be applied in its decision on the new rate increase case.

By now there was a strong momentum building up in favour of "equalization" or of "ending discrimination" in freight rates, and the railways faced with the urgent problem of obtaining additional revenues were showing a readiness to take some positive steps. In their application to the Board for the 20 per cent increase, they stated their intention to submit "a plan by which certain class and commodity rates may be equalized as between Eastern and Western Canada in an attempt to assist the Board in its inquiry and to eliminate, so far as is reasonably possible, the complaints which have been made with regard to so-called inequities in the freight rate structure."[46] The stage was now set, from coast to coast, for the actual attack on the freight rate problem, the prelude to which was the Mountain Differential Case, for which hearings began in Vancouver on November 1, 1948. The main performance – the Royal Commission – was still to come.

The Mountain Differential Case, 1948-49

The Mountain Differential had been the most conspicuous landmark of regional inequality in treatment of freight rates since at least 1907, when John Oliver convinced Premier McBride of British Columbia that if he wanted to pick a quarrel with Ottawa the freight rate issue was by far the most effective weapon. It was responsible for British Columbia's long interest in the issue, its assumption of the leadership among the provinces in this respect, and its contribution to the ideology and the ideological attitudes that came to characterize it. Only the memories of the ideas and exploits of Oliver, Gerry McGeer, and the Vancouver Board of Trade needed to be called upon by *The Vancouver Sun* in 1945 to unite provincial opinion solidly behind a new and final campaign to get rid of "freight rate discrimination." It should be noted for future reference, however, that the glue holding this body of opinion together so tightly was the underlying appeal to regional patriotism and a general feeling of resentment against the central part of the country. The majority, including many who might have been expected to know better, had not the slightest understanding of the nature of the freight rate problem or what its real effects were, and were hardly interested in knowing about it. All that was needed was a grasp of the mathematics of addition, subtraction, and calculation of simple percentages to give the feeling that one possessed all that one needed to know about it. As William Aberhart used to say in persuading Albertans to turn to Social Credit, it wasn't necessary to understand it, but only to vote for it; the experts would take care of everything else.

Not the least interesting aspect of our investigation is in seeing how the experts tried to solve the problems that were handed to them. Whenever they got down to the nitty-gritty level of analysis, the problem had the distressing habit of either evaporating into thin air or becoming inextricably associated with a number of other factors, many obviously more important than freight rates. Thus, it became difficult to predict any noticeable effect at all from the removal of the discriminations most easily visible to the public eye. At this point, the realization would dawn that to begin to satisfy the public expectations that had been aroused would have required a fantastic amount of overkill in which thousands of innocent, "theoretical" discriminations would have been marked for slaughter with subsidy ammunition to be wheedled from the federal government. This is not to say that it was either wrong or useless to try to get rid of those visible discriminations that had no justification consistent with modern views of the rate structure. Due to the geographical nature of the rate structure, the particular institutional position of the railways, and the public's susceptibility to respond to regional slogans (which is not to imply that there were no legitimate reasons for regional dissatifaction), the campaigns to remove the offending aspects of *the* rate structure resulted in a strong ideological buildup that became cohesive enough to survive long after the removal of the original causes for the complaints.

Whether it be credited to the province's skill and experience in these matters or to the luck of timing, British Columbia was able to repeat its celebrated coup of 1925, when it had brought pressure on the Board to announce its decision on the extension of the Crow's Nest rates for grain exported via the Pacific Coast barely in advance of the opening of the General Freight Rates Investigation. With the revival of the freight rate issue in 1945, British Columbia acted more purposefully than the other Western Provinces. It had a major grievance in freight rates to concentrate upon, one easily identified and understood by the public. Not the least of its merits as a grievance was that it seemed to be aimed directly at the province, almost as if it were a deliberate case of discrimination. Premier Hart moreover had not taken an unconditional stand against a freight rate increase; he had merely said that the Mountain Differential had to go first. While not achieving this objective, it still could be regarded as a victory that the application to remove it had been made before the Board announced its judgement in the increase case.

As in the past, the efforts of British Columbia to get rid of the Mountain Differential opened up differences of opinion in the West. While Alberta had become an enthusiastic supporter, Manitoba remained opposed. Saskatchewan was able to mask its indifference or opposition by joining the others in seeking to have the subject included in the general rate investigation. The Prairie Provinces, however, were on weak ground here, since they were pointedly ignoring the very same investigation and could hardly argue before the Board that the matter be turned over to a royal commission.

One of the consequences of the Board's long evasion of the equity issue was that even when it took a step in that direction – the reasons for which always seemed to hang in the air unsupported by the usual flock of precedents from earlier judgements – it was given little credit for its actions. Often it was quite the opposite. The public merely searched behind the scenes to find out who might have applied the political pressure and gave credit accordingly. This hardly enhanced the prestige of the Board, but for this the Board itself had some responsibility: it had never left a quotable sentence in judgements acknowledging the importance of an underlying basis of equity in the rate structure. Any phrases tending in that direction were promptly erased by a qualification such as "under similar circumstances and conditions" or "there is no unjust discrimination shown." Oblivious of the long-term effects of the smugness of its reasoning, the Board had been carefully tending a culture of germs of the ideology so that now not only did they infect the comparatively minor areas of rate inequity but also their contagion was spread like wildfire to the concomitant rate increase application, which proved to be a catastrophe for transportation policy and the transportation industry.

Although the Mountain Differential Case was strenuously argued on both sides, there hardly could have been any doubt but that the Board would declare in favour of abolishing it. Political pressure behind the scenes, even if there had been any, was surely superfluous at this stage. The Board, now under a new chief commissioner, was still reeling from the stinging attacks of seven angry provincial premiers who had gathered in Ottawa for the expressed purpose of letting the federal Cabinet know their feelings on what they regarded as the Board's incompetence, and on what little confidence they had in the Board's readiness to deal with the classic rate grievances. At last, in the Mountain Differential Case was a chance for the Board to show that it could do the job and restore some of that lost confidence.

The case itself was argued in a somewhat different fashion from the earlier cases on the same subject. Costs in the Mountain Region naturally formed the backbone of the railway argument, but the provinces of British Columbia and Alberta brought a wider range of argument into play. They were able to show that because of the higher proportion of main line track in the mountains, revenues were substantially higher than in the Prairies, thus offsetting differences in costs. The rather loose manner in which the differential was applied – by increasing the mileage in Mountain Territory by a quarter – gave anomalous results with little relationship to actual costs, since on the longest hauls the extra mileage meant little in additional charges, while on the short hauls it was naturally much higher due to the tapering effect of the rate increments with mileage.

Alberta, however, went further in offering a theory of the rate structure that justified a basic equalization subject to exceptions for reasons which would be applied in a reasonable manner, such as differences in service, volume of shipment, and competition.[47] Briefly, the argument was that because of the generalization of rate structures required by both the public and the railways and the great difficulty in segregating costs by individual shipments, the proper concern should be with a positive balance of revenues over costs and a system of rates that gave effect to an acceptable principle of equity. To apply certain factors arbitrarily would give rise to feelings of injustice and was not necessary to assure the carriers of adequate revenues. In other words, the inherent logic of the rate structure, which had long been evident

160

within each region, should simply be extended to cover the whole system, since revenues from all parts of the system were pooled in the company treasury and the sources of that revenue might vary widely from year to year, for which it was totally impossible to adjust rates.

The Board found several good reasons for abolishing the differential without having to commit itself to Alberta's theory, but its decision was tacitly in accord with it.[48] Perhaps most significant of all, from the point of view of the importance attributed to the issue, was the information that only a small portion (about 16 per cent) of the traffic moving in Mountain Territory was bearing any part of the differential. The Board identified this partial application of the differential with unjust discrimination and thus was able to dispose of the issue both in terms of its old criterion as well as the newer factors. The relatively slight impact (Canadian Pacific claimed that it accounted for only four per cent of its revenues from provincial and interprovincial traffic in British Columbia) should be contrasted with the exaggerated language and the open appeal to regional animosities that had been the feature of the newspaper campaign in 1945. This shows as well as anything can the degree of ideological inflation to which the issue had been subjected. Feelings based on much deeper matters than freight rates had been aroused, and consequently the reduction or disappearance of the discriminations in British Columbia and elsewhere did not see the flames die out. They had now spread to other timber.

In retrospect it is possible to see the final Mountain Differential Case as the last peaking of British Columbia's interest in the freight rate question, but in view of the public stances taken and the continuing, though declining, political value of the issue, it took several years for the province to wind down. Participation in the Turgeon Royal Commission and the succession of rate increase cases was continued on the basis of fighting for the interests of the long-haul shipper and the consumer. The initiative, however, was let pass to other provinces, and British Columbia's participation seemed more in the general interests of Western solidarity, as if by remaining associated with the issue it was reassuring itself and others that it was fundamentally "Western" at heart; so closely had attitudes in freight rates become the touchstone of an authentic Western attitude.

161

CHAPTER 8
The Turgeon Royal Commission

The pressure that had been brought to bear on the federal government to have the freight rate problem turned over to a royal commission ensured that the subject would get the most complete airing in its history. The terms of reference of the Turgeon Commission, contained in P.C. 6033 (December 29, 1948) were much broader than those for the General Freight Rate Investigation of 1927 and constituted an open invitation to all and sundry, "if you have complaints, prepare to air them now."

The provinces entered the investigation under a heavy onus to speak out. There was a feeling that the time had come for the issue to be cleaned up once and for all; moreover, there was a popular feeling that the change could and must be done. The degree of ideological contamination was largely unrecognized since the debating points seemed to be about actual anomalies within the rate structure. For the most part, even the most righteously indignant attacks asked no more than a reasonable degree of equity in rates. Whether the complainants believed it to be or not, the request for equity was actually quite moderate. But the ideological elements had the capability of imparting eternal life to the issue, and these began to surface. Protests about horizontal percentage increases and regional economic disparities became more pronounced as it become obvious to those grappling at close quarters with the issue that the economic benefits of "equity" would be so slight as to be imperceptible to the general public, who by now had been led to believe that economic miracles would follow from the removal of "rate discrimination." Paradoxically, this obsession was strong enough to nullify even the anticipated psychological benefits of equity as freight rates come to be regarded as containing not just some surface imperfections but something deeper, almost a kind of original sin. The Commission was given six terms of reference, of which three constituted the main thrust of the enquiry:

(a) to review and report upon the effect, if any, of economic, geographic or other disadvantages under which certain sections of Canada find themselves in relation to the various transportation services therein, and recommend what measures should be initiated in order that the national transportation policy may best serve the general economic well being of all Canada;

(b) to review the Railway Act with respect to such matters as guidance to the Board in general freight rate revisions, competitive rates, international rates, etc., and recommend such amendments therein as may appear to them to be advisable;...

(f) to report upon any feature of the Railway Act (or railway legislation generally) that might advantageously be revised or amended in view of present-day conditions.

References (c), (d) and (e) referred to Canadian National Railways' capital structure, railway accounting and statistical procedure, and the results of the Canadian National/Canadian Pacific Act of 1933, subjects that had been raised during the 30 Per Cent Increase Case.

The desire of the Government to have the issue settled in an authoritative and acceptable manner was evident in the composition of the Commission. The chairman, W.F.A. Turgeon,[1] who had proven himself a highly useful chairman on previous royal commissions, was given leave of absence from his post as Ambassador to Ireland to undertake the job. His experience and knowledge of the grain trade and transportation made him a logical choice. He also doubled as the French-speaking member of the panel. As if to remove all doubt over how the Government wanted the issue to be investigated, the other two commissioners were prominent academic economists – Harry Angus of the University of British Columbia and Harold Innis of the University of Toronto. This meant that two of the regions that felt the most aggrieved – the Prairies and the Maritimes – were not represented on the Commission. Professor Innis, however, had been a member of the Jones Commission in Nova Scotia and had not made any enemies for his part in that, and Professor Angus' proximity to the Prairies and the strong campaign that had been waged by British Columbia on freight rates seemed to justify his representation of all the West. As it turned out, it was the member from Toronto who showed greatest sympathy with the regional positions, and the member from Vancouver who demonstrated considerable skepticism regarding them.

The fanfare and agitation that preceded the formation of the Commission ensured that it would be greeted by a record number of petitioners. The Commission reported that 214 witnesses had appeared before it supporting 143 formal submissions. Hearings were held in all provinces, including the new province of Newfoundland, which thus received a very early baptism into the freight rate mysteries. Comprehensiveness was the main feature of the investigation, and the aggregate shopping list of the parties appearing before it swelled to fantastic proportions. Every lost cause in freight rates since the formation of the Board of Railway Commissioners got another day in court; every long-standing favourite project of a province, town, or board of trade, as well as products of more recent ingenuity, stood in line hopeful of obtaining the blessing of the three wise men. This was done not so much in a spirit of excessive optimism for the relief to be obtained, but rather as a precaution: if one were to fail to at least register the grievance with the Commission, one might somehow lose proprietory rights to it through the operation of some unwritten statute of limitations on freight rate grievances. In future years it might be seen that to have failed to bring a matter to the attention of the Turgeon Commission might effectively disqualify the grievance from receiving any further serious consideration.

The size of the Commission's report reflects the number and variety of the submissions. There were five questions alone arising out of the concurrent freight rate increase applications; particular freight rate problems numbered twenty, not including equalization; other matters of national or local concern were no less than twenty-eight; and twelve more chapters were devoted to other major issues. An analysis of this range of problems is beyond the interest or purpose of this study. I propose merely to select those aspects of some of the provincial briefs which seem to record most faithfully the progress and state of health of the freight rate ideology. To go further would be to follow the brief writers, whether lawyers or rate experts, up the laborious barren paths leading to their respective *culs-de-sac*. The specific rate grievances, no matter how clearly they could be demonstrated technically, for the most part lacked sufficent intrinsic importance to support the scale of demands for relief that were made. Of the provincial briefs, the most interesting aspect was the manner in which they tried to solve the problem of producing evidence and argument that would serve to hide the vacuity of much of the impassioned rhetoric of regional members in the House of Commons and in provincial legislatures and the regional press.

The milieu in which the counsel and experts on freight rate cases worked was quite different from that of the politicians and the press. The free-wheeling, hit-and-run style of the latter, if it could be used at all in the courtroom, had to be kept within certain limits, the margins of which continually had been probed and tested by counsel such as Gerry McGeer and J.J. Frawley. It was not that the politicians were unaware of the technical complexities of the subject, for speakers in the Commons were continuously referring to its abstruseness. This they consigned to the experts, thus justifying their own concentration on the tub-thumping and remaining serene in the faith that the experts would produce the corroborative detail. But the lawyers and experts had to have more exacting standards. A counsel did not want his argument unravelled by failure of his witnesses to provide the necessary evidence nor dismembered by questioning or argument of opposing counsel. Experts called as witnesses had to be able to support any assertions made in a plausible manner and not be discredited by being confronted with contrary evidence that could not be refuted. Moreover, provincial counsel had already had more than two years of experience in sparring with railway counsel and in meeting questions put by the Board, and so had acquired a shrewd sense of the possible and the plausible. Like chess players they had acquired a knowledge of the principal opening moves. The result was that the provincial briefs, considering the passions that had been aroused by the issue, took a moderate tone and a cautious style of phrasing and of subject.

The Provincial Input to the Commission

Because of the insistence with which the provinces had pressed for a royal commission that would discuss fundamental principles, freed of the cramping limitations of the Board's powers and precedents, they were under a moral obligation to present their most comprehensive views to the Commission. There was a certain competitive atmosphere in the West among the experts of the various provinces, much like contesting which could put the best float into the Grey Cup parade.[2]

The provinces' insistence on a Commission also meant that there were many subjects on which they may have had no strong views or any fixed views at all, but which they had to cover for the sake of completeness. This explains the heavy padding of the briefs (only exceeded ten years later in thinking up matters to be brought before the MacPherson Royal Commission). This problem became acute with the steady fading-out of the equalization issue, although it had been the tinder used to start the fire in the first place. By that time, even the railways agreed in principle that regional differences in certain basic class rates should be eliminated. Commodity rates reflect unique market conditions in the individual markets. As for competitive rates, the rapid expansion of highway transport was causing higher-valued commodities either to shift to trucks or to be retained by railways only at competitive rates, which by common consent were outside the scope of regulatory control. The amount of traffic being carried at class rates was consequently declining, and with it, the importance of the equalization issue. Alberta presented a formal argument in favour of equalization, based on the reasoning that had been developed in its brief on the Mountain Differential. It was largely superfluous. The Commission itself did not have to commit itself to any doctrine to support its recommendation of equalization. It simply made two statements to the effect that the fullness of time had now arrived:

> It would appear, from the foregoing [the positions of the provinces and the railways] and having regard particularly to the terms of Order in Council No. P.C. 1487 [April, 1948], that the broad general principal of equalization throughout the country is now accepted....
>   ... it appears that Canada has reached a stage in its development when former methods of making regional rates must give way to a uniform rate structure that, as far as may be possible, will treat all citizens, localities, districts and regions alike.[3]

That marked the end of a sixty-year argument. Beyond this point the freight rate issue entered into a state of degeneracy. But a glance at the provincial briefs will be of value to indicate the state of the art of freight rate agitation under these changing circumstances.

By 1949, the Transportation Commission of the Maritime Board of Trade had completed fifteen years of continuous operation since its reorganization in 1934. Working full-time over this period, its executive-manager, Rand Matheson, had explored every corner of the freight rate structure and had followed its changes on a day-to-day basis. Thus, Maritime positions on freight rates had reached a fair degree of stability, and in successive rate cases or transportation investigations it was largely a matter of reiteration, varying only the degrees of emphasis. The foundation for this position was a "charter" – the Maritime Freight Rates Act. Of prime concern was its protection from the "encroachment" by establishment of competitive rates in Central Canada and its extension in area, rate of advantage, and mode of transport. Its scriptural canon consisted of the Duncan Report and the preamble to the Maritime Freight Rates Act, to which there was appended an apocrypha comprising the documents and papers supporting and propounding the Patterson thesis on pre-Confederation promises. Into this pattern, the issue of horizontal percentage increases naturally fitted, and, together with the later-to-be-developed theme of regional economic expansion, gave the Maritimes an unfailing spring of unsatisfied demands that could be attached to the popular issue of freight rates. While this would appear to set no limit to possible demands, the Maritime brief presented to the Turgeon Commission was moderate both in demands and language. It conceded the questionability of the Maritime Rights interpretation of London Conference Resolution 66, observing only that many Maritimers were convinced of its essential accuracy.[4] It also conceded that "government policy, as reflected in the rate structure, appears to have been reasonably maintained until about 1912."[5] However, the Maritimes did not subscribe to or support the equalization of freight rates.[6]

This point had been overlooked by those Western spokesmen who had lumped the Maritime Provinces with the West in demanding the end of rate discrimination. The Maritimes, having already obtained "equalization minus 20 per cent" with Central Canada, did not want their rates to be tied to any upward revision of Central Canadian rates in the course of being equalized with the higher Prairie scale. Since this, according to Canadian Pacific, would have required an amendment to the Maritime Freight Rates Act, to which the Maritimes were opposed, no government would have had the foolhardiness to trifle with the charter in this fashion. When equalization was put into effect, the Maritime rates were left untouched. The cooperation between the eight provinces came more naturally in the opposition of horizontal percentage increases and in the emerging theme of regional development.

Manitoba's dark secret during the Turgeon Commission period was that it really didn't have any freight rate complaints that were worthy of the laments being made by its provincial and federal politicians. Ever since it concluded the 1901 Agreement with the Canadian Northern, Manitoba had been in a defensive stance at freight rate hearings, striving to maintain the advantage its early presence had gained for it and to resist the persistent attempts of the three more westernly provinces to reach a position of equality with it. It had joined in the campaign rhetoric of the other Western Provinces, but had tended to vote with the railways, keeping the ballot as secret as possible. Only a few months prior to the opening of the hearings, Manitoba had unsuccessfully opposed the British Columbia application for the removal of the Mountain Differential.[7] With the Mountain Differential removed, the Fort William terminal rates, based upon a reduced mileage between Fort William and Winnipeg as a result of the 1901 Agreement, were the last vestige of Manitoba's advantage over the other provinces except that of geographic position. But this had greatly declined, in whatever importance it ever had, with the quieting of the long struggle between the distributors of the principal Western cities. Winnipeg had no chance of recovering its former dominance in the Western distribution trade because the other cities had successfully established their own distribution trades and the larger units in the business maintained branches in all the principal centres and were becoming largely indifferent to comparative freight rates. At the Turgeon Commission, Manitoba supported equalization and let the constructive mileage issue go by default. On the major stances – such as the acceptance of the disadvantages of distance,[8] the neutral roles of freight rates,[9] the freedom of the railways to publish rates to meet competition,[10] and equalization,[11] – Manitoba, Alberta, and British Columbia were in general agreement. In fact, in its summary of the regional complaints in the Prairie Provinces, the Commission had no occasion to make any reference to any particular Manitoba complaints at all.

Saskatchewan's position is interesting in that its scope for complaint reflected the gradation in its geographic position between Manitoba and Alberta. In any given grievance based on distance the chances were that Saskatchewan could complain slightly more than Manitoba, but not as much as Alberta. This in-between position had been reflected in the history of freight rates by Saskatchewan's stance on the Mountain Differential, the transcontinental competitive rates, and equalization at the General Freight Rates Investigation in the 1920's, and on other occasions. In 1949, Saskatchewan, like Manitoba, lacked any clearly defined, let alone shocking, examples of freight rate grievances. Therefore, its problem of what to say or what to ask for was different only to a slight degree from that of Manitoba. Each province solved this problem in a way that is curiously in accord with the provincial temperament sometimes ascribed to it. Manitoba settled for a scholarly discussion of principles from which neither the province nor the Commission was able to derive any solid residue of recommendations after the excess words had been boiled off. Could this be traced to the underlying conservatism Manitoba derived from the economic and political dominance possessed by the early wave of settlers from Eastern Canada? In Saskatchewan, on the other hand, this same dominance tended to be in the hands of immigrants and their descendents coming from the British Isles, which may explain the earlier and deeper penetration of ideas linked to the philosophy of the British Labour Party than elsewhere on the Prairies. To such people and the provincial CCF government, words alone were hardly enough – some tangible reform proposals were clearly called for. In the absence of any precise definition of the problem in the public mind, it was up to the lawyers and experts to come up with one. The workings of their minds were almost transparent; they cast about for a suitable proposal and quickly discovered the Maritime Freight Rates Act with its reduction of 20 per cent on rates within preferred territories. The application of this type of assistance to Saskatchewan traffic – and other Prairie traffic as well – was estimated to cost $40 million annually, an amount that surely should have been enough to convince the most stubborn skeptic that there must be big freight rate problems in that area!

Manitoba and Alberta refused to go along with Saskatchewan's proposal, giving the Commission (had it been necessary) an easy means of dismissing the idea. How could a subsidy of that magnitude be justified if two-thirds of the beneficiaries are not even asking for it? Indeed, the other Western Provinces were inclined to look down on Saskatchewan's action. In the rather puritanical economics of the time, asking for a subsidy was as unsporting as upsetting the chess board. The other provinces regarded the proposal as a breaking of the rules of the game and a sapping of the high moral stature the freight rate issue had acquired. The goal was still justice, not subsidy. In retrospect, however, what seems to have meant failure for the Saskatchewan effort was that it was merely ten or twenty years ahead of its time.

It fell to the patriotic duty of Professor George Britnell of the University of Saskatchewan, the "economist-laureate" of the province with a high national reputation for studies on the grain economy, to present the provincial brief. All went soberly until it came time for railway counsel to cross-examine. Thereupon there ensued a hilarious chase, in the classic style of Elmer Fudd and Bugs Bunny, as Britnell nimbly and in the most unlikely fashion leaped out of every trap that railway counsel, pursuing him with lumbering gate, tried to put together out of some of the more extravagant statements in the brief. It was all good fun and the audience in the courtroom, consisting mostly of provincial counsel and their advisers, enjoyed every minute of it. But by the time Britnell stepped out of the witness-box two points had become very clear: he was not going to let himself become involved in a serious defence of the Saskatchewan proposal, and the proposal itself was not one that could be taken seriously. The epilogue is even stranger. Innis, after having signed the Commission's Report, which gave short shrift to the proposal, included a memorandum (not described as a dissent) which he called "an elaboration of the basic argument behind the conclusions of the Report." This elaboration ended with a page in which he advocated in some detail nothing less than a very similar proposal! I will return to this point shortly when I discuss the confrontation between the professors and the freight rate issue.

Although it created little attention at the time and was soon forgotten, the Saskatchewan brief nevertheless acquires some interest in retrospect. It represented the prototype of the arguments that were later put forward as the ideology. This was a new breed of ideology, freed from concern with the trivialities of actual freight rate anomalies, which began to paint a sweeping picture of regional disparities. The connection with freight rates or transportation policy was largely imaginary. The generally orthodox ideas in the briefs of the other

Western Provinces indicated that they were not yet ready to take off with Saskatchewan, into the wide blue yonder, but it was only by such a strained interpretation of the role of freight rates that the Western premiers were able to relaunch the ideology in the late sixties. The Saskatchewan brief must be regarded as a trial flight. Later and more streamlined models would be able to dispense with some of the concessions to logic that impeded its take-off.

The brief demonstrates a selective, or elastic, logic, often present in ideologies, which closes gaps in the argument by question-begging and rigorously excludes awkward incompatibilities that would weaken the argument. It is a fascinating exercise to put together the links in the argument. First, there is a very frank statement of the problem of the brief-writers, that the effects of mere equalization in rates will be inconsequential:[12]

> In the opinion of this Province, relatively little can be achieved through modifications of the rate structure as such (p.73).... It is conceivable that insofar as equalization of class rates is concerned, desirable adjustments could be made without materially affecting railway revenues. The same is probably true of the proposed replacement of distributing rates of town tariffs. Any alleviation from these sources would, however, by the same token, be *relatively slight.* (p. 95)

Then there is a statement of the main premise, based on popular opinion on the subject:

> It has, nevertheless, long been *the contention* in the western region that as between East and West there has not been an equality in the matter of railway freight rates. More specially *it has been alleged* that rates are higher in the West than in the East and that there is no reasonable ground on which this differential can be justified. (p. 79)

Allegation slides directly into fact. The Western credo parallels the Patterson thesis in the Maritimes and rests on a similar foundation in the clouds:

> Aside from such *possible* grounds of complaint as the one noted in the preceding paragraph [differences in the levels of distribution and town tariffs, a specific grievance] there is a *broader and much more deeply-rooted belief in the West* regarding rate differentials. *We believe – and there seems to be little doubt about the facts* – that freight rates have been at a higher level generally in western regions than in the East. (p. 80)

Yet we are then told:

> It will be conceded at once that a compelling statistical proof of this allegation cannot be made. Not all western rates are higher: some are lower. Moreover, a higher stated rate in a majority of instances is not conclusive without reference to the volume of freight moving under various rates and without an analysis of the distances involved. (p. 80)

The brief goes on to state that Saskatchewan is in no position to make an accurate study and that even the Board or the railways could not do so without a long period of preparation. Even so, the brief states: "Nevertheless the history of the decisions by the Board of Transport Commissioners and official pronouncements of the Dominion Government are consistent with the position here taken and indicate the *existence of a factual basis for this contention.*" (p. 80) But the examination of these decisions and pronouncements discloses that they are all referring to specific differences in actual rate scales whose removal is dismissed as being inadequate.

> It has been urged [in the brief] that ... equalization of certain standard and class rate levels and the more comprehensive control of competitive rates, while desirable in reducing inequalities in effective rate levels between regions, *will not and cannot solve the fundamental* problem arising from the disproportionate burden for national transportation which falls upon Western Canada. (p. 92)

There remains only to take the death-defying leap: "It has been demonstrated in this Submission that equity to the West demands *drastic reductions* in freight rates." (p. 95) Subject to only one important qualification: "The Government of Saskatchewan wishes to emphasize that this relief is quite separate and distinct from the Crow's Nest grain rates." (p. 93)

When the talk is about rate levels in general, it can only mean an averaging of the amounts paid for the movement of all traffic in any given area. A vast number of unlike and unrelated items with different conditions of carriage are going to be heaped together to derive these averages, but a major distortion would be involved in excluding the traffic having the largest volume, greatest distance, and lowest rates in the area. The formidable task of the brief-writers, compelled to find some rational basis for the ideology by such means, can thus be easily appreciated. It involves deriving from units conceded to be roughly fair to begin with, or with differences such that their removal would have scant effect, a basic and very sweeping inequity when these units are combined in, say, an annual traffic volume. (Since the Saskatchewan proposal was first made, data in the form of the Waybill Analysis have been regularly compiled, making it possible to test some of the hypotheses in the proposal.)

Compared to the Saskatchewan brief, the several briefs submitted by the Alberta government appear distressingly orthodox in tone. Apart from a short dissertation on horizontal percentage increases, the items in the Alberta case are based on references to actual rates in the tariffs, in the classic manner of the briefs in the Western Rates Case and the General Freight Rate Investigation. The fact was that Alberta, located at "the apex of the rate structure," alone of the Western Provinces had sufficient items on specific rate situations to make up the bulk of its case. As a result, the Alberta experts had a feeling of superior virtue such as a clergyman may have when looking down on the actions of some brethren whose sermons are not based on texts from the Bible. The Alberta position on the subject of equalization was an elaboration of what had already been submitted in the Mountain Differential Case. A new element was the coining of the concept of "regional discrimination," to be distinguished from the "personal discrimination" that was identified with the "unjust discrimination" used so often by the Board to dismiss applications for equalization. It was a pure verbalism, of course. There was, however, this to be said for it, that just as a set order of words may create problems or frustrate their solution, so a new distinction in words may be able to lead to the solution of problems. In any event, at this point agreements of any kind were no longer necessary to bring about class rate equalization.[13]

Alberta also made a massive attack on the transcontinental competitive rates, or rather on the comparatively high intermediate rates that were maintained simultaneously. This was, and continues to be, the most spectacular of the alleged discriminations in the rate structure and has been called in as evidence for all manner of general discontents. Much was made of the suggestion that in some cases it might be cheaper for Alberta to have the freight hauled two ways across the mountains, paying a combination rate rather than the direct rate from Eastern Canada to Alberta. If the railways were prepared to charge such rates, the implication was that the intermediate rates by comparison were exorbitant. The argument of the railways, which had always been accepted by the Board, was that these were no different in nature from any other competitive rates. If the railways could realize some net gain from the low-priced transcontinental traffic, it was better to accept the traffic than to forgo it.

While businessmen may have found this acceptable, the rates were a standing target for the wrath of politicians. Alberta's request was for the Board to have something comparable to the Interstate Commerce Commission's "Spokane principle," which made the coast rate the maximum for rates to intermediate points. There was an important difference between the American and Canadian cases. The American railways were competing with high-cost American-flag water carriers who, in general, were subject to governmental rate regulation. Water competition, or the threat of it, for Canadian carriers came from low-cost Commonwealth shipping at the much lower and wholly uncontrolled rates of world shipping. This was a subject dealing with competitive rates, and it is difficult to see how the Board, if the argument had to have been addressed to it, would have been prepared to infringe on its long-standing hands-off attitude to competitive rates. With no such impediments to its actions, the Commission recommended a direct intervention in the form of a statutory prohibition against a railway charging an intermediate point more than one and one-third times the competitive rate to the coast. The justification given was largely on compassionate grounds since the Commission did not directly challenge the position of the railways and the Board:

> As long as the competition exists, the railways should be permitted to meet it. But when meeting the competition creates anomalies of the character indicated above and causes such long-standing grievances, it is desirable that a solution be found which will enable the railways to meet the competition and at the same time eliminate, at least to a substantial degree, the anomalies created. [14]

Another Alberta brief dealt with the more complex subject of raw material and finished products rates, suggesting that the relationship should be such as to favour the processing of raw materials in the province of origin. This had been raised twenty years earlier at the General Freight Rates Investigation and was to be raised again twenty years later by Alberta in connection with rates on livestock and meat products. The complexity of the problem, which had caused the Board to bypass it, was still such that the Commission promptly sent it back to the Board, noting that there seemed to be no doubt that the Board had the power to deal with it. Of the other Alberta grievances, little need be said except to note that a deep dredging of railway tariffs brought to light an anomaly whose existence until then had apparently not been suspected. When it was discovered that the standard class rates – which were reputed to be as little used in actual transactions as an automobile dealer's list price – made up the Canadian component of international combination rates across the Western Canadian gateways, it was regarded with the same pride as an angler's prize catch, having been as unpredictable.

British Columbia entered the Turgeon investigation in a state near to satiety, scarcely having digested the results of the abolition of the Mountain Differential. There were a few rate complaints outstanding, such as the difference between export and domestic rates on grain, but these were hardly stressed. Like some of the other provinces, British Columbia's problem was what to find to say to the Commission. With the Mountain Differential a thing of the past, B.C. was now prepared to accept its geographical disadvantages as they were, with the proviso that it might want to reconsider if other provinces obtained relief from their disadvantages. All that was left was to endorse equalization and to decry horizontal percentage increases. As had been the case for the other provinces, this had to be enveloped in a suitably impressive matrix of principles, considering the high professional competence of the members of the Commission, who might be expected to respond to such an approach. The writing of the British Columbia brief could therefore be assigned almost on a random basis, and the senior civil servant to whom the lot fell confessed privately that he knew little about freight rates and so decided to stay close to the textbooks and keep clear of controversy. The result was that British Columbia's brief was an advocacy of the cost of service as the main principle of rate-making. (There was evident confidence that it would not lead to a restoration of the Mountain Differential.) Only a defence of motherhood could have offered a less controversial approach. The brief's limitation was that it was meant only to be looked at and admired but not touched, much less picked apart. When that happened it dissolved into a sticky mass of qualifications and contradictions. In its Report the Commission gravely remarked that the definition of the words "cost of service" did "appear to be a difficulty of a fundamental nature" and concluded that the proposal had not been shown to be a practical one. But perhaps the Commission took too narrow a view. It did, however, have a practical value in giving British Columbia a respectable exposure before the Commission; one comparable to that given other provinces.

The Professors' Presence in the Commission

The Turgeon Commission's function as seen by the federal government is revealed by the presence of two of the top-ranking Canadian economists – Professors Harry Angus and Harold Innis. Thus the profession had a numerical majority unusual in such bodies. It was as if the Government had decided that a cross-section of opinion quite different from that which the Board itself could ordinarily provide was essential. The expertise of the Board's membership, where it existed, was almost always in law, which served to reinforce its conception of itself as a strictly judicial body. Appointments for political or particular representative reasons generally yielded personnel who seldom challenged in any consistent manner the advice of the legal and traffic departments that was buttressed by long experience and precedents. It may have been the Government's hope that two such eminent economists might be able to make recommendations to set the Board on a new course more acceptable to those parts of the country where public opinion had become highly sensitized to freight rates. Moreover, there was general agreement that the Commission had been summoned to deal with what basically was an economic problem.

The significance of the Turgeon Commission is not that it recommended tearing down the old house and building a new one, but that it went through the house, inspecting it thoroughly, throwing out some of the junk that had been accumulating for years, recommending a few minor repairs here and there, and then pronouncing it fit for further habitation. It didn't fire the janitors but gave them a few new duties, relatively speaking. It wrote a business-like report, a bureaucratic achievement filled with the methodical disposition of the more than sixty separate subjects that had been brought to the Commission's attention. Some were accepted. Some were put aside regretfully. Some were sent to the Board, hopefully for action. Others were sent to the Board, hopefully for oblivion. Some were the subject of interesting chats in lieu of action. But the greatest number were simply dropped quietly out of sight.

There is some reason to suppose that the economists may have become bored with all this detail and left it to be processed in conveyor-belt fashion by the chairman and the staff. In the 280-page Report there was only a final chapter of seven pages entitled "National Transportation Policy," and this was given over to a discussion and recommendation of a "central authority" to co-ordinate the regulation of all modes of transport under federal jurisdiction. But this was more of an engineering-type of proposal and didn't really reflect the presence of economists on the Commission. Consequently, when the economists present their respective "Reservations and Observations" and "Memorandum" at the end of the report, one senses them as men taking fullest advantage of the few minutes allowed to stretch their legs and catch a breath of fresh air on the platform after spending hours on a crowded train. A striking difference in approach between Angus and Innis is revealed in their remarks in the Report and even more in their notes made during their sojourn on the Commission. These notes have been preserved in the Public Archives.

The principal item preserved in Angus's notes is an uncompleted and, so far as I am aware, unpublished essay entitled "Notes suggested by the Regional Hearings."[15] It is a frank document in which sympathy and skepticism are seasoned with irony and wit. He sees that the ideological formulation of the problem, which came out abundantly during the original hearings, is unsatisfactory and he is sensitive to the psychological, social, and political aspects. As indicative of the trend of his reflections on the problem, Angus noted:

> It may as well be admitted at the outset that the Commission cannot discover any general principle of justice applicable to such a situation as has been described [the distance factor]. In practice, fortunately, the difficulties are not so great. Discontent is, of course, always latent when one part of the country is less prosperous than another. But it comes to a head when increases in freight rates are made, or when hard times are experienced. An industry which finds itself in difficulties is quick (or astute) to look on an increase in freight rates as a cost which is unjustified; an industry in search of relief is quick to ask for cheaper services from others. (p. 4)

The growing emphasis on the alleged evils of horizontal percentage increases attracted his attention and understanding beyond the single mathematical arguments on which they were established:

> To recapitulate: It is because geographic and economic disadvantages are thought of largely in terms of vulnerability to the impact of a recession, because it is feared that rates determined in years of prosperity will remain as a charge on industry in years of adversity, because industries wish to retain as normal the level of prosperity which they have attained as a result of fortunate contingencies, that discussion has concentrated on the timing of changes in freight rates. There is a universal desire to postpone the moment of increase which is quite consistent with the admission that an increase will be necessary; much as the desire to postpone the moment of death does not imply a desire to live forever. (p. 9)

In his "Reservations and Observations" in the Report, Angus commented "on the desirability of clarity and intelligibility in Canadian railway policy."[16] The parties should be conscious not only of their conflicting interests but also of their common interests. Angus went further in his notes, pointing out the difficulty created by the "unintelligibility" of railway rates:

> It is at this point that the unintelligibility of railway rates is most

significant. It seems true to say that no one seems to feel any responsibility for asking for lower rates or for better service because it is utterly uncertain who will have to meet the ultimate cost. As often as not it may seem as if the cost might be imposed on shippers who are at present escaping too lightly. The unintelligibility of freight rates also makes it easy for some (or perhaps even all) shippers to nourish a sense of injustice and of victimization. It stands in the way of sound public relations and in the long run the railways are probably the greatest sufferers from it. It is, in a sense, the core of the railway problem. (p. 12)

The difficulties are summed up in a final question: "It is desirable that rates should not only be fair but that they should also appear fair: But is it practicable?" (p. 17)

The clarity and detachment exhibited by Angus as he observed the events taking place before the Commission is in marked contrast to the rather uncritical enthusiasm and confidence with which Innis plunged into the melee to extract, as he saw it, an economic solution to an economic problem. Throughout his career, Innis was a captive to a methodology that generated contradictions he did not seem always to be aware of. This may partly explain the turgidity and the Rube Goldberg-like structure of his chains of reasoning. Each link was bound to the next in a tenuous string of "incidental to's." He once described his method as essentially Marxist, meaning that economics was to be considered the prime explanatory factor in society, but he was never in any sense a political Marxist.[17] This accounted for a certain economic scientism in his views. Society was seen as a complex polyhedron of forces, each one exerting itself on all the others in an eternal push-pull contest. Hence, the recurrence of physical metaphors in his style, such as stresses, strains, and collapses of structures as the contending forces measured their strengths against each other. It might be supposed that such a methodology would hold out the possibility and even the obligation to conduct quasi-scientific investigations to confirm the objective nature of these factors and thereby the validity of the method. But, as is common knowledge, in the social sciences, of which the freight rate problem could be as good an example as any, such detailed and systematic attempts to pin down these factors often result in their vanishing from view altogether. As in an oil painting, the scene viewed at a distance may seem to be extraordinarily clear, but when the painting is examined at close range, square centimeter by square centimeter, all that can be discovered is a meaningless mass of brush strokes. Innis's solution to this dilemma seems to have been not to question the certainty of the methodology, but to evade its implicit obligation to prove certainty by a style that became increasingly impressionistic in tone. Facts were linked by that ambiguous phrase "incidental to," which could stand for everything from a firm causal connection to a mere passing reference to a coincidence in time or place.[18]

Angus was able to perceive psychological, social, and other classes of causes playing a part, yet Innis's lack of flexibility led to a dead area in his reception of data from the outside world. According to the presuppositions of the economic interpretation of history, social, political, and psychological factors were part of a superstructure, the true explanation of which was to be obtained by examining the underlying economic factors. No matter how real their disguises appeared, they were still only masking economic realities. When, in the freight rate issue, the reverse occurred – social, political, and psychological discontents adopting an economic guise to explain themselves – Innis was not tuned to the wavelength and did not pick up the signal. This is not to say that he was lacking in a sense of humour, although he did take his own presuppositions quite seriously, or that he could not recognize rationalizing self-interest or sheer humbug when he saw it. But such cases he seemed mainly to dispose of by dropping into a trash can labelled "politics," as an impurity in the sample that must be removed before serious analysis could take place. Unfortunately, his methodology here simply gives another spin around the circle, for even the crudest political nonsense is part of that same superstructure that had to be explained in terms of the underlying economic realities. The more irrational the outcry, as with the patient suffering great pain, the more serious the diagnosed economic cause could be held to be. There can be "econo-somatic" causes of ailments just as there are psychosomatic causes, particularly if the methodology has captured the popular mind to the extent of impressing on the populace the basic nature of economic explanation. Naturally, one would espouse the most acceptable or convincing explanation of one's case to ensure that it is taken seriously. Five hundred years ago witchcraft might have seemed a more effective diagnosis, but today economics is regarded as the universal therapy.

Innis's notes from the Turgeon Commission proceedings consist of a lengthy number of brief comments, probably jotted down during the hearings. Not being produced for any ulterior purpose such as publication, it can be assumed they give his real impressions and convictions, although not necessarily as they would be after reconsideration. They provide indications only and are not something that could be used as chapter-and-verse citations to prove some particular point about his ideas.

In the first place, there are some references that indicate his awareness of the emotional or ideological element. He could hardly have been oblivious to it: "Problem of antagonism to the CPR – responsible for opposition to horizontal increases and to Board's decisions – involves an element of distortion in the problem of railway finances and rates." And again, "I am certain that if rates had been equalized between Eastern and Western Canada, much of the objection to horizontal increases would have disappeared."

By and large he seemed to take seriously the numerous complaints about horizontal percentage increases, as the Commission itself did in its Report. For instance, he noted:

Alberta poultry producers complain of blanket increase in longest distance shipments – another anomaly of blanket increase – penalizing areas with longer shipments.

Possibility of putting large-scale blanket changes under control of Parliament rather than the B.T.C.

Query: whether the Canadian Pacific as a yardstick is worth the disturbance to the whole economy incidental to blanket increases?

Perhaps the best indication of Innis's determination to regard the problem as purely economic is given in his ideas about the future duties of the Board. These add up directly, and by implication, to a formidable list requiring a performance that could hardly be expected of any department of government. As Innis saw it, the problem was to free the economists from the thrall of the politicians so they could get on with the task of providing a solution. Their ability to do this is not doubted:

Neglect of Board of problem of the economy as a whole – left to Parliament and political agitation.

Need for Board to develop more intensive interest in economic analysis to check tendency to resort to political solutions and to avoid necessity of sudden changes – i.e. blanket increases, large wage increases.

The possibility of strengthening the Board to the point that it could handle problems previously left to the political field.

The neglect of the B.T.C. on economic problems of prices or on economic analysis.

Difficulty of securing a Board capable of making flexible rates in relation to the problems of business cycle.[19]

These comments voice the conviction that if only the Board – even a superhuman Board with a superhuman staff – would come up with the proper economic solution, the whole problem could be removed from "politics" and solved. They indicate little feeling that the ideological nature of the problem would negate even the miracles that such a Board might produce, nor that the more radical solutions coming to the surface, such as the Saskatchewan proposal, represent the beginnings of attempts to break the issue free of any economic moorings.

Mention has already been made of Innis's rather surprising endorsement of the Saskatchewan subsidy proposal in the guise of elaborating the basic argument behind the conclusions of the Report. A few sentences from this part of the memorandum fully illustrate the disastrous effects of elaborating patterns of elementary theoretical economics with properties taken from the real world and totally ignoring the *ceteris paribus* clause which remains the only thread connecting theoretical reasoning with reality.

> A reduction in class rates on traffic in the Western region and westbound would offer the greatest immediate relief. Such a reduction would encourage long haul and local traffic in Western Canada producing the greatest revenues. An increase in this traffic would be of the greatest advantage to the railways in the utilization of equipment and the reduction of expenses. It would be of advantage to producers and consumers in the Western provinces and to producers in the St. Lawrence and Maritime regions.[20]

Such an answer might get high marks in a first-year examination paper that asked: assume that there is great suffering in Western Canada; show how a reduction in freight rates would provide immediate relief. The sobering thought is that had the Commission recommended this, the political influence of the ideology, reinforced by the prestige of a Commission that was regarded as having a high economic competence, would probably have forced the government to accept it. This is indeed what happened, on a much smaller scale, with the Bridge Subsidy that the Commission recommended. It would seem that in the economic theorizing of the freight rate ideology, Innis noted an affinity with some of his own theses on Canadian economic history, thus providing a sort of updating and confirmation of his ideas. At any rate, the Turgeon Report yields very few indications of any meeting of minds; the body of the Report is largely a staff document and from the nature of the addenda the professors could have spent most of their time on the Commission each talking to himself.

The Commission's Solution

The Turgeon Commission's recommendations represented about the greatest length that one could go under Canadian conditions in eliminating "freight rate discrimination" if one merely aimed to establish a practical application of a principle of equity in which the costs would be paid by the users. Beyond this point the demands for something more than equity could only be satisfied by subsidy, for the Crow's Nest Pass method of a simple statutory freezing of the rates, regardless of the consequences, was not likely to be repeated.[21] The Commission recommended, and the Railway Act was amended in 1951 so to provide, that the class and commodity rate scales be equalized (outside the Atlantic Region), that the one-and-one-third rule be attached to the transcontinental competitive rates to mitigate the spread between them and rates to intermediate points.

In two other respects the Commission attempted to satisfy the popular discontent that had been translated or interpreted by the provincial governments during the 30 Per Cent Case into specific grievances. In the matter of competitive rates, the Commission tried to tighten the regulation and surveillance by the Board even though this only resulted in statutory provisions that could be little more than admonitory. It was agreed by all that competitive rates could be established by the railways on their own initiative and at a level based on their estimate of what was needed to meet the competition. The Board's usual avenue of approach through the complaint of a shipper, however, could obviously not serve in this case as the shipper either was satisfied with the railway rate or was using the competitive carrier. Possible complaints were limited to two: either that of a shipper who felt that he was in some way injured by the rate or by not getting a comparable rate, as in market competition, or the much vaguer complaint the provinces had now pushed to the forefront, that whole levels of competitive rates in one region might be lower than necessary to meet the competition, thrusting an added burden of a rate increase on non-competitive areas. Why the railways might knowingly establish rates lower than necessary to meet competition is difficult to explain, except that competing carriers may tacitly have abandoned rate competition without attempting to raise the rates. Something clearly had to be done to remind the Board that it had a responsibility here, even though it proved impractical to try to discharge. Knowledge of the competing carriers' rates and services would have been required for a serious investigation, but these were not under the Board's jurisdiction. The section remained in the Railway Act as mostly a dead letter until swept away by the very different provisions of the National Transportation Act in 1967.

181

Another concession to Western opinion, as it was intended, was the Bridge Subsidy, which was paid to the railways in compensation for lowering their non-competitive rates between Eastern and Western Canada. Such a proposal had not been given much prominence in the representations to the Commission. It was mentioned at the hearings only by the United Farmers of Alberta Farm Cooperative but had been previously put forward by Walter Tucker, a Saskatchewan Liberal MP and later opposition leader in the Saskatchewan legislature. The Bridge Subsidy was a mini-version of the Saskatchewan subsidy proposal, in that it required $7 million as opposed to $40 million. The actual justification for it was that the rates on the long-distance traffic were too high and unduly burdensome on the Western shipper and consignee. However, for reasons into which it would be fascinating to inquire, it was not considered adequate just to leave it at that, for the allegation had been repeated boldly over the years, working up to a crescendo starting in 1945. The rates had to be found defective in some concrete way, so that there could be some semblance of an economic justification. It had to be a demand, not just because the West wanted lower rates, but because the rates were already too high for some quite other reason. The Commission evidently decided that Tucker offered the best myth for this particular purpose. According to him, the reason why the West was being penalized by the high level of the interregional rates was the existence of a long stretch of unproductive territory between the two regions (from Sudbury to the Lakehead) that the railways had to cross but which yielded them no traffic. Relief was to be given to the West by compensating the railways for the cost of maintenance of these portions of their tracks. I will not go into the complications that arose in trying to derive a connection between cost of maintenance and a reduction in rates in the tariff, as I have covered that elsewhere.[22] It will be sufficient here to note it was one of the curious byways into which policy is forced in order to accommodate itself to ideological pressure.

Had something like the Turgeon Report plus the Mountain Differential judgement appeared as a result of the General Freight Rates Investigation in 1927, there could have been at least a slight chance that the subsequent ideological growth would have been nipped in the bud. For in 1927 and for many years after there was no complicating factor such as a general rate increase to keep the home fire burning. But this is perhaps to overlook the high political value the freight rates issue had acquired even in the absence of any major concrete grievance. The impassioned pleas for nothing more than equality proved to be easily transferable to new and bigger demands based on the alleged harm from horizontal percentage increases, than from any increase whatever, and finally in the absence of any increase to the ultimate generalization of attacking regional economic disparities. One can see the shift starting in the speeches in the House of Commons on the amendments to the Railway Act implementing the Turgeon Report recommendations. The theme is one of "yes, but ...," as some speakers realized that equalization was actually going to make little difference in conditions and started to adjust their targets and aim in order to continue to use their favourite weapon. The impending rate increases made this a relatively quick and easy operation. It changed the nature of the game, however. Henceforth, it was to be played almost entirely with symbolic counters rather than with hard factual data. The real economics of the case had become of secondary importance, and where it was obviously inadequate a new economics was created where the importance of freight rates was inflated to whatever degree necessary to sustain the politically satisfying changes that were being made. In the hands of the politicians the freight rate issue became an instrument of political regionalism. The problem has become not one of discovering, by massive studies, the supposed link between the actual freight rate situation and the overblown value of regional protest, for it is simply not there, but one of locating the true, or at least the more plausible, causes of that regional discontent. It must be assumed that they were not created *ex nihilo*.

The Minister of Transport, Lionel Chevrier, expressed the hope, in introducing the second reading of the Bill, in October, 1951, that it would give "relief to the Board from those regional controversies from which it has never been free in all the 48 years of its existence." He went further:

> In my opinion the final advantage to be derived from this legislation lies in the removal of a persistent source of regional grievance. In this country, made up as it is of widely differing regions, no state of affairs within the power or responsibility of Parliament, and which is a source of friction and grievance between regions, should be permitted to continue. So long as regional grievances remain unsolved they encourage thinking exclusively in terms of regional interests rather than in terms of national interest.[23]

As is well known, the Bill failed to fulfil such hopes, otherwise the implementation of the Turgeon Report recommendations would have been the logical place to end our own story, with everybody living happily ever after. However, much worse was still to come, not deterred in the least by two decades of unparalleled prosperity in all regions.

CHAPTER 9

The Takeoff of the Ideology from Turgeon to MacPherson

Although a few changes were made in the rate structure after the General Rates Investigation of 1927, the freight rate issue subsided in importance for a time. After the Turgeon Commission Report and the implementation of its recommendations, however, there ensued a steady rise in the pitch of the discontent that culminated in the 1959 decision by the Diefenbaker government to pay a subsidy to the railway companies rather than permit a further rate increase. The period to be covered starts from a point at which there was some reason to think the old problem of "discriminatory freight rates" had been finally disposed of. Like all good movie serials, it ends with the hero falling into a bottomless pit of perpetual subsidization, and with a royal commission rushing – but probably too late – to effect a miracle by snatching him back to solid economic ground at the last moment. One can hardly wait for the next chapter.

The period marks a change in government attitude toward the freight rate issue, and with it, introduction of a new factor to upset the freight rate balance. Under the ordinary working of the econo-political system there are checks and constraints intervening at all times to keep the system in a rough balance, although they are not strong enough to prevent longer-term shifts away from a former point of equilibrium. These forces permit the system to keep functioning with minor adjustments and changes in direction. As these limited moves seemed helpless to stop the impending crash, it is significant that talk about "transportation policy" became prevalent. But it was, and indeed has remained, a collection of confused and contradictory concepts rather than one having a clear, unambiguous meaning. "Transportation policy" has the meaning for each individual that he wants to give it.

On the grounds that it would be wearisome to the reader to go step by step through the development of the different themes and their interrelations during this period, I have attempted to give a panoramic view of the whole in Table 1, which constitutes a composite chronology

Table 1. Railway Wage and Freight Rate Increases in the Post-war Period

Wage Increases*	Freight Rate Increases	
July 16, 1948 (after Cabinet intervention)	March 30, 1948	21%
	September 30, 1949	8% interim increase
	March 1, 1950	16% interim increase replacing previous one.
	May 11, 1950	20% final increase granted
January 30, 1951 (after Parliament ended strike)		
	July 4, 1951	12% interim increase
	January 25, 1952	17% final increase granted
	December 30, 1952	9%
February 7, 1953		
	March 6, 1953	7% application
	February, 1954	7% dismissed by BTC
February 24, 1955 (after threat of intervention) May 16, 1956		
	July, 1956	7% interim increase
	December 26, 1956	11% replacing previous one
	December 27, 1957	15% increase increased a further 4%
	January 7, 1958	above increase postponed until March
	February 18, 1958	increase further postponed until May
	April 29, 1958	4% additional increase rescinded by PC 58-601
	September 16, 1958	19% applied for
	November 17, 1958	17% awarded by BTC
November 26, 1958 (on basis of 17% increase)		
	July 8, 1959	Freight Rate Reduction Act passed to provide subsidy
	August 1, 1959	10% increase decreased 7% under subsidy of FRRA
	April 27, 1960	8% increase decreased further 2% under FRRA subsidy
	July 28, 1960	rate freeze extended until April, 1961
	August 1, 1960	FRRA extended until April, 1962, subsidies increased $20 million
May 11, 1961 (act passed to postpone strike)		
	June 8, 1961	FRRA extended until April, 1962, subsidy increased $20 million.
	June 30, 1961	Rate freeze extended voluntarily until April, 1962
November 2, 1962 (after conciliation board gave small increases) July 17, 1964 (settled after government agreed to provide assistance)		

*Increased holiday, vacation, and other non-wage benefits are not shown.

of the period. This may give a general understanding of the whole period and serve as a map that can be consulted by the reader whenever he becomes lost in the course of the following discussion. It will also permit me to confine myself to the general trends pinpointed by some of the more significant or illustrative details.

If it were necessary to track through the complex series of events shown in the table to a basic cause, the choice would fall on the inflationary conditions that persisted through the period. We have already had occasion to note the role of inflation after the First World War in unsettling the freight rate situation. In the late forties and throughout the fifties rising levels of wages and prices inevitably affected the levels of freight rates. The ideology, reinforced by the statutory limits on the Crow's Nest Pass grain rates and its attribution of a hypersensitivity to any changes in freight rates, could not fail to see economic disaster in any region subjected to higher freight rates, even though the price increases had affected all other goods and services. And, as we have had ample experience to know in later years, inflation justifies one's own price increases but, at the same time, also justifies a complaint against the legitimacy of other price increases.

To the effects of inflation on the freight rates issue must be added another causal factor of a general nature – the widespread attitude of regarding railways as social institutions rather than as economic enterprises. This dates back many years, in the first instance to the Intercolonial Railway in the Maritime Provinces and then spread across the country with the formation of the Canadian National Railways. This attitude has amounted to a playing down or rejecting of economic decision-making in railway matters in the interest of wider "social" objectives. The latter in turn have served as a cover under which different groups have pursued their own narrower self-interests. When the railways' ability to conform to such demands has been exhausted there has been no hesitation in calling upon the federal government to assume the responsibility by compensating the railways for the costs that have been thus thrust upon them. The dismantling of the economic factor as the governor of the system has left very inadequate defences against pressures backed by specious social and humanitarian arguments. There is the rapidly weakening force of conscience to inspire a detached and overall appraisal of the issues, but this is all too often swamped by a flood of ingenious rationalizations equating one's self-interest with other people's responsibilities.

There are also the limits of the federal budget, but to say the least these are quite elastic, and appeals involving the support of railway services have generally been able to push themselves to the head of the queue bearing quotations from all too many economists who have talked loosely about the cardinal importance of railways to the Canadian economy and nation. They are important, like any other industry, as long as they are economic; otherwise they become a burden on the economy, which their institutional role may disguise for a while. In their non-economic role the railways sustain an ever-widening circle of other non-economic enterprises. Such institutional thinking about the railways provides a vastly greater scope for demands since it widens the gap between what exists and what is believed could exist. This in turn is made equivalent to what one is entitled to have. If it becomes the reasonable thing to pay a subsidy, then all demands can be cloaked in the garment of reasonableness. The greatest pressures on the railways under the process of institutionalization do not come, as with a normal industry, from the actual customers, but from railway labour, politicians, and the general public in some areas, who all believe that certain benefits can be extracted from the railways which have little relation to their efficient and economic operation. The powerful image of the railways as they were in the twenties on the eve of their displacement from their monopoly position by the highway carriers has persisted in the form of an ideology. This is shared as much by railway labour unions, striving to freeze their duties and operating conditions as they were under steam power, as by the public insisting on regarding railway freight rates as having the significance that they still possessed at the time of steam power.

A further consequence of institutionalization has been the enlarging of the reference groups that involve themselves in labour, services, and rate matters affecting the railways.[1] Every time it is said that the railways are the most important economic structure in the country, these groups say they should be represented in a whole range of decisions on how the railway is to be operated – the running of passenger trains, the closing of stations and branch lines, and of course, freight rates.

Braybrooke and Lindblom point out that as a reference group in the decision-making process becomes more inclusive the policy itself becomes more inclusive, with the result that policy-making becomes cluttered with extraneous matters, even to the extent of paralyzing any action whatever.[2] In Canada we seem to have come perilously close to this point in the discussions on branch line abandonments and freight rates. What might be expeditiously decided between the railways and the actual shippers involved, with the help of some adjudication on the part of the regulatory authority, becomes endlessly ensnarled in arguments brought forward by those located on the outer edges of the reference group whose direct interest is either marginal or non-existent. Evidence that an issue has fallen prey to an excessively large reference group is a succession of studies, proposals, investigations by commissions of inquiry, concurrent truces, or indefinite freezing of the status quo. This often raises what might have been dealt with by a small reference group as a local matter to a national issue on which it may be almost impossible to reach the smallest decision, and then only by agreeing to compensate the many groups who have asserted an interest. If transportation policy is paralyzed and "in a mess," the principal reason is that too many people have been persuaded that they have a direct interest in it. Table 1 shows the effects of institutionalization and the resulting enlargement of the reference groups that took place following the Second World War to the present time.

We have unearthed here perhaps the basic reason for the "contaminating" effect of government involvement in certain economic decision-making. It is not so much that the government is irremediably "socialistic" or inefficient. Generally, an enlargement of the reference group, of which institutionalization is only a more extreme case, creates pressure groups whose direct interests may be minuscule, but who acquire the power to delay and complicate decision-making and enforce claims for compensation or relief at the expense of the government. The Canadian National Railways, as the "people's railway," has thus felt pressures that Canadian Pacific has escaped, although Canadian Pacific has felt pressures of another sort. One might put it best by saying that in the popular mind Canadian National is there to be exploited while Canadian Pacific is there to be fought.

The Labour Factor

It will be noted from the table that labour settlements in the railway industry came at two-year intervals throughout the period. Here, the effects of the institutionalization forced on the railways are most clearly evident. The collective bargaining process had been reduced to formalities since on the one side the unions were prepared to carry matters to a general strike before making concessions. This created an inflexibility on the part of the railways because there were no corresponding advantages to be gained by compromise. Changes in work rules were either refused or could be bought only at a prohibitively high price and would take effect at a snail's pace. Instead of their receiving any kid-glove treatment, the high importance universally attributed to the railways merely attracted a horde of privilege-seekers. Almost in routine fashion, labour disputes, like rate increases, were left to be finally decided by the Cabinet. Rate increases had clearer sailing, however, since the government only escaped difficult labour impasses by permitting the increases. This left little basis for appeals of the rates by the provincial governments.

The record indicates the nature of the crisis that was building up in the fifties. A strike was averted in 1948 only after the Cabinet gave in to labour's demands. A strike did take place in 1950. It was ended by the Maintenance of Railway Operations Act, passed in a special session, which again conceded the essential demands of the unions. Perhaps the preamble to the Act had only the effect of reassuring the unions of their "invincible" bargaining power. " . . . and whereas the vital interests of the people of Canada and the welfare and security of the nation are imperilled by the suspension of operation of the railways, particularly in existing international conditions...."

Government intervention was again required in 1953 and was threatened two years later. A settlement was made in 1956 solely with the assistance of a conciliation board, but the railways never did get their final installment of the rate increase – it was rescinded by the new government. The first major labour negotiations after the Diefenbaker government assumed office culminated in another full-scale crisis in November, 1958. This was solved, not without heartburn on the part of the Cabinet, by the Board's granting of an immediate increase of 17 per cent in freight rates. The new government, which when in opposition had unreservedly declared freight rate increases to be the greatest evil, was made distinctly unhappy by having to deal simultaneously with both sides of the question, the wage increases and the rate increases, for it could not be reasonably denied that the one was the cause of the other.

In the following year, as if to atone for the sin of having permitted such an increase with almost no provision for argument, the Government passed the Freight Rates Reduction Act, which "rolled back" the increase to 10 per cent, and then to 8 per cent, and dumped the whole problem into the lap of another royal commission on transportation. In the next round of wage negotiations, in 1960, the Government held off as long as possible, as if to show that it was not infinitely pliant, until forced to pass another act to postpone a strike. In 1962, the settlement was reached between the parties directly concerned, the ease of settlement perhaps reflecting the current worsening of economic conditions. By 1964, however, labour was back with the hard line and, with the rate freeze that had been imposed in 1961, the Government found itself a party in the negotiations. The wage settlement was obtained on the promise of the Government to provide the railways with the necessary financial assistance to sustain the increase. These events already run beyond the period under consideration but it might be noted in passing that on two further occasions, in 1967 and 1973, Parliament was forced to pass legislation to stop railway strikes.

The labour question during the period had completely escaped from the normal restraints of economics. The unions had been pursuing the wage levels said to exist in the durable goods industries, and when that goal had been achieved a newer one was substituted. At the same time a minimum of concessions in operating practices was granted, but then only at heavy cost. Our table shows the frustration of even fairly obvious management decisions in two particular cases – the "run-through" issue involving the bypassing of divisional points no longer necessary with the switchover from steam to diesel traction, and the removal of firemen from diesel locomotives. The social issues involved were the fates of many small railway divisional points and of the firemen's union. Despite elaborate proposals for compensation and attrition, solutions were only reached after lengthy negotiations, investigations, and even more generous terms.

The Economic Factor

The pressure of railway labour and the resulting need for a steady series of rate increases naturally had pronounced effects on the railways as economic operations. In retrospect, the fifties appear as a decade of transition in transportation in Canada, made possible in large part by a fairly unbroken series of prosperous years. The railway strike of 1950 had a traumatic shock effect upon users of transportation and may be said to have given an impetus to highway transport that was lasting in effect. Traffic lost to highway competition during the strike was never wholly recovered as highway transport successfully established itself in the long-haul as well as the short-haul market. The subsequent completion of the Trans-Canada highway made rail-truck competition nation-wide. The benefits of new technological developments on the railways, such as the diesel locomotive, were eroded by rising wage levels and rigid operating procedures. Others, including the inter-modal developments such as piggy-back and containers, seemed to be possible means of recovering some of the high-paying general merchandise traffic the railways had lost to the trucks. Much traffic of this type developed but the inter-modal picture was blurred by the railway ownership of trucking lines, which allowed the railways to opt for a highway mode solution instead of risking the capital and operating complexities in a true inter-modal operation at that time.

The combined effect of these factors was to accentuate the speed and thoroughness of the "shakedown" of traffic between the competing modes. The economic choices forced on the railways favoured the heavy-density traffic of industrial materials and fuels that moved in large volume, in carload weights, or in trainloads. The inability to control labour costs where their impact was heaviest – on small volume, erratic, or occasional movement requiring expensive terminal, transshipment, and delivery costs and also a very high quality of service – led to a quick and silent disappearance of the railways from most of this business. By 1960 the railways, but not their trucking subsidiaries, had substantially retrenched railway services for the short inter-city hauls within Central Canada, and from the distribution to the small centres in both the West and the Maritimes. These rather fundamental changes in the role of the railways in the distribution of general merchandise and in the service to the small towns and rural areas seemingly passed unnoticed by those who still found the freight rate ideology as their most satisfying form of public service. For such people life went on much as it had in the twenties, when every Western farmer might be a customer of the railways and all the inbound supplies were delivered three times a week by way freight. That was a time when the distributors and boards of trade in each Western city carefully noted every change in the freight tariffs that might indicate some rival city was expanding its distributing area by negotiating a small reduction in the freight rates.

The common-carrier truck and the private truck, with their flexible patterns of distribution, had long since ended this practice, and while a resolution on railway freight rates might survive over the years in the annual report of boards of trade, it had become an empty gesture for which the time had not quite come when it could be completely dropped without stirring up old controversies. The small shipper, long the prime concern of freight rate analysis, was also changing. Less and less was he locating on the railway, finding that for his comparatively small volume, highway transport was more than adequate. When we add to those changes the fact that by 1958 the Board had almost completed its assignment of equalizing the class and some commodity mileage rates, one might have supposed that the issue would simply have subsided because of the combined efforts of satisfaction and irrelevancy. After all, Diefenbaker had told the House of Commons in 1948 that there could be no objection to necessary increases when the discrimination was removed.

The ideology, however, proved to be far too deep-seated to be exterminated by a few relatively modest technical adjustments in parts of the rate structure that were applicable only to a small part of the total traffic being carried. When we turn next to the ideological factor we are to see that its vehemence increased directly as the old regional discriminations were removed and as the advantages of the fixed statutory grain rates increased.

The Ideological Factor in the Courtroom

From the first post-war railway rate increase application in October,

1946, rate applications and hearings were almost continuous for more than twelve years. When these were not in progress there were closely related events such as the Turgeon Royal Commission, rate appeals, the Canadian Pacific application to the Board for the establishment of a rate base, and the second Turgeon Royal Commission on agreed charges. Throughout this period the same group of provincial counsel appeared in every case and became a rather closely knit team unavoidably developing a procedural ritual for dealings with railway counsel. After the protracted battles in the first two increase cases, procedures and standards had been worked out that tended to sanction the increases despite the repeated protests of provincial counsel that the Board was out to become a mere rubber stamp in such matters.

Leadership among provincial counsel, in terms of activity and persistence, went to Alberta counsel, J.J. Frawley, who had a certain advantage in this respect. Frawley was not in private practice. Throughout his career, he remained a member of the staff of the Alberta Attorney-General's department, and from the time of his assignment to the 30 Per Cent Case he was almost wholly devoted to freight rate matters. Locating himself in Ottawa where his duties embraced the somewhat wider responsibilities of the provincial agent, he appears to have had a completely free hand in determining provincial strategy on the subject, since the positions actually taken were of lesser importance to the provincial government than was the desire to ensure a high profile in opposing freight rate discriminations and increases. With great energy and persistence he led the charge in nearly every battle. While other provinces may have felt a waning of their enthusiasm from time to time, they could not afford to desist, leaving Alberta and their own opposition parties in full possession of such a highly valued political issue.

Frawley's colourful personality set the tone of the freight rate battles of the fifties much as had McGeer's during the twenties. But Jimmy Frawley was a much gentler soul that Gerry McGeer. Whereas McGeer could alternate charm and orneriness in a calculated manner to advance his point, Frawley preferred to rely on wit, verbal dexterity, and a rotund rhetoric to press the attack and keep opponents off balance. Railway counsel found it was risky to trade ironical barbs with him, since he might draw attention to their comments as expressing their true indifference to the problems of the "sovereign people of Alberta," and the same comments, stripped from their ironical context, might appear next day in cold print on the front pages of some Prairie newspaper. As a result of the freedom of action that he was given, Frawley may be said to have been a major force in pushing the freight rate ideology to its furthest point. Every plausible argument was unearthed, and a bullpen of American professors of economics, accounting, and transportation was available to carry the provincial colours in the individual trials of strength between opposing experts. Yet the differences between the freight rate battles of the twenties, when the ideology was founded, and those of the fifties are considerable. McGeer had kept his permanent war going mainly by his own initiative and ingenuity and never had reason to depart from his basic texts, the freight tariffs. In contrast, provincial counsel during the fifties appear to have been whirled along helplessly by the rapid succession of wage and freight rate increases without any opportunity to take the initiative. To an ever-increasing extent the freight rates themselves as published in the tariffs became irrelevant. The ideology moved to newer and more general grounds.

While the Turgeon Commission had recommended equalization of rates this could not be instantly put into effect since the Board of Transport Commissioners was charged with the task of determining the shape of the new single scales that were to replace the separate regional scales then in use. It was not until 1959 that the Board decided it had carried out equalization to the greatest extent practicable. In the meantime, however, the freight rate increases were applied to the existing levels of rates, disparities and all. The provinces made some attempts to have increases delayed until the discriminations were removed, and there were repeated references to this in the freight rate debates in the House of Commons. Nevertheless, the promised settlement of the long-standing equalization issue made it necessary to bring forward additional arguments to oppose the successive increases in freight rates. To this course the provinces were committed both from their initial eagerness to open up the freight rates issue and from the uncompromising stand they had taken in the first rate increase case. They were compelled to follow the logic of their position that if one freight rate increase threatened them with disaster, by how much more could a second or a third increase? Had the inflationary and the union pressures relaxed after 1951 it is probable that the issue would have subsided again as it had in the twenties, and after a lapse of time during which the equalization program would have been completed, a subsequent revival might have been in a much lower key. But there was no such respite, and every new increase seemed to redouble a sense of grievance.

The basis of the protests against the later increases was reduced almost entirely to the alleged evils of horizontal percentage increases and the effects they would have on long-haul traffic, which both the West and the Maritimes held to be the most important characteristic of their traffic. Beyond this, all that could be done was to probe into the nature of railway expenditures to try to uncover some evidence that its needs had been exaggerated, and to protest that the adoption of a rigid formula of railway needs would turn the Board into a rubber stamp.

It was not surprising that among the experts – in the courtroom of the Board of Transport Commissioners – the freight rate issue came to be treated almost in a spirit of philosophical calm and resignation as the increase cases succeeded one another. There was no way that the provinces could detach themselves from it but there was little left to be said about it. This was in sharp contrast to the sustained fiery oratory on the subject in the House of Commons, which received more attention from the press and public. Discussion before the Board was no longer about specific freight rate anomalies but based on the broadest generalities. The inequalities due to competition, which had provided a strong argument during the first increase cases, were rapidly diminishing as highway transport took advantage of the many thousands of miles of new, paved highway. Thus, the MacPherson Commission in 1961 was able to declare, with very little gainsaying, that competition in transportation was the predominant feature in nearly all parts of the country. The purely general nature of the provincial position in opposing the increases was noted in 1953 by MacPherson when he represented Saskatchewan in the 7 Per Cent Case:

> We are here representing the governments of our respective provinces. We are not representing individual shippers. On principle, having regard to the provincial economy of our provinces, we have resisted the increase, but we have never pretended that we could speak for the individual shipper.[3]

In so interpreting their role, provincial counsel limited themselves to those areas where the effects were most thinly spread out and thus of least consequence. In this area where statements are as difficult to prove as to disprove, the key question which seems never to have been asked, was "what was the actual significance of any particular point raised?"

Battle-weariness was clearly in evidence during the concluding arguments to the 15 Per Cent Case in October, 1956. In beginning his argument MacPherson remarked that it was the eleventh occasion since 1947 that he had been involved in a rate case before the Board.[4] Frawley, when it came his turn, also remarked that it was his eleventh rate case, adding: "and I hope, Mr. Chairman, that when my epitaph comes to be written that someone will be kind enough to record that it was in spite of and not because of the efforts that I made on behalf of Alberta that the freight rates went up so far and so fast."[5]

F. M. Smith, counsel for the Atlantic Provinces, spelled out the prevailing mood:

> I am sure that I express the sentiments of all of us here in the Board room when I say there is a general feeling of weariness which pervades these proceedings. I know that we, in the provincial side, do not relish our constant role of respondents, and I would presume that my railway friends are not wholly happy in having to come to the Board time and time again to ask for further increases in freight rates, and I am convinced that each successive case makes it more difficult for the Board to adjudicate upon the issues involved.[6]

It is a picture of all parties being trapped in their roles and forced year after year to go through the same rituals with very little to add to the old arguments. The drive and initiative in the freight rates issue was no longer in the Board's proceedings but in the capacity of the politicians and the general public to remain highly emotional about the issue. The experts had been left behind and the campaign proceeded without their further intervention. Despite their close cooperation, which enabled each to specialize on some aspect of the cases, provincial counsel continued to present some variety in approach. C.W. Brazier, Q.C. for British Columbia, in contrast to his Prairie colleagues, always added the statutory grain rates to the competitive and agreed to charge rates as involving an added burden on the remaining traffic in rate increases. He also continued the line taken by British Columbia before the Turgeon Royal Commission that freight rates must be more closely related to costs, without, however, drawing what implications this might have for rate increases.[7]

C.D. Shepard, Q.C. for Manitoba, defended the grain rate and traced the seriousness of the railway problem to two root causes: railway labour and competition. As to remedies, he was forced to conclude that "there can be only one solution and that is increased efficiency."[8] Smith and MacPherson held closely to the condemnation of horizontal percentage increases on which there was throughout the decade a continual buck-passing between provinces, the railways, and the Board. Ian Sinclair, counsel for Canadian Pacific, claimed that the only alternative to the horizontal percentage increase in securing additional revenues would be individual rate adjustments that would make it impossible to deal expeditiously with such cases.[9] Frawley sought to shame the railways into producing a new method:

> It does seem to me a sad commentary on the state of things in the railways today when, notwithstanding the invitation of the Board ...

that the railways who are possessed of all the knowledge of these matters cannot come before the Board with some suggestion as to something different than the routine, permissive authorization of horizontal percentage increases.[10]

A few years earlier Chief Commissioner Kearney, speaking about the same problem, had said:

> I think ... that our only hope was to hold out for an equalized scheme, so that if horizontal increases came they would fall with some equity throughout the whole of Canada; and until that can be done, frankly, gentlemen, I don't think we can do anything and we will just wait, I suppose until someone perhaps develops some better scheme.[11]

The issue thus remained stalemated. Even the railways attempted no thorough examination of the significance of the effects, while provincial counsel confined themselves to the simple mathematics of the theoretical case with frequent references to the comments of the Duncan and Turgeon Royal Commissions, which had been based on equally theoretical arguments.

The Ideological Factor: The Public Exposure of the Issue

What is written in briefs or said in the courtroom of the Board or a royal commission on an issue of such strong ideological content tends to differ greatly from what might be written in a newspaper editorial or said in the House of Commons. Whatever the differences the two remain closely related, supporting and influencing one another. The history of the issue is a fascinating story of the complex interplay between the experts and the public, between the facts and the emotions, both of which could at any particular time be either real or simulated, and the leading position being assumed now by one, now by the other. It may help to make clear the public attitudes during the fifties if we trace again briefly the main features of this plot.

In the beginning, there was in Western Canada a deep sense of regional grievance – alienation as we might say today – springing from a number of causes. These were in themselves by no means imaginary, but as the grievances more or less coalesced into a Western attitude or state of mind the resulting amalgam loomed much larger than any of the individual causes, leading perhaps inevitably to an exaggeration of the effects of those causes in order to make them appear as plausible sources for the grievances. Otherwise, credulity would be strained at the claim that a mouse had given birth to this mountain. These grievances in time assumed a life of their own independent of the real status of the original cause-effect pairs. At the beginning they were enlisted by the "experts" of the interested parties to add weight to their case. The boards of trade, dominated by wholesalers and merchants, were the original freight rate experts and were concerned with the relative positions of their respective cities as the Western economy began to take definite form. Winnipeg had acquired an advantageous position by reason of its early appearance on the scene, while Vancouver found itself starting with many disadvantages. In between, cities in Saskatchewan and Alberta fought to lower Winnipeg's initial advantage and joined with Winnipeg in opposing any concessions to Vancouver. In seeking lower rates on a national railway before a federal board it helped to be able to point out the difference in rate levels that existed between East and West.

As a result of the freight rate wars of the twenties, the public formed the strong impression that not only were freight rates of the greatest importance but also that the rate structure continued to contain many basic injustices to Western Canada. In the General Rates Investigation and at other times before the Board and before the Turgeon Commission the experts set forth in detail such "rate discriminations" and the public identified the obtaining of equalization as the final solution of the freight rate problem. But before this time the experts had come close enough to the problem to realize that equalization would have little more than nominal effects. This was apparent as early as the General Investigation in 1927. It was also frankly acknowledged in the brief of the Province of Saskatchewan to the Turgeon Commission. But public opinion had become deeply committed to its particular view of freight rates, and the politicians, even if they were able to see beyond it, had no desire to scrap so satisfying an issue, much less to hand it over to their opponents. It had become almost a badge of loyalty to Western aspirations. The Turgeon Commission had recommended equalization and from this point on the experts lost the initiative to the public clamour, for not only did this mean that the historic basis of complaint was in the process of being removed, but that the historical attitude of complaint could only be sustained by recourse to theoretical arguments of the widest generality, and therefore of minimum relevance.

All they could do was run to keep up with public opinion, first condemning horizontal increases because they were imposed upon unequal rates, then because they were bad in themselves, to finally arguing that any increase in rates, regardless of how justified were the railways' needs, was more than producers or consumers could bear. The "afterlife" of the ideology that began in the late sixties has placed impossible strains on the ingenuity of the experts to build a case in the style the public expects because of their inability to use any of the classical "rate discriminations" or horizontal percentage increases arguments. Many metaphors would illustrate their predicament: that of the sorcerer's apprentice comes first to mind. Our task will not be finished until we have an explanation of why the experts, after walking the dog for many years, finally let him get off the leash. In other words, why were there no common-sense correctives or restraints to ideas on the rampage?

As a result of the agitation beginning with the first post-war rate increase application and leading up to the Turgeon Royal Commission the popular mind had come into possession of a series of propositions that ensured that freight rates would remain the focal point of regional dissatisfaction for some years to come. These largely involved a gross and often tendentious over-simplification of the complexities of freight rates and traffic data that had defied the best efforts of the experts to make a *substantial* case of freight rate discrimination or injustice. Their combined effect was to suggest such a monumental degree of unfairness or injustice that the regional opinion was easily aroused to see in it, at the very least, a typical indifference or lack of understanding on the part of the Central Provinces, and at the worst, a conspiracy between the railways and "Eastern interests" to keep the rest of the country in economic subjection.

These simplifications may be set forth as follows. (1) Railway freight rates reflect monopoly conditions such that the West must pay the freight both ways. (2) The Central Provinces benefit from competitive conditions that enable them to escape from the burden of increases in freight rates. (3) There are still basic differences in rate levels that are accentuated by the application of horizontal percentage increases. (4) As a result the burden of increases in freight rates falls entirely on the outer regions of the country. (5) Horizontal percentage increases, even on equitable base rates, are discriminatory to the regions because they widen the actual differences in rates with distance. (6) Finally, increases are bad in themselves since regional producers and consumers cannot afford to pay higher freight rates.

The time has not yet been reached when we can look closely at whatever substance these propositions might contain, but it may be clear already from their nature that they represent a collection of theoretical ideas whose connection with the facts is simply taken for granted. The developing freight rate crisis of the fifties was incited by the seemingly self-evident nature of these propositions, which came to fill a role similar to that of religious dogma. The believer was not interested in the technical details or props of the dogma but merely relied on a few selected elements that served to exemplify, and therefore justify, the claims he was making. During the parliamentary debates on the freight rate question it is a fascinating sight to see the ways in which the propositions were cited, combined, and subjected to shifts in meaning and inaccuracies compounded by misinterpretations. This, in itself, is not surprising, for the average member of Parliament, like the man on the street, no more claims to be able to give expert analysis of the intricacies of freight rates than of the doctrine of the Trinity. But that doesn't prevent him from being an enthusiastic supporter of either dogma.

We start with an early example, from William Bryce, the MP for Selkirk:

> The second matter I want to bring up is the discrimination against the prairie provinces under the freight rates as they exist today. For many years Western Canada has been forced to pay freight rates from 15 to 18 percent higher than rates for similar commodities in Ontario and Quebec.... I want it to be perfectly clear to Hon. members that if the railways need additional revenue to meet increased expenditures caused by higher costs and wages, that is quite all right; but why make the West the scapegoat? If we must have increased freight rates let us all bear our share, and not have the prairies foot the entire bill.[12]

We see exemplified the maxim that a little knowledge (in this case, statistics) can be a dangerous thing, particularly here where it is combined with the fourth assumption that the West is paying all the increase. The freight rate case continually called for documentation of the injustices people said they felt long before they had any actual knowledge of them. For polemical purposes it was best to have it all in a nutshell – one striking illustration. I have not been able to find the actual source of the 15 to 18 per cent cited by Bryce, but it is a well-known figure and was probably offered by a railway witness, either during the 30 Per Cent Case or possibly twenty years earlier during the General Rates Investigation, when pressed to give some summary statement of the aggregate relationship between the scales. All that is said, however, was that as a very rough *average* of those comparable class *scales* of rates (and it is problematical how meaningful an average of scales can be when they vary widely between themselves and over the whole range of distances covered) the scales applying in the West were that much higher than those in the East.

However, this is not talking about actual traffic or rates paid but only about the structure of the published scales, of which possibly 80 per cent of the separate rates for the various mileage blocks never were used for any traffic. The same scales applied to class rates and many

199

commodities mainly of a bulk nature. The former represented no more than 10 per cent of the total revenue and were declining, while the overall share of both categories could hardly have been more than 25 per cent. If one wanted to make comparisons there were two main choices. Either one talked about differences in collections of rates independent of any traffic that might move under them, in which case the figures did not have any necessary relationship to a concrete grievance other than offering a *prima facie* case for equity in the abstract, or one talked about the average level of rates paid per ton-mile for all traffic. In the latter case the Western level was depressed by the low-revenue-yielding statutory grain rates, and the compression of all the facts into single figures gave no basis for drawing any inferences whatever from them, since every shipper is buying a different package of transportation services.

In 1950, after a 20 per cent increase on top of the earlier 20 per cent increase had raised rates by 45 per cent, Diefenbaker made one of his many slashing attacks on the evils of "freight discriminations." Taking up that very useful figure of 15 per cent and dispensing with the qualification "as between similar commodities" that Bryce had made, Diefenbaker compounded the injury done to Western Canada by means of a mathematical howler and by citing alleged effects for which he apparently confidently relied on the economists for support:

> In view of the fact that discrimination is taking place and is intensified by horizontal increases, the continuation of freight rates at this present level strikes at the economy of the western farmer and farmers of the Maritimes as well. It strikes at the expansion of industry in Western Canada as it does also in the Maritimes. The horizontal increases have been imposed on the original unfair discriminatory rates of 15 percent and as a result the provinces of Manitoba and Saskatchewan are now paying 21.78 percent higher freight rates than are paid in the two central provinces of Ontario and Quebec. It was 15 percent three or four years ago, and by reason of the horizontal increases the difference is now 21.78 percent.[13]

In recalling attention to minor incidents of this nature the purpose is not to strike a blow for mathematical accuracy but to illustrate the interpretations – complete with their exaggerations, misapprehensions, and falsities – that the regional public were invited to accept as the simple and definitive explanations of the freight rate issue. There was very little said to the contrary and consequently no serious debate ever took place. The sensitivities of the Westerners and the Maritimers had become such that the subject, like religion, tended to be avoided in mixed company. It is perhaps indicative of the mood that no one in the House, whether blinded by sympathetic indignation or somnolence, rose to correct Diefenbaker's statistics or calculation, and it may be assumed that the other users of the figures likewise were unchallenged. Those who might have done so were not sufficiently interested, and for the rest it was too much like what they were ready and willing to believe in any case.

Another feature that became more prominent as the issue was carried forward through the fifties was a shift in the meaning of the basic term "freight rate discriminations," which constituted the body of the complaints in Western Canada. From the earliest days this had meant the differences in the respective scales of class and commodity rates between East and West, which were easily discernible since they were printed in the tariffs. This was made clear on different occasions by Diefenbaker himself. For example, in speaking in the debate on the transport estimates in 1950:

Sir, I repeat what I have said on this and on other occasions. No one has any objection to an increase in freight rates to permit an efficient operation and a fair and reasonable profit. We take that for granted. But what we do object to, and what the legislature of Saskatchewan unanimously object to, was the loading of the western provinces with still a greater burden of freight rates by reason of unfair discrimination being intensified through the increase.[14]

This was made even clearer in his remarks the following year on the publication of the report of the Turgeon Royal Commission:

I welcome this report, first because it at least recommends the removal of discrimination in freight rates. It does not refer directly to discrimination but it recommends equalization of freight rates which indeed is just another way of saying the removal of discrimination which we in the western provinces, as well as those in the Maritimes, have suffered from over the years.[15]

The obvious conclusions from these statements and those of many others were that the equalization of freight rates would effectively dispose of the issue and that there would even be no objection to further freight rate increases if found justified on the basis of need. However, by the time the amendments to the Railway Act implementing the Turgeon recommendations were introduced in the House, some of the members were already expressing reservations on this inference. The remarks of Howard Green (Conservative, Vancouver) in this debate indicate how the issue might be kept alive by stretching the meanings of the existing terms:

> ... we will be inaccurate if we describe this as an equalization bill. I think the minister will agree with me when I say that it is perhaps a start on equalization, but it can be more truly described as a step toward improving the freight rates structure of Canada.... I suppose that the only true equalization in Canada would be to have a freight rate structure such that you paid the same to have a car brought from Oshawa to Vancouver as you paid to have it carried by rail from Oshawa to Montreal. That is the kind of equalization that would appeal to me. If we had that sort then we would have what could be properly called equalization. However I guess that is a long way in the future, too. Or we might have equalization by a wider system of subsidies. It may prove to be a good policy for Canada, through her federal taxation to subsidize freight rates in different parts of the country so that Canadians would pay the same rates no matter where they live.[16]

What Green in a speculative mood did to "equalization," many others were to do to "freight rate discrimination," which became a sort of floating or generic term to refer to anything that one did not like about freight rates. There was an opportunity for this to happen since equalization took time.[17] But throughout this period, rate increase cases were being heard almost continuously. Hence, it was still possible to argue that the increases were being imposed on the rate structure that had not yet been equalized, and therefore to that extent the discrimination was being aggravated. Even more important in the shift was the fact that the main arena of conflict in freight rates in the fifties was the freight rate increase case. While both provincial counsel and some politicians strove painfully to maintain a distinction between "good" increase applications and "bad" increase applications there was an inevitable blurring of these distinctions. *Horizontal* increases were not just bad when applied to inequitable rates but became bad in themselves. Increases *in general* were not just bad when applied "horizontally" but also became bad in themselves. This ambiguity was enhanced by the practice of demanding on the part of Members of Parliament and provincial premiers that rate increases be denied or rescinded without making any fine distinctions between good and bad. A few examples will suffice:

> Hazen Argue (CCF, Assiniboia): Does the minister not agree that the recent increases in freight rates of 7 and 4 per cent are discriminatory against the prairies?[18]

J.A. Smith (SC, Battle River-Camrose): I ask that the government institute a thorough investigation into the whole freight rate structure with a view to eliminating the discriminatory rates which are now in effect in Western Canada.[19]

Mr. Argue: Can the Minister say whether the cabinet has given consideration to disallowing under Section 57 of the Railway Act the 3.6 per cent horizontal and therefore discriminatory increase in freight rates recently allowed by the Board of Transport Commissioners?[20]

Mr. Diefenbaker: There are inequities in the freight rate structure. They have been aggravated through the years.[21]

Mr. Hees (Minister of Transport): Consideration will be given to means of further relieving the unfair discriminatory burden of the freight rate structure.[22]

The "discriminatory freight rates" were becoming ever more elusive, however doggedly the politicians proclaimed their continual existence. When, with the MacPherson Royal Commission, the experts were once again turned loose to track them down, the bag of game they were able to snare was rather meagre, as we shall see. The biggest ones, if they were indeed there, continued to get away.

We now come to a decisive factor in the political evolution of the freight rate issue, one which provoked and made inevitable the final crisis of 1958. This is what might be called the lopsided nature of the issue as the ideology gained in strength in the Maritimes and the Prairies and became identified with loyalty to regional aspirations. By "lopsided" is meant the condition created by the political necessity of every one to get as far as he can to the one side of the boat regardless of what it might do to the stability of the craft. In part, the situation reflected the already lopsided balance of power between the major parties in Parliament. For nearly eight years, the Liberal government of Louis St. Laurent was one of the most solidly entrenched governments in Canadian history, so much so that there seemed to be no possibility of ever upsetting it. In the circumstances, with the responsibilities of power seeming to be so remote, the Opposition grasped tenaciously at any issue that offered the slightest hope of improving its status. The freight rates issue was a godsend in that it evoked nearly unanimous support in East and West without arousing any reaction in the politically dominant Central Provinces. There was everything to gain and nothing to lose by exploiting it to the limit. This alone will explain the need to be able to refer to "freight rate discriminations" that existed beyond all attempts to discover them.

So it was that with every new freight rate increase application the Opposition would demand that it be denied or that the Board's decision to grant it be rescinded. For many years the St. Laurent government was able to stand firm against such demands, although always carefully avoiding any direct confrontation on the issue. Its position was that with the adoption of many of the recommendations of the Turgeon Royal Commission the Board was actively engaging in removing the main cause of discontent. The Opposition, for its part, hesitated for many years to accept the full logic of its position and thus relieved some of the pressure on the Government. There were yet few responsible voices urging subsidies instead of freight rate increases and no one proposed that the bargaining power of railway labour be curbed, the CCF in particular being in the awkward position of simultaneously having to applaud wage increases and condemn rate increases.

Ordinarily the extreme consequences of the lopsidedness of a political issue can be averted in a changeover in the government by the parties simply taking opposite sides in the boat, the new opposition striving to tip the boat and the new government accepting its responsibility for keeping it aright. This happens normally, even under strong ideological commitments, so long as there are no occasions where decisions must be made which the government is powerless to either prevent or evade. On issues like tariff policy or Senate reform, governments can retain the initiative either to act upon or ignore their previous positions on the matter. Such flexibility, however, was not possible when the Diefenbaker government came into office in 1957; the freight rate issue refused to become dormant but almost immediately confronted the new government with the same situation that its members had spent the past ten years castigating in the strongest terms. The Board had awarded the railways an interim increase of 11 per cent in December, 1956. The Government took office in June, 1957. In December, 1957, the Board authorized a final increase of 15 per cent (3.8 per cent over the current level) to take effect on January 15, 1958.

In terms of previous increases, which by now had aggregated to 100 per cent above the pre-1948 level, it was little more than a token increase, but it nevertheless demanded, under the bright glare of publicity, that the Government give a token response affirming its own sincerity on an issue to which it had attributed such an overriding importance. There was no quiet way in which such a decision could be sidestepped. Argue, the CCF spokesman on the subject, took every opportunity, and in the most extravagant terms, to remind the Government that the West expected every man in it to do his duty:

I think the 3.6 per cent increase now allowed by the Board is an abomination. I think it is a miscarriage of justice. I think it is a shame that in this period of widespread unemployment and distress in so many industries, at this time when thousands of people engaged in agriculture are considering whether they can remain in the business or whether they are going to have to close up shop and leave their farms, the Canadian Pacific Railway, probably the wealthiest company in Canada, with a record of extremely high profits, should be handed a Christmas present in the form of a 3.5 per cent increase in freight rates.[23]

As if this were not enough to move the Government, he had another argument that touched a sensitive spot:

These people (in the Western and Maritime provinces) are coming to the conclusion that the attitude of this government is merely a continuation of the attitude of the previous administration in allowing such tremendous increases in freight rates and this is causing a severe strain on confederation itself.[24]

Four days later, on January 7, 1958, a week before the increase was to take effect, the Government bought a little time by postponing the effective date until March 1, but was soon faced with the approach of the new expiry date.[25] On February 18 the effective date was set back two months to May 3. This served to keep the issue quiet until after the election, in which the Government was returned with a record majority.

The final plunge was taken on April 29, just four days before the effective date, and the increase was rescinded.[26] This rather hesitating series of decisions, however, sealed the Government's commitment to take action in any future freight rate increase, for if a 3.8 per cent increase was too much to be tolerated, the typical increase required by the recurring wage demands would almost automatically be ruled out. But it enabled the Prime Minister, looking back on it some months later in the midst of a much graver crisis, to cash its political dividends: "They talked about inflation, but they took no action. They allowed freight rates to be raised. Last spring when we met this problem ...."[27] However, even here the tribute that politics pays to economics still had to be paid: "We disallowed that increase because we said it was based on a wrong principle. It was based on a principle regarding depreciation into which I am not going to go now, but on that basis we said the increase was not permissible."[28]

The Big Crisis

The stage was now set for the big crisis – the clash between the irresistible force of union demands and the immovable object of the Government's tacit moral commitment to turn back any more freight rate increases. Negotiations between the railways and the unions on a new contract to apply for the calendar years 1958 and 1959 dragged on into the fall of 1958, ensuring that the railways would be liable for a heavy lump sum payment for wage increases retroactive to the first of the year. Events conspired to create a situation of maximum frustration and embarrassment for the federal government and the provinces attacking rate increases. A conciliation board recommended a settlement that would have meant an expenditure of an additional $67.8 million for the two major railways over the remaining fourteen months of the contract period.[29] Unlike some earlier conciliation board reports that had been rejected by the unions, this one was accepted by them giving their case an added moral advantage. The railways' alternatives were reduced to two. They could reject the conciliation report and face a national railway strike or endeavour to obtain assurances from the Board that an increase in rates would be granted in the event they accepted the report. Rejecting the strike alternative, the railways applied on September 16, 1958, to the Board for an immediate increase in freight rates of 19 per cent.

The position of provincial counsel appearing yet again before the Board to contest a rate increase was that of men who suddenly had been deprived of all the arsenal of weapons they had been using for more than ten years. The logic of the situation was coercive in the extreme to them. The union's position was buttressed by their acceptance of the conciliation board report, and it could not be denied that a national railway strike would immediately follow a rejection of that report by the railways. The provinces had no wish to get involved in the labour argument and counsel struck a pose of virtue in abstaining from that conflict.[30] But this left them face to face with the unpleasant consequences of labour's action: freight rates would have to be increased substantially and immediately. There was no real argument left. The railways, however, felt unable to accept the conciliation board report until they had firm assurance that they would be permitted to increase their rates sufficiently to cover the cost of it. All that could be said by the provinces was that the Board should not be put in the position of having to endorse a "conditional" application and that the railways should first incur the increased costs and then come to the Board. But even Manitoba counsel, A.V. Mauro, replied under questioning by one of the Board members that "it was one of those instances where the principle, I admit, perhaps appears to be based somewhat narrowly on technical grounds."[31]

From the point of view of the provinces, everything had to be decided in haste. There was no time or occasion to make the usual protests about horizontal increases, no time to probe closely into the railways' statements of needs. The application was made on September 16 and the hearings took only four days, from October 6-9. The Board rendered its decision of a 17 per cent increase on November 17, 1958, to take effect at the end of the month. At the hearings there was time only to insert the usual procedural roadblock: a motion to dismiss the application for lack of jurisdiction, which the Board rejected.

The following day the provinces fired their remaining ammunition in a salvo of futility in the form of a petition to the Governor-in-Council, requesting that he rescind the Board's ruling that it had jurisdiction, that if an interim freight rate increase were granted it should be rescinded, and, finally, that if the first request were granted the Board should be ordered to desist from a further hearing of the railways' application. All that this served to accomplish, however, was to transfer the embarrassment to the Cabinet, which now had to deal with the petition and publicly arrange itself either on the side of the Board and the railways or on the side of the provinces. One choice meant the acceptance of the increase or payment of a subsidy; the other meant a national railway strike.

The freight rate battles of the fifties thus culminated in a spectacular climax, with a most unpredictable of endings: a government led by a long-time foe of "freight rate discriminations" and with almost solid support in Parliament from the areas where freight rates were a burning issue was led by circumstance to acquiesce in the largest interim increase ever granted to the railways and after the briefest of hearings. The decision was not easy. The Cabinet deliberated for a day and a half, split between pro and con factions, with the Prime Minister himself absent on an extended tour of Asia. But at noon on November 26, 1958, with the strike only five days away, the Acting Prime Minister, Howard Green, announced that the provincial appeal had been rejected. Moreover, he was reported as having "flatly turned down the provincial suggestion of a subsidy to cover the increase."[32]

The issue, however, had not yet cooled to a point of rest. The Government could not afford to ignore the strong feelings, which were also its own, of the eight provinces in the matter of freight rate increases nor turn its back on its own brief record of dealing with freight rate increases – the rescinding of the 3.8 per cent increase – of which the Prime Minister was so proud.[33] Thus, simultaneously with its rejection of the provincial appeal, it announced the establishment of two Cabinet committees, the first to study the impact of the increase on the hardest-hit sections of the country and the second to study the general field of railway problems and policy. But there was no time for a quiet study of the problem. On the day the new increase was to take effect Lester Pearson, trying out his still rather unsteady political wings as leader of the Opposition, was reported by the *Ottawa Journal* as having said that he opposed a freight rate increase and that the railways should have been given a subsidy instead. By the rules of the political game, the Liberals as the "outs" had the right to exploit any promising issue unmindful of their positions. Even if the Government had not already made up its mind to take some action on its own initiative, this statement would have closed the door against any stand-pat position, since there was no way that Pearson could be permitted to steal the freight rate issue from under its nose.

A subsidy was the path that the government eventually took. However, before such a move could be made a number of questions had to be answered. The main questions were how much subsidy should be paid, how the Government could extract itself from this obligation within a reasonably short period of time, and, not least of all, what the official justification for the subsidy should be. It is from the decisions made at this point that the origin of the "mess" in transportation policy dates, as a Minister of Transport some fifteen years later was to describe it. The size of the subsidy, if based on the alleged need, would have had to have been sufficient to cover the entire amount of the increase, which was roughly estimated around $60 million for one year only. The actual amount, in the Freight Rates Reduction Act, passed in the summer of 1959, was the round figure of $20 million, which represented the maximum amount that could be extracted from a very reluctant Minister of Finance. This was estimated to be sufficient only to "roll back" the increase from 17 to 10 per cent, although after a harder look at the results the Board was able to authorize a further roll back to 8 per cent. At the same time, every indication had to be given that the subsidy would only be paid for a very brief period. It was described as "short-term" and was to extend only for the next calendar year, but possibly into the following year, by which time the experts might be ready with a "solution."

The Government's assurances on this point were received in many quarters with a skepticism that was abundantly justified by the outcome. Comments by *The Globe and Mail* on the short-term nature of the subsidy were right on the mark: "These words, these assurances, have a sadly familiar ring about them. How often, in our Canadian history, a "short term" subsidy has proved to be as durable as granite. If we may go by past experience, Ottawa has saddled itself with yet another long-term handout."[34] The Government, in fact, as a result of our ten years of whipping up public opinion with irresponsible talk, had boxed itself into the tightest of corners, from which the only means of even temporary escape was both inelegant and costly. The subsidy, said *The*

Globe and Mail, "is, to be blunt, a political sop thrown to the West and the Maritimes in a mood of desperation."

With regard to the reasons to be stated for the payment of subsidy a cover-up job was necessary. It would never do to admit the bald truth that the Government was financing a wage increase for railway workers rather than face either a railway strike or an offended regional opinion. For a brief moment, it even went through the motions of abhorring such a step. In rejecting the provincial appeal the Government expressed its intention of providing "an immediate alleviation of discrimination," and a few weeks later announced its intention to pay a subsidy to reduce the impact of a horizontal rate increase and to have a commission of experts consider a long-term solution to freight rate inequities. The speech from the throne on January 15, 1959, said: "My ministers will recommend to you action to alleviate the discriminatory effects of the recent horizontal increases in freight rates."[35]

Nothing will illustrate more clearly the semantic shift that we had earlier commented upon than the example of how terms like "discriminatory freight rates" had degenerated into buzz words whose mention justified the drawing of the most absurdly exaggerated conclusions as to their effects. Clearly Diefenbaker had never made any "in-depth" study of the freight rate issue, but he invariably showed a firm grasp of its political potentialities. In the position of embarrassment into which the Government had now foundered, the only hope of maintaining some credibility was to conjure up a frightening image of the size of the "discrimination" that was claimed to exist, for this (if it could be believed) represented the only plausible explanation for the Government's actions. Equalization over the years had been subject to conflicting judgements in Western Canada. The experts had kept clear of making any exaggerated claims for it,[36] but this caution did not register with the politicians. Thus in his election campaign of 1957, in a speech at Drumheller, Alberta, Diefenbaker was quoted by the Canadian Press: "On freight rates, he said, that a rate pattern discriminatory to the west had been made worse by recent increases. 'This had struck an almost paralyzing blow' to industrial development in the west." And in *The Globe and Mail*: "He said a Conservative government would equalize freight rates as far as possible to help both agriculture and industry on the prairies to compete with the rest of Canada."[37]

This trend was telescoping "equalization" and "horizontal percentage increases" in a single vague generality of "freight rate discrimination," against which Lionel Chevrier, the previous Liberal Minister of Transport at the time strove vainly, if only in the interest of historical accuracy.[38] The transition was complete when the Minister of Transport, George Hees, offered the resolution on the Freight Rates Reduction Act "as an interim measure designed to alleviate the burden of the authorized increase in rates."[39] He went on:

> . . . the government has indicated its intention of proceeding with a comprehensive inquiry into matters affecting the railways. The proposed legislation therefore limits the assistance to a 12-month period, where it is hoped a report will be available to the government. Consideration will then be given to means of further relieving the unfair discriminatory burden of the freight rate structure.[40]

The Freight Rates Reduction Act turned out to be "interim" only in the sense that it carried on until the National Transportation Act took over the authorization of the payments in 1967. Payments under this act in turn were to be phased out by the end of 1974. Subsidy payments in 1975 reached a new high of $252 million. The same provinces were still loudly protesting about "freight rate discrimination."

As might have been expected, the Government's recourse to an annual subsidy in lieu of freight rate increases only resulted in its sinking deeper into the mire. It had now made itself a principal in the wage negotiations that continued at two-year intervals.[41] The rate-freeze was to last only until the report of the Royal Commission had been received. But the final part of the MacPherson Report was dated December, 1961, and the recommendations called for a legislation of such a seemingly radical nature that more time was needed by the Government to digest its contents. The embarrassment of having to keep extending the expiry date of the rate-freeze was relieved when the railways "voluntarily" agreed to maintain the freeze pending legislative action. This presupposed that the Government would continue to foot the bill for the original and for any subsequent wage increases. The wage contract for 1960-61 was not settled until May, 1961, after the Government had been forced to pass the Railway Operation Continuation Act on December 2, 1960. This had postponed a strike for six months. The contract for the 1962-1963 period gave little difficulty since a conciliation board made a unanimous recommendation for a comparatively small increase, but for the following contract period the Government had to ask for six months of time to estimate the cost to the railways before accepting the majority report of the conciliation board. The 1966-68 contract negotiations ended in a strike in August, 1966, and once again Parliament had to be called to legislate the railwaymen back to work, eventually acceding to their demands. The following two contracts were successfully negotiated through Department of Labour mediators, but legislation was again necessary to end a strike in connection with the 1972-1974 contract. Of much more lasting significance for the course of development of the freight rate issue was the Government's promise of a comprehensive inquiry, to which we now turn.

CHAPTER 10

Exorcising the Ideology: From MacPherson to the National Transportation Act

[This chapter was not written by Howard Darling, but has been put together from portions of his manuscript, other of his works, and an assortment of primary material he had specifically selected. The emphasis on the MacPherson Commission is deliberate. We had reviewed all of the testimony and submissions for Mr. Darling, who was developing a scheme for presentation at the time of his death. The only serious departure from chapter outline is the omission of discussion of the key personalities and what influenced them. Mr. Darling knew and had worked with many of the principal characters. He often told anecdotes about them, but prepared no notes that could be used. The analysis of the issues has been drawn from Howard's notes, resulting in a shorter chapter than Howard would have written, since we have not added in missing interpretation. Eds.]

Although the Government had indicated its intention of putting the freight rate problem into the hands of yet another royal commission in November of 1958, the appointment didn't come until May of the following year. The appointment was in the nature of a defensive reflex motion on the part of the government, whose own premises for action had led to an insoluble contradiction. If one is in favour of – or at least not opposed to – higher wages for railway workers, opposed to an increase in freight rates, and instituting a subsidy that was only to be of a "temporary" nature, one's problem is in the class of eating one's cake and having it too. There was no possibility of satisfying these three exigencies. Clearly, something would have to give and it is not surprising that the "temporary" nature of the subsidy proved to be the least resistant of the three.

At this critical point, however, such a possibility could not even be hinted at, no matter how inevitable it seemed to be. As a result, the Royal Commission was conceived and born in an atmosphere of deliberate double talk and confusion. The nature of the real problem with which the Commission was to deal could not be stated openly, even in its terms of reference. Clarity and explicitness had to be avoided since they only led to calls for explanations that threatened to compound the contradictions already present. In language that was curiously reminiscent of the terms of reference of the Turgeon Commission ten years earlier, the new Royal Commission was instructed to inquire into:

(a) inequities in the freight rate structure, their incidence upon the various regions of Canada and the legislative and other changes that can and should be made, in furtherance of national economic policy, to remove or alleviate such inequities;

(b) the obligations and limitations imposed upon railways by law for reasons of public policy, and what can and should be done to ensure a more equitable distribution of any burden which may be found to result therefrom;

(c) the possibility of achieving more economical and efficient railway transportation;

(d) whether, and to what extent, the Railway Act should specify what assets and earnings of railway companies in businesses and investments other than railways should be taken into account in establishing freight rates; and

(e) such other related matters as the Commissioners consider pertinent or relevant to the specific or general scope of the inquiry.[1]

In paragraph (a) is the phrase often used by the Prime Minister in the 1950's, "inequities in the freight rate structure," which made clear the "official" reason for the investigation – that the freight rate issue was, by definition, about inequities in the rate structure. As already pointed out, however, the increasingly shadowy nature of this argument and the rate struggle had found other means of survival in the absence of its original causes. This had been done by focusing attention on horizontal percentage increases. As former Minister of Transport and acting Leader of the Opposition Lionel Chevrier suggested in criticizing what he called the "inadequacy" of the terms of reference, these horizontal increases had become the main point of contention that provoked the provinces to appeal the latest rate increases. Chevrier saw clearly the purpose of the Commission – to find a solution to the problem of the provinces wanting lower freight rates, "greater relief from ... the horizontal percentage method," and wanting also "to retain any existing advantages ... enjoyed by the shipper and the consumer";

at the same time, Chevrier surmised, the railways want to preserve the horizontal rate increases, which "is their way of obtaining relief from the increasing costs of transportation." The Prime Minister's only reply was to ask whether paragraph (a) was comprehensive enough to cover it.[2]

In the course of the ensuing debate, Chevrier drew a perhaps unwitting but nevertheless important distinction between inequity and equality, a distinction that would not be forgotten:

> My suggestion is this, I doubt very much whether there are inequities in the freight rate structure in the sense mentioned here. What I am saying is that there are inequalities.... I doubt very much if there are inequities in the legal sense of the word. There may be inequalities in the freight rate structure and I think there probably are serious ones, but how could there be inequities ....[3]

Again without specific references, paragraph (b) of the instructions to the Commission applied by common consent to the growing losses of branch-line and passenger services and the burden that these losses placed upon freight shippers. But by implication, this also included the statutory grain rates, the burden of which was entirely left upon the railways, and by transference, to shippers of other commodities. The Prime Minister, when announcing the Commission, of course had been careful to conclude his remarks by strongly emphasizing that Western farmers would not have to pay higher rates on export grain as a result of the Commission's review. His dilemma was that it was imperative that the Commission have the highest possible public stature in all areas of the country. This meant it must have the fewest possible restrictions on its freedom to investigate anything it chose to do under the broad authority of the terms of reference. A specific restriction, either in the terms of reference, or imposed later, was out of the question. At the same time, the last thing the Government wanted to see was the Commission probing into this sensitive issue. But it would not do to state this openly. Thus, after proclaiming that the previous Liberal government never had intention of changing the rates, we have another interesting interchange between Chevrier and the Prime Minister:

> Mr. Chevrier: ... Am I correct in the assumption that I have made that the royal commission on transportation is not to give consideration to the Crowsnest rates?

> Mr. Diefenbaker: I have not challenged the honourable member's interpretation.[4]

It was thus a calculated risk, and the Government could only hope that the Commission might be ingenious enough to find some suitable pretext for sidestepping the issue. But the Commission had its own independence and credibility to protect and could not afford to be influenced by the Government's clear meaning – couched as it was in the ambiguous language favoured by politicians – and so, over the protests of Western representatives, the Commission boldly announced its decision to investigate this hitherto tabooed subject.[5] The Prime Minister is reported to have stormed privately with the Commissioners, but so high were public expectations, he could not risk any interference and was quite helpless to alter the course of events.

The Government obviously wished to take the pressure off its own actions by appointing a high-profile commission composed of seven rather well-known men. Many had been involved in the freight rate debate in the past. The chairman was Charles P. McTague, QC, former Justice of the Ontario Supreme Court. Representing the interests of British Columbia was Herbert Anscombe, for many years the provincial Minister of Finance. From the Maritimes was Howard Mann, the secretary of the Maritime Transportation Commission. The Quebec member was René Gobeil, a consulting forestry engineer. From the Prairies came M.A. MacPherson, one-time Attorney-General in Saskatchewan, who had represented provincial interests at earlier freight rate hearings, and Arnold Platt, immediate past president of the Alberta Farmers' Union. As if to give protection to the railway workers whose wage demands were often blamed for the freight rate problem, the seventh commissioner was Archibald H. Balch, chief agent and legislative representative of the Brotherhood of Railway Trainmen and member of the Canadian Labour Relations Board.

Four of the seven commissioners were prominent members of the Conservative Party, a fact the Opposition did not let escape unnoticed. McTague had been national party chairman in the forties. MacPherson had contested the Conservative leadership in 1938 and again in 1942, outpolling the then newcomer John Diefenbaker. Gobeil was a party organizer in Quebec early in the 1950's, having unsuccessfully contested the Quebec South seat.

Apart from the favourable time at which it was constituted, the Royal Commission was fortunate in other ways. The retirement for health reasons in December, 1959, of the original chairman, Mr. Justice McTague, was followed by the appointment of MacPherson as his successor, coming from the heart of the ideology's "Bible Belt" – Saskatchewan. A Commission under MacPherson's chairmanship could be expected to inspire confidence in those sensitive areas of the country, but at the same time it was reasonable to expect that his

214

personal probity would more than offset his partisan background in his desire to be fair and impartial on all matters. This was, in fact, the way it turned out. When the report came out there was a predisposition to accept it favourably and, despite its rough treatment of some sacred cows, it aroused almost no *odium ideologicum*.

The Commission's hearings in some ways were anticlimactic as the old briefs prepared ten years earlier were dusted off and brought up to date. Many submissions changed in language, but not in substance, and to a large extent the same group of provincial and industry experts and counsel who had been doing continuous battle over the rate increases for the past ten years provided the nucleus of the proceedings. Among the principals were Fred Smith for the Maritimes, J.J. Frawley for Alberta, and C.W. Brazier for British Columbia. Even more submissions were received by the MacPherson Commission than the record number presented ten years earlier to the Turgeon Commission, and there were numerous new faces, as if many of the earlier petitioners felt they had sufficiently documented their complaints or, perhaps, they were tired, ten years and equalization having not produced any appreciable results.

Although many of the presentations before the Commission were reiterations of old positions, there was a slight, but noticeable, shift in emphasis to matters beyond simple equity in freight rates. In this category were submissions which dealt with goals related to transportation only incidentally, submissions which served primarily as means to other goals. These included the diminution or removal of regional disparities, the promotion of regional development, and the relief of the small shipper and consumer. These were not new goals, transportation policy having always been tied to broader national policies. As we have seen, such wider goals had already penetrated the freight rate issue, with the Duncan Commission recommending as early as 1927 that the Board take initiatives in furthering regional development by ordering more favourable freight rates. Similar demands were rejected by the Turgeon Commission. As time went on, these regional demands came more to the forefront to cloak the argument as specific freight rate grievances were removed. Aside from the odd anomaly all that remained was the issue of horizontal increases, one which was, after all, a general grievance inseparable from non-transportation grievances.

Broader economic arguments were used directly and indirectly by representatives from all regions or industries outside of the mainstream of the Canadian industrial base. They were especially prevalent at hearings in the Maritimes and in the Prairie Provinces (this was before the time of the new Western resource-based prosperity).

215

The Maritimes, however, provide a tidy package that illustrates how the freight rate ideology had grown.

In Charlottetown, Prince Edward Island, Premier W.R. Shaw summed up his province's problem with freight rates as one of survival of local industry over the disadvantage of distance:

> The distance which we are from our markets is a tremendous deterrent in the light of increased freight rates to our farm people, and I do say that if these increases continue, or even remain as they are at the present high rates, it is going to seriously affect the whole of our main industry – the industry on which we are mainly dependent – and, subsequently, the economy of our Government and every other department, social and economic, of the province.[6]

In its written brief, the province repeated an earlier suggestion for nationalization of the Canadian Pacific, not that it "believed in state control for the mere sake of state control, but the best reason for nationalization is that the present system does not work."[7] The question raised was "Who is going to pay the bills?" Implied in this question, of course, was that shippers would not, or could not, pay through higher freight rates. What was needed was a transportation policy tailored to the economic needs of each of Canada's regions.

While not offering any set solution, the P.E.I. counsel, Mr. Campbell, at least put the whole freight rate problem, and the immediate problem of that year's railway wage demands, in a perspective that shows the regional feeling of the times. Noting that the commissioners sat at the same table that the Fathers of Confederation had used, he commented: "I don't suppose any body of men has ever done such a momentous thing as you are expected to do." In reply to MacPherson's warning not to expect miracles, he added, "if you find a solution ... I believe the pages will be torn from the Bible!"[8]

The next day Nova Scotia Premier Robert Stanfield took much the same line as his counterpart from Prince Edward Island, but he amplified the statement of regional problems to include those of more far-reaching importance: "there are times, however, when a close and searching examination of what appears to be simply a regional demand, prompted by self interest, will reveal that the whole matter is one of national interest and that there is no conflict."[9] The actual written Nova Scotia brief was a repetition of the Maritime position at earlier hearings, sprinkled liberally with quotes from the brief to the Turgeon Commission and from the Duncan Commission on Maritime Claims. Most of the brief was given over to a discussion of the province's economy and the importance of transportation to the health of its industries. Much was made of the need to market Maritime steel in the southwestern Ontario market, which had local suppliers 1,200 rail miles closer.

Nova Scotia's freight rate complaint, said to be still unsolved despite the work of the Turgeon Commission, was that the province was squeezed by the effects of competition in Central Canada: "The competition afforded by the motor trucks to the railways on traffic into and out of Nova Scotia is not as pervasive as in other areas of Canada. As a result, a greater percentage of such traffic must bear the full or a larger part of the impact of the freight rate increases."[10] The pure effects of applying increases to a shrinking base, combined with applying them horizontally, had a detrimental impact on the Maritime economy because "instead of being afforded 'the largest market of the whole Canadian people,' [the raison d'être given in the preamble for the Maritime Freight Rates Act] they are limited to the restricted market of the Maritime provinces. Owing to the small size and dispersed nature of the market, freight rates cannot operate effectively as 'a tariff wall.'"[11]

Thus, Nova Scotia called for a restructuring of the Maritime Freight Rates Act in such a way as to re-establish the effectiveness of its original purpose. Concurrent with this, there was a need to revise the rate structure so as not to put more than a "justifiable" burden on Nova Scotia shippers. Rejecting the solutions of Turgeon, the brief echoed those of the other Maritime Provinces in calling for a policy based on the economic needs of individual regions; one which "precludes development of a uniform national transportation policy based absolutely on equalized freight rates."[12]

The theme of regional economic development and broader national policies was not limited to the provincial experts and political leaders. Representatives of small shippers, producers, and boards of trade came in good numbers to the Commission's regional hearings in the Maritimes and eastern Quebec, complaining that the horizontal price increases and the lack of competition, which would preclude competitive rates, were bad for business and the region. A number of the complaints echoed the sentiments of New Brunswick fish packers who declared that geography should not be allowed to interfere with business and competition. Likewise, the Fredericton Board of Trade accused carriers of developing only the profitable traffic and ignoring their "moral obligations" to carry less profitable traffic. With a few exceptions, little attention was paid by the businessmen to Patterson's constitutional arguments. A few referred to the erosion of advantages previously expected to be generated by the Maritime Freight Rates Act, but by and large the arguments were based on the impact of high freight rates on business and the local economies.

If measured solely on the basis of the transcript, the Commission's decision to delve into the Crow's Nest Pass grain rates proved to be the hottest issue at the public hearings. More than half of the participants took advantage of this first formal opportunity to air their views on a subject that, as it turned out, would remain controversial for at least the next twenty years. Not surprisingly, opinion divided along regional and occupational lines. On the Prairies both provincial governments and agricultural organizations were opposed to any interference with the grain rates, and there was often bitter resentment that the Commission was even listening to arguments of the subject. Had not the Prime Minister promised them that their "charter" would remain? Two threads pervaded much of the Western arguments. First there was a genuine opinion that the Crow's Nest rates were remunerative, and did not place any additional burden on other shippers. Second, there was a general opposition to subsidies, in particular any subsidy that might be construed as a subsidy to the Western grain farmer.

In British Columbia, Ontario, and Quebec, on the other hand, much of the blame for the whole freight problem was laid at the doorstep of the grain rates. The St. Catherines Chamber of Commerce, for example, referred to them as the "most glaring inequity" of the whole freight rate structure, but like so many others, was not about to provoke the West by suggesting the Crow's Nest rates bestowed any special privileges and should be altered. The usual response was that any loss on grain should be paid by the national treasury, not by other railway users. Provincial governments apart from the Prairies for the most part stayed away from the issue, although both Ontario and British Columbia mentioned it tangentially in discussion of the general problem of the squeeze between railway costs and competition. But the Commission's most important contribution to the Crow's Nest debate lay not in airing the rhetoric, but in examining the costs of the export grain traffic.[13] The methodology used in these three sets of studies of the grain traffic – by the railways, the Prairie Provinces, and the Commission itself – represented a substantial advance in railway costing. Day after day of hearings were devoted to detailed examination and cross-examination of a parade of costing experts. This soon spread to other areas, most notably passenger services and light density lines. As well as adding to what previously had been imprecise, almost subjective, arguments over the possible losses incurred by the railways in these broad areas, it was also now possible, in theory at least, to determine some measure of costs, however ambiguous or generalized, applicable to selected segments of the railways' operation. Costs would find their place in the Commission's rate regulation philosophy and in the freight rate agitation that still lay ahead.

One of the more striking conclusions that can be drawn from an examination of various submissions to the Commission is a well-developed analysis of the problem – that competition had rendered the value-of-service pricing system obsolete – and the widespread acceptance of what would turn out to be the final solution. Stripped of the political rhetoric and opening statements designed for public consumption, we can find the thread of what became the Commission's position woven into many of the provincial and railway briefs, although the interpretation of the intricacies was not always what the brief-writers must have intended. The process by which the Commissioners sifted through this wealth of proposals and the extent to which the arguments of the railways and provinces influenced them unfortunately remain a mystery.

After a year of hearings, events conspired to put the Commission in a position where it had to act boldly. The existing situation of the rate freeze could not continue indefinitely. Yet the scale of subsidization was such that it could not be substantially reduced within a short time without requiring massive freight rate increases, which, given the freeze, would have then been economically and politically infeasible. The pressure on rates and subsidies was building as the Commission deliberated. The non-operating workers' contract was due to terminate in December, 1960. The union demanded an increase of 25 cents per hour, which the railways said would cost $60 million. A conciliation board recommended a 14 cent increase, but the railways said a rate increase would be necessary. The union announced its intention to strike. The strike was prohibited until after May, 1961, but the hint of additional subsidy had already been given. This wasn't the end, however. Looking forward to the summer, negotiations with the engineers were expected to open, and a new contract with the non-ops would have to be written.

Fortunately, the Commission was equal to the task, and thus has come to occupy a permanent and conspicuous place in Canadian transportation policy. It came at a point in time when the long-dominant ideology had become bankrupt. In a few short pages of the first volume of its report, it swept them away and forever shifted emphasis to what would be a new ideology – competition.[14] Railway deficits were found to be due to the collective burdens of uneconomic services and unremunerative rates, which could no longer be covered by all shippers in a competitive transportation environment.

Thus, the horizontal percentage increases, described by some as the most glaring inequities, were not simply a problem but merely a symptom of a deeper problem that had been building up gradually with the expansion of the alternative means of transportation. As the **Report from the MacPherson Commission explained:**

In terms of equity the most serious regional outcome of the effects of competition upon the railway rate structure arises from the fact that the railways, because they can only be certain of applying their fully allowable increases to a constantly shrinking area where competition is weak or non-existent, are forced to ask for greater percentage increases than they would if the increased rates could be applied more broadly. As a consequence, the regions where competition is weakest are being called upon to pay a larger and larger share of the revenues required to cover railway costs. To put it another way, it would appear that an attempt is being made to preserve the traditional railway rate structure, based on differential pricing and cross subsidization, by means of the profits obtained by increasing the level of rates in the residual monopoly areas of the transportation system and not, as was originally done, from the profits derived from high rates on high-grade traffic. Thus, the divisive effects of distance and other geographic and economic factors which the railway freight rate structure in Canada has traditionally sought to mitigate are, under present competitive conditions, being aggravated by that selfsame freight rate structure.[15]

Increasing general railway subsidies such as those authorized as part of the rate freeze, or the specific ones such as the Bridge and Maritime Freight Rates Act payments, were not the direction of solution:

Measures such as these, while they help to alleviate freight rate inequities, cannot by themselves solve the underlying problem. Moreover, in the form in which they have been applied, they may tend to distort the competitive market in transportation with resultant adverse effects upon the transportation system as a whole.[16]

While on one side competition was seen as one of the driving forces of the railways' problem, it was also central to the solution:

Our investigations have led us to conclude that the potential environment is considerably greater than their actual performance in recent years would seem to indicate. To unleash this potential is, in our view, the solution to the railways' financial dilemma and, thus, the sine qua non for a solution of the freight rate inequity problem which is, essentially, a projection of this dilemma.

The competitive position of the railways has been seriously weakened, we are convinced, because of the burden which the railways continue to carry as a legacy from the monopolistic environment of the past. It is a burden which, in our view, derives in part from public policy and in part from policies pursued by the railway industry. This burden, which bears upon the plant, the rate, and the regulatory structure within which the railways operate, prevents them from adapting fully to the new competitive environment and it must be lifted if the railways are to take their proper place in a transportation system which adequately reflects the needs of our Canadian society.

In brief, the broad aim of public transportation policy should be to ensure – consistent with the other goals of national policy – that all the various modes of transport are given a fair chance to find their proper place within a competitive system. The application of such a policy is, we believe, essential if we are to obtain – at a minimum cost – a balanced and efficient transportation system which is fully adequate to meet the nation's transportation requirements. [17]

As a measure of relief, the Commission recommended that the railways be permitted to rationalize their networks. This meant abandonment of uneconomic passenger services and light density branch lines. It also meant compensation was to be paid to the railways for continued operation of any uneconomic services deemed to be in the public interest. A system of temporary payments was also recommended to dampen the shock of transition.

In the matter of its charge to remove or alleviate the "inequities in the freight rate structure," the MacPherson Commission took a bold new line. Since the more obvious of the old discriminatory features had been removed as a result of the Turgeon recommendations, there was little left to work on and its importance was dwarfed by the magnitude of the general problems it had to face. So traditional discriminatory complaints were left on the shelf. In the Commission's view the combination of competition, the burdens of uneconomic services, and horizontal price increases tended to create an inequality in freight charges, but it also took a strong but sympathetic stand on the inequalities in freight rates due to distance and cost:

In submissions from all over the nation complaints were brought before us concerning the increasingly onerous burden of rail freight rates with predictions of disastrous results which would follow any further increase in these rates. We are impressed with the seriousness of these complaints. . . . The complaints, while differing in other respects, were unanimous in condemnation of the device of the "horizontal" percentage rate increase. . . . The problem of securing additional revenues arises because the pace of technology on railways has, to this moment, been unable to increase productivity sufficiently to offset price and wage increases. If any commercial enterprise is to survive, cost increases must eventually be passed on to the users of the company's product. No one denied this before us. Dissatisfaction arises because of the inequitable manner in which the increases are passed on. . . .

There is nothing inequitable about a high freight charge *per se*. Distance and other factors in transportation costs make it necessary that the long-haul shipper will have a higher freight bill than a short-haul shipper, other things being equal. This simple axiom is self-evident by itself but often it is obscured in the complex of factors which beset an industry or a region facing serious market competition. . . .

No shipper can justly complain if, in using rail services, he is asked to bear his fair proportion of increasing costs. If, on the other hand, he is fortunate enough to be situated in the competitive sector and the railways do not feel that they can increase his rate in the light of potential competition, then this is a locational benefit accruing to some shippers but not to others. . . .[18]

The Commission made competition the cornerstone of its new philosophy of rate regulation. This proved to be a master stroke, for, as we have seen, competition had long been the most vulnerable part of the ideology. In the formative period of the ideology, there had been little or no competition to the railways, and the type of rate regulation and the concept of that regulation, such as unjust discrimination and undue preference that represented the goals of transport policy, were all directed toward serving the public interest under conditions of monopoly. Competition, when it began to appear, lay outside this picture and there did not seem to be any way of integrating it into that picture. The exception always sanctioned departures from the ideal rates and procedures. As competition grew, departures from the ideal system eventually became much more important than the remnant that conformed to the original conception of that system.

All the Commission had to do, therefore, was to draw attention to the obvious fact that competition was almost everywhere; hence, the old methodology of setting and regulating rates had lost its raison d'être. Thus it would be safe to move away from regulation and let competition do the job. For anyone who was prepared to recognize the facts as they were, there was really no argument against such proposals. All that was left was a feeling of nervousness about venturing out alone into such a world, much as a timid person might look forward with dread to his first ride on a Ferris wheel. However, the Commission was suggesting an elaborate system of safeguards to cut the harm and the risk to a minimum by providing a system of maximum rates in areas of little or no competition and minimum rates where cutthroat competition threatened. Both minimum and maximum rates would be based not on informed judgement and considerations of equity, but on a more mechanistically determined cost base. These safeguards, as it turned out, have been gathering dust due to relatively little usage.

Moving away from formal rate regulation was also a master stroke in other ways. With the elimination of applications for general freight rate increases, the constant public airings of grievances were eliminated and political involvement neutralized. Without the mechanism of public hearings, there was no longer a strategic need for provincial governments to take a strong stand in opposition to increases, a process which had kept the issue burning for so many years.

The attention given in the Commission's report to the Crow's Nest Pass rate issue was small in proportion to the arguments made by railways, provinces, and shippers in the hearings, and by Members in the House before the Commission began its work. The Commission found that the railways did in fact lose money on export grain transportation, and this placed a burden on other shippers, but having listened to the various arguments, the Commission was careful not to become embroiled in controversy over either the existence of or the level of the grain rates. Using skilful, pointed language, the Commission left the determination of the rate in the political sphere, but with an important caveat:

> We will recommend that losses associated with the obligation to carry grain and grain products to export positions at a rate set by statute, which must of necessity be recovered from other shippers, should in future be borne by the Parliament of Canada, who in its wisdom sets the statutory rate. In this way Parliament remains the sole judge of whether or not the grain industry can bear rates higher than it presently bears....[19]

After making what it saw as an important distinction between the railways' light-density lines and passenger services, which were "uneconomic," given the "economic realities of a competitive environment," and railway movement of grain, which, given rationalization, was a means "more economical than any other," the Commission indicated that the railway grain movement should be encouraged and made remunerative, repeating its admonition to Parliament: "Since the payment received from work performed in the movement of grain achieves its special distinction by virtue of the fact that Parliament has taken the responsibility for setting the rate, we shall suggest that the

Parliament of Canada, the authors of the statutory rates, ensure that the railways receive sufficient remuneration...."[20] This cautious wording is indeed interesting when compared with some of the Commission's strong statements on other rate issues, but then, the issue was still politically charged, with the West unlikely to accept any suggestions.

There was no unanimity within the Commission, but surprisingly not from the directions one might expect given the regional backgrounds of the Commissioners. In their "Reservations and Observations," Anscomb and Balch were not convinced that the "Western grain growers were not able to pay a greater proportion of their export freight charges." They suggested that Parliament should review the grain trade and "when conditions record obvious improvement the freight rates to the Western growers should be increased over those now in effect in order to ensure that at the earliest possible moment the burden now imposed on the Canadian taxpayer and/or the railways be removed."[21] Gobeil, in a Reservation nearly a quarter the length of the main report, took the opposite view, unconvinced that a subsidy was necessary:

Firstly, I believe that the Canadian Pacific Railway, having obtained certain very real advantages when it undertook – in perpetuity – to accept a ceiling on these grain rates, became party to a contract which is still in effect and which must be abided by. Secondly, I do not believe that the grain cost studies which have been brought before this Commission have succeeded in their attempts to measure the extent of the loss which, it is alleged, the railways incur in the movement of grain under statutory rates. I am not convinced, furthermore, that the studies in question have been able to establish that there is any loss whatsoever. Thirdly, I believe that, if there is a loss associated with the carriage of grain it is due to the cost of maintaining light density lines rather than the cost of carrying grain.[22]

Unlike the aftermath of the Turgeon Commission, there was considerable delay in the eventual implementation of the MacPherson Commission's recommendations. Of course, the circumstances were different. While the rate increase problems were every bit as pressing as ten years earlier, the solution was much more radical, with certain aspects not fully acceptable, or even understood, by those who had complained the most. As well, the subsidies of the Freight Rates Reduction Act had opened the floodgates and it was possible to stall forever by approving additional funds. The six years that elapsed before the National Transportation Act gave effect to the proposals was a period of the most lively and meaningful discussions in transportation policy that the country has ever experienced. Perhaps the mood of the country on the eve of this debate is captured in an editorial which appeared in the *Winnipeg Free Press* a few days after the first volume of the Report was made public:

> [It] can be said that the commission report has found some constructive answers to the railways' problems and to the historic grievances of the western and maritime provinces. . . . Everything now depends on the willingness of the government and the public generally to undertake the radical surgery that Mr. MacPherson and his colleagues have prescribed. Nothing can be more damaging to the commission's objectives than for the government to adopt some of the simpler remedies and ignore the more painful ones.

After noting that the findings of a loss on the export grain traffic were "not a final answer" since even the experts disagreed, the *Free Press* had "nothing but praise" for the Commission's main findings and announced victory in the fight over discrimination: "The condemnation of horizontal rate increases substantially confirms what the western and maritime provinces have been saying at every freight rate hearing since 1946." Optimism also ran high in the Maritimes, where the *Halifax Chronicle-Herald* greeted the Report with an eight-column editorial on the Commission's "realism" and its "welcome change in principle."[23]

Of course, reservations were expressed everywhere over specific points in the recommendations, most notably those pertaining to grain, but given the development of the ideology, reservations had to be expressed. Saskatchewan Premier T.C. Douglas was "deeply concerned" that the grain rates were even "an issue requiring a solution," while Manitoba Premier Duff Roblin, perhaps taken by surprise, was "disappointed with the majority report." In Alberta, Premier Manning went further, stating that "it must occasion grave public concern" that a subsidy of such "magnitude" be taken from public funds. He thought that putting labels on components of the railway deficits was "staggering and completely unjustified."[24] As it turned out, however, the reaction to the Commission's finding of uneconomic services tended to divert attention from its more sweeping proposals to scrap the existing structure of rate regulation.

In general, the freight rate proposals were misunderstood. Where the Commission recommended temporary payments to lessen the shock of change and a few payments in respect of imposed public duties, the newspaper headlines blared "Subsidy!" The attention paid to costs and competition, and to earlier calls for cost-based freight rates, led many to believe the Royal Commission had actually proposed a cost-based freight rate structure, when costs in fact played a minor role in the regulatory philosophy.[25] Others were more careful and recognized the proposals for what they were, but their doubts only served to delay the inevitable.

The government's reaction was a non-reaction. The first volume of the Report had been tabled in the House without comment on April 11, 1961. When pressed, Prime Minister Diefenbaker was noncommittal, indicating only that "After study has been given thereto, the question as to whether legislation shall be introduced will be determined and the House will be advised."[26] The Opposition took every opportunity to press for comment on the Report and possible legislation, especially when extensions to the Freight Rate Reductions Act became necessary and when the second volume of the Report was tabled the following January. In the spring of 1962, just before the general elections returned a minority Conservative government, the Minister of Transport again warned the House not to expect early action. The Throne Speech in September promised legislation to remedy the "unfair burden" of the rate increases, yet none had been introduced by the time a minority Liberal government was elected in April, 1963. Meanwhile, the rate freeze continued and the subsidies had to continue, subsidies that were angrily denounced as "the cost of evading the railway problem."[27]

The Liberal government didn't fare much better. Although the new Transport Minister, George McIlraith, announced in July, 1963, that the Government was preparing legislation and consulting with the provinces, first reading of Bill C-120 did not take place until September of the following year, after a change in portfolios saw Jack Pickersgill assume the transport post. Because of Western opposition to some of the provisions, the bill was allowed to die on the order paper with the general election in the fall of 1965. The new bill, Bill C-231, essentially the same as the first in regard to freight rate provisions,[28] was introduced the following year as part of the Government's package to end the 1966 railway strike. In January, 1967, the National Transportation Act and amendments to the Railway Act were finally passed after years of debate. In the sensitive sections dealing with freight rates, the Government was punctilious to the point of adopting a maximum rate formula that apparently only had been meant by the MacPherson Commission as a suggestion for further development. The literal application of these provisions to various classes of traffic would produce some rather obvious anomalies, but this was a small cost to pay for getting rid of the obsolete features of the traditional rate regulation.

The only major change from the Commission's position was the removal from the Act of the provision for review of the Crow's Nest rates. The loss of this point was a temporary political embarrassment, but the Government did not insist since the money was needed anyway and it became simply a matter of finding another heading under which to classify it. Even so, the Crow's Nest issue was put on the back burner, only to boil over again ten years later as this book is being written.

CHAPTER 11
Freight Rates and the Constitutional Issue

Why do the Westerners rage, so furiously together?
And why do the Maritimers imagine a vain thing?
The premiers of these provinces have taken counsel together
Against the prime minister and against his minister of transport.

[This chapter was written in 1976 by Mr. Darling as a paper to be submitted to one of the public policy journals. Although it is not structured along the lines of his original work plan, it contains the points he had been planning to make in the concluding section of this book. Eds.]

The curious thing about the constitutional problem in Canada, which is now threatening to boil over, is that it has taken more than a hundred years for it to acquire the status of a live public issue. There have been flare-ups, such as the King-Byng issue in 1926, but these have been concerned with what might be described as technical issues in the everyday functioning of government and interpretations of the statute. Now, however, it seems Canadians have got around to asking themselves those fundamental questions the Americans faced and answered *before* they ratified their constitution. After living comfortably and uncritically under the British institutions that had been transplanted to the new environment, we are now facing questions and problems that simply cannot be answered by any appeal to inferences or judicial interpretations of those institutions, which had reached their final form before having to come to grips with the problem of federalism.

Now that the problem has surfaced so boldly, it is possible to look back and recognize its subterranean presence in many places and at all times in our history. Its identification is both surprising and enlightening, for it seems to give meaning to issues that have hitherto been puzzling and too easily dismissed as due merely to the inveterate habits of politicians. Such issues have become accepted as nothing more than ineradicable nuisances, much like mosquitoes at the summer cottage. Being currently engaged in a study of the nature of one such issue – the freight rate controversy – I have become convinced that this long-lasting and often bitter controversy with its many puzzling aspects can be best understood as a spontaneous and symbolic portrayal of the constitutional problem as it most deeply affects Western Canadians. If you like, it is a morality play in which the West tries to explain to itself its plight in the Canadian confederation.

That the actors may have not grasped the symbolism – in other words, that they really "believe" the mythology it contains – only goes to explain the depths of feeling that are aroused by what to an outsider and nonbeliever is simply a religious ritual demanding some naturalistic explanation to be intelligible. Just as plays or novels ostensibly about the Greeks or the Romans may refer with varying degrees of subtlety to contemporary political and social issues, so the freight rate issue, having been one of the earliest vehicles of regional self-conciousness and self-assertion in the West, persists as the most readily available and understood means of expressing regional resentments that are directed against the central part of the country symbolized by Ottawa, Toronto, and Montreal.

The freight rate issue is, of course, equally prominent in the Maritime Provinces, and though they have been for some time singing the same tune as the West, the words are still somewhat different. For reasons of space, I confine myself here to an analysis of the Western phenomenon, although much of what is said could equally be applied to the issue as it exists in the Maritime Provinces. It will suffice here to mention some of the more puzzling aspects of the freight rate issue that make one wonder whether the causes or the effects of the problem can be fully understood if confined within the narrow range of manipulation possible in the freight rate structure. Some of these anomalies are:

(1) Its unresponsiveness or even imperviousness to treatment. A long succession of investigations and decisions by the Canadian Transport Commission and its predecessor boards, several royal commissions, as well as new legislation, subsidies, rate freezes, and other direct action by the federal government have come and gone like waves washing over a rock, leaving it unmoved. The tone of the complaints heard by the parliamentary committee making the first freight rates investigation in Western Canada in 1894 was not appreciably different from that heard by the Prime Minister and his col-

leagues at the Western Economic Opportunities Conference in Calgary nearly eighty years later.

(2) The increasing disparity between the magnitude of the complaints and the apparent capacity of freight rates either to have generated them or, on the other hand, to provide a remedy that would come anywhere close to satisfying them. A credibility gap has appeared and is widening.

(3) The gradual detachment of the issue from the everyday problems of shippers and carriers. At one time, shippers, through their boards of trade, used to approach the provinces for help in achieving their freight rate objectives. Today the reverse is the case: the provinces try to induce shippers to supply some "corroborative detail" to support their own inflated demands.

(4) The disproportion between cause and effect in the freight rate grievances has led to a shifting of ground to broader and more general causes and demands. Regional development and the removal of regional disparities have taken over as the main themes, and provincial premiers marching four abreast from East and West converge on Ottawa to demand a transportation policy designed to cure these bigger and better causes for regional complaint. In this new and strange company, the freight rate issue rides like King Billy at the head of the Orangeman's parade. It is there solely as a link with the past and not as a definition of current problems. It just wouldn't be a parade of regional differences without it.

(5) Nor is the cause of the present discontent anything revolutionary in the economic sense. It is not a starving and oppressed proletariat that the East is grinding under its heel. The barefoot boys from Jasper Avenue have plenty of "bread" and are only looking for a piece of the action, a respectable share of the national decision-making. The West has been experiencing a sustained period of what by any standards should be called prosperity. All the more reason to believe that any further manipulation of freight rates or expansion of federal subsidies to railway transportation, even though designated by such a catchy title as a "new transportation policy," could have anything more than a slight ripple effect on the pool of discontent that has been building up. After all, the federal government is now well into its third billion of dollars in direct railway subsidies in lieu of freight rate increases over more than fifteen years without a single new industry having stepped forward to attribute its existence to this wise and enlightened policy.

This rather incongruous association of prosperity and freight rate complaints drives one to look elsewhere for the explanation. The **final clue is the almost indissoluble link between freight rate protest** and strongly felt antipathy to Central Canada, personified by the federal government, Ontario and Quebec, the greedy Eastern interests, Bay Street, and, of course, the Canadian Pacific Railway. The latter gives the bite to the former. Transportation matters that escape this "Ottawa connection" seem also to be immune from the type of criticism usually connected with the freight rate issue. The trucking industry, for example, has largely displaced the railways in service to small shippers and communities, in the intraprovincial distribution of general merchandise traffic, and on a growing volume of east-west traffic. Yet their rate increases have not been identified with regional collapse and so far as I am aware have not been protested because of being "horizontal percentage increases" untapered for the long hauls. The motivation to challenge this is absent here, despite the similarity of the arguments that could be used, because Ottawa is not involved. This might change if the federal government ever carried out its threat to take over the regulation of interprovincial trucking!

In short, the trail of the probable culprit leads right to the door of federal-provincial relations and one should not be thrown off the scent by all the fine-spun arguments in transportation economics that have been thrown at us. My diagnosis of the complaint, then, which I offer only as a first approximation, is that it is due to the defective working of the *federal* part of the constitution. There has been much attention given to the relations between the federal government and the provinces, and while these have been important in themselves, they are not responsible for the general malaise now being felt. In fact, it is plausible to claim that the ineffectiveness of the federal part of the constitution has created problems we have been forced to try to solve through the awkward process of federal-provincial confrontations and negotiations. It is not difficult to see why this source of the trouble should have been largely overlooked. Federal-provincial disputes provide occasions for litigation and force the attention of the courts and constitutional lawyers on these aspects to the neglect of all others. Lawyers are interested in what is in the statute and how it is to be interpreted. To go beyond this to speculate on what might be done, by incorporating other principles, would take them outside their usual field of operations. But to lead up to this point it might be useful to observe first some of the historical background to the West's problem.

Societies meet their problems by the use of tools – physical, institutional, and conceptual. Many of these tools are handed down from previous generations, others are borrowed from societies which have been dealing with similar problems, and still others may be fashioned on the spot, "custom-built" for the particular matter in hand. Confederation offered many unique problems of government, which we were satisfied for the most part to meet with political and economic tools borrowed from a parental home – Great Britain. In most cases, we would have to say, they have served us well, and our political history, while lacking any spectacular achievements in originality, has at least not been marked by breakdowns and fresh starts and compares favourably with the performance of most other nations of the world. But obviously the present is no time for self-congratulation or complacency when the system is experiencing the building up of problems whose source we have had difficulty in recognizing, and which the system itself seems poorly equipped to handle. It even seems to be stiffening under pressure instead of showing a flexibility and resilience that would absorb or dissipate the shock.

The society of the Canadian West when it rose from the bare prairie already had its political and economic tools chosen for it. Already functioning was the British parliamentary system of government established by the British North America Act of 1867; likewise the economic system of laissez-faire capitalism with its emphasis on individualism and the abstention of the government from interference in economic affairs. Both of these systems had evolved in the relatively compact area of the British Isles and both suffered in effectiveness in being stretched over a distance of more than 4,000 miles to cover a sparsely populated country, in the greater part of which settlement and economic development were only at the most rudimentary stage.

The West was not in a position to absorb without serious difficulties the laissez-faire economic philosophy. The homesteader could not be identified with the entrepreneur of classical economics. The severity and vagaries of the climate, the lack of any basis for living off the country as in the mixed farming areas of Eastern Canada, the dependence on a single cash crop, the distance from market and from sources of even the most ordinary supplies, such as fuel and building materials: all of these factors put the Western farmer not only at the mercy of the swings in the economic cycle but also of the stronger bargaining power of almost every individual and company with whom he had any business transactions. It was no accident that the West pioneered in co-operative enterprises and in social welfare legislation in Canada: the environment enforced a strong sense of solidarity. But when he sought to apply these qualifications of the free enterprise society to matters under federal control, the Westerner found that his political power was woefully weak. The only areas in the economy where the federal government felt free to intervene were in tariffs and transportation. But tariffs were the opposite to everything the West wanted, and while the government was ready to build and overbuild in railways, it was very reluctant to lay down any effective principle of equity in freight rates. The Board of Railway Commissioners conceived its duty to be to act simply as a referee in disputes involving a shipper and a railway, and in the best tradition of the British common law strove to limit as much as possible the generalization of its findings, so that it was over fifty years before the last – by now inconsequential but still exasperating – differences in rate scales between East and West were eliminated. But long before this, freight rates had become almost indissolubly linked with Western aspirations. Equally frustrating was the federal government's long reluctance to recognize the need for centralized wheat marketing. A Wheat Board functioned during the First World War but it was dissolved on the return to "normal" conditions. It took fifteen years of Western agitation to restore it.

Experience in trying to get along with the shortcomings of the main economic tools soon led Westerners to question the adequacy of the political tools and the structure that sanctioned them. The main problem was how to make the provinces' views count in Ottawa where the Western members were always greatly in the minority. Both the national parties had their centres of gravity in the Central Provinces and the West and the Maritimes could only hope to influence matters decisively in periods of minority government, as they did in the unsettled period from 1921 to 1926. Four different solutions have been tried over the years since 1921 without having done more than perhaps aggravate the feelings of helplessness and alienation. At any rate, the persistence of such feelings has kept the freight rate issue in prominence as the stick to beat Central Canada despite its rapidly declining relevance to either the economic or political problems of the West.

The first proposed tactic was by far the most interesting, and had its definition of the problem been kept clearly in mind it might have served to stimulate an indigenous school of political economy, not only in Alberta where it originated but throughout Canada. Unfortunately, the possibilities were not seen and only the most impractical of its proposals were given attention, which naturally led to the discarding of the entire definition. The ideas in question came from the philosophical meditations of Henry Wise Wood who, from 1916 to 1931, was President of the United Farmers of Alberta. An American by birth and nearly fifty years old on becoming a Canadian citizen, Wood reflected for many years on the problem of the political ineffectiveness of the Western farmer in national policy despite his forming one of the most important groups in the economy. He was always in the minority in either of the national parties, and from this Wood went on to draw his main conclusion that the two big parties with their basic support in the populous Central Provinces merely reflected the business and financial interests of that area. Against this, Western opinion had little leverage and then only under unusual circumstances, such as minority government. This led Wood to denounce the party system as such as the principal negator of democracy because the parties were always under the control of the dominant interests. In its stead Wood preached the gospel of "group government," by which he meant a government carried out by negotiation between groups representing the various economic interests throughout the country. Although there was no connection between them, Wood's ideas bear a resemblance to Mussolini's theory (which remained on paper only) of the corporate state, except that Wood regarded the groups as actually holding the power rather than being the facade of an advisory council. Wood's ideas were enthusiastically taken up by the UFA and against his own better judgement the organization plunged into provincial politics, sweeping into power in the election of 1921. Group government, a difficult concept to make workable even at the federal level, was practically meaningless at the provincial level because the farmers found when they tried to apply it that they were the only group in the legislature and were left to talk to themselves. They settled, as did Social Credit some twenty years later, for giving the province "businesslike" government. This aborted Wood's project, for his purpose had been to apply the concept federally where the Western farmers could deal with the groups of the greatest importance to them – the Eastern industrial, commercial, and labour interests.

Although the memory of Wood may have long since faded in his own province, his ideas set a stamp on Alberta politics which is still quite visible today. How else to explain the fact that Alberta for more than twenty years sent an almost solid block of Social Credit members to Ottawa where they remained on the farthest opposition benches as a small but cohesive minority group? The distrust of national parties became a characteristic of the Alberta voter, an attitude that gradually spread to the other Western Provinces. Even today, when Albertans wholeheartedly support the Conservative Party, it is an adherence with a difference. The Alberta caucus at Ottawa is not swallowed up in the party caucus but retains its distinct approach and attitudes, and its members possibly would not entirely reject the suggestion that what has happened is not that Alberta has joined the Conservative Party but that that party has joined Alberta.

In the years following the attempt to apply Wood's ideas federally, the West took up two more political tools in its attempt to solve the political problems it saw for itself in Confederation. Unlike Wood's ideas, which were the result of meditation on local conditions, they

234

were borrowed from abroad and the attempt was made to apply them to Western conditions in defiance of the central insight of Wood, namely, that national parties would always tend to be dominated by the numerical superiority of Central Canada. Thus, Social Credit, a product of the despair of the thirties, to be effective even on its own estimation, had to have control of the central government, and when this was seen to be impossible it subsided, as had the UFA government, into the routine business of keeping shop, aided immensely by the oil boom. Almost at the same time, the Cooperative Commonwealth Federation took root in Saskatchewan, importing the ideas of the British Labour Party and the Fabian socialists. Again, these ideas, which may have gains to their credit at the provincial level, were largely irrelevant to the problems of the West in Confederation for they, too, presupposed the capture of power in Ottawa. But in this they condemned themselves, as did Social Credit, by ignoring Wood's dictum that any government in power in Ottawa will, except for brief interludes and under extraordinary circumstances, depend on Central Canada for its main support. Thus, a Social Credit government would have been dominated by Social Credit members from those provinces, and the same would apply to a CCF government, and the West would still be in a minority. In discarding Wood's ideas of group government they had also thrown out his insight into the reality of federal politics. The baby got tossed out with the bath water.

Since the defeat of the Diefenbaker government in 1963, the West has been again on the outside looking in, and has been brooding over the problem with increasing restiveness. It was perhaps to have been expected that the familiar symptoms of the old sickness should reappear, namely a new outburst in the old style on freight rates, just a few years after everything was thought to have been settled by the passage of the National Transportation Act in 1967. As I have already said, a rational interpretation of this phenomenon today leaves a wide credibility gap, which suggests that it may not be meant to be understood in this way but rather as a ritual war dance or even a college yell. This may be only a succession of meaningless sounds, but it certainly builds up the enthusiasm and support for the team on the eve of the big game. If there is such a secondary intent in this, there is also a deepening confusion of thought. The mindless ranting on freight rates of otherwise very intelligent people resembles nothing so much as the confused yelping of hounds that have lost the scent. This confusion of mind extends to those who suppose that some new and elaborate recasting of transportation legislation is going to work like a tranquillizer. It is more likely to be criticized or rejected in its turn *because* it is handed down by Ottawa.

The most ominous development of all, however, is that the West, and also the Maritimes, seem to be picking up and testing a fourth tool, namely, using the provincial governments to act both as the official opposition and as the pressure group to achieve their ends in federal policy. This type of federalism has been tried before, and experience shows that there are really only two possible results: either the dissolution of the federation or the dissolution of democracy by the rule of the strongest member of the federation.

The Holy Roman Empire, which governed Germany from the time of Charlemagne to Napoleon, was one such federation – a loose collection of states of all sizes whose rulers paid nominal allegiance to the Emperor but who went their own way as much as they could. Pulled tightly together by the armies of strong and able emperors from time to time, it was for the most part an amorphous mass without any collective policy or rule whatever. What strength the Emperor had came to him by virtue of those lands he ruled directly in his own name; the rest was like foreign territory where his presence or authority was resented as an intrusion. The result was that when finally dissolved it was little more than the title, the shell of the structure, that had to disappear. The other extreme of this form of federalism was the German state created in 1871 under the dominance of Prussia. This was a very strong federal state indeed, mainly because it was not a democracy but was ruled directly by the Emperor who was also King of Prussia, by far the largest and strongest state in the federation. The representative assembly, the Reichstag, lacked any effective power. It is not difficult to imagine something similar to either of these alternatives taking place in Canada if the federal part of the constitution continues to display its deplorable shortcomings and the provinces succeed in establishing a claim to be the true and only representatives of the people. At the one end there is no loyalty to the federal government and no legitimacy to its authority, at the other end there is an enforced loyalty and legitimacy together with the sacrifice of democratic control and autonomy.

However, there is another type of federalism in which we do not have to look to earlier centuries or other parts of the world, but only to observe what has been going on for 200 years just below our southern border. There is a very strong taboo in Canada against coveting any particular part of the American political system, so strong that it hardly ever has to be mentioned; it just comes naturally for us to avert our eyes from the American experience. True to our counter-revolutionary origins, as the American sociologist Seymour Martin Lipset calls them, we sit before the spectacle of parliamentary institutions with the same attitude of reverence and with the same expectation of having them speak to us as Mr. Mackenzie King must have sat before the portrait of his mother. There has been no need to warn us about the tree with the forbidden fruit, and any serpent would have long since given up his assignment as a hopeless job. Even in Western Canada there seem to have been few who have dared to peep over the fence to see why there haven't been comparable screams coming from the states of Montana or North Dakota about freight rates and the dictator in Washington. But then the West has been confused by people like Diefenbaker who combine a fervent devotion to Western Canadian aspirations with a fulsome and uncritical praise of Parliament and its ways. Who would suspect, after that, that the ways of Parliament might be the root of the trouble?

Yet the criticism of the way in which Parliament operates is rising on every hand, not just in parts of Canada but in Great Britain itself. We find ourselves with a monolithic form of government in which power is concentrated in the hands of the Prime Minister and is only delegated, and no more than delegated, at his discretion. The historic convention that the government must have the support of Parliament has been interpreted and put in practice as requiring implicit obedience on the part of all government party members both on the most inconsequential as on the most controversial measures. The members have become voting automatons. Legislation comes down from on high, polished into final form by bureaucrats and ministers before being introduced to the "lawmakers." Changes are difficult to make because the prestige of the minister and of the government is on the line. Unless the government is given its own way, it will resign and force an election. Naturally, there is a little more give and take in the ordinary business of Parliament, but the power and the responsibility remain concentrated at the top.

Such a system is obviously something less than perfect in a federal state, such as Canada, where there are great differences in population density and where distance itself creates differences in views. This is especially so for regions outside the central area, which find themselves in the situation of permanent disadvantage or minority, as Wood pointed out. But Wood missed the target in singling out the party system as the source of the grievance. A party system is essential for the effective working of a modern democracy; it is the vertebral column of the constitution that gives leadership and organization to the process of government. Where there are no parties, a power vacuum is created which, if it doesn't lead to the destruction of the system, leads to government by a one-party system where democracy is abolished or exists on sufferance in a very limited capacity. Wood's target should have been the monolithic system of party government at which parliamentary institutions in their present form have arrived. A minority can never hope to act like a majority but there are techniques open to it, whether of a geographical, racial, linguistic, or any other type. It should be possible for representatives of regions or minorities to belong to a national party without losing the freedom to vote as they see fit on any issue. This type of voting happens so seldom in Canada that it becomes the subject of a formal announcement, as in the debate on capital punishment, although even here the Government was accused of having brought pressure on some members to support a position it had refused to acknowledge openly as its own.

Yet when we look at the American Congress in action we see a democratic institution operating, it is true, on a well-established party system, but with a flexibility that enables it to keep tuned to and respond to views coming from many directions. Here it is possible to be a member of a party but to vote independently of party on a regional issue, or indeed on any other issue. The members of Congress have real power and real responsibility. The administration does not treat congressmen as so many rubber stamps. The administration works closely with its own party members in Congress, but it must request Congress to pass the laws, and if in their final form they are not what the administration wants, it has no power to force compliance by threatening to resign. It must accept, subject to some veto powers, the laws that are passed by Congress. It seems logical to conclude that the apparent absence of any endemic regional alienation, at least on a scale anywhere comparable to the Canadian case, can be explained by this separation of powers and resilience in the constitution. Regions find it possible to achieve their objectives by negotiations or "log-rolling" in Congress. Regional members are not required to compromise themselves on local issues, and share, to the extent that their interest and ability warrant, in the actual making of the legislation. Legislation made in this way has a legitimacy in all parts of the country. Congress, of course, like any democratically elected body, has its full quota of deadwood. While it may accept the guidance of the administration on many matters, it retains its powers. It would be a very inefficient body if it tried to use them to the full, but that is not required of it. It is sufficient that it possesses them and can respond when the need is felt, for rarely does it divide on strict party lines.

In the United States, leadership on regional issues is provided by prominent and influential members of Congress. One has only to mention senators of smaller states, of both parties, such as Mansfield of Montana, Church of Idaho, Magnusson of Washington, Goldwater of Arizona, Aiken of Vermont, and Muskie of Maine. On the other hand, in Canada, upward progress in a political career means gradual absorption into the central establishment and a cutting off at the roots, from which the only way out is to resign. The enforced silence of government party members, the confidentiality of caucus, and the unanimity of Cabinet leaves a gap which permits the Opposition and the provincial premiers to appear as the only plausible champions of regional positions. As long as major parties were fairly even in strength, the changes in government tended to correct this lopsidedness, but lately there seems to be a semi-permanent assignment of roles which in the long run could seriously damage the legitimacy of the federal government, supported as it almost always is by a preponderant strength in the Central Provinces.

One can speculate on what would have happened, say, to the bilingualism legislation in Canada, had it to be passed by a body with powers similar to the United States Congress. One can imagine an Alberta member explaining to a constituent that he had supported in the first place a bill sponsored by Western members and had taken part in the work of final consolidation of all the proposals into a single bill which naturally was based mostly on the government's own draft bill. "We sat down with some of the Quebec members to explain our position and to find out what theirs was. We were able to get this and this, but there was no way we could get enough support for that and that, so we had to accept the bill as it was passed. But we did make some points, and we understand better the other side, so I guess it is the best to be hoped for under the circumstances." A bill on such a controversial issue, passed in this manner, would have acquired a stamp of legitimacy in all parts of the country that a bill handed down from the Cabinet in basically non-negotiable form could not equal. The Opposition members, having had no part in the drafting of the latter, and no hopes of amending it, are driven to a negative and irresponsible attitude toward it.

In our system, such a sense of grievance is allowed to collect along with others, and they become merged together in a sort of generalized regional grievance. With this the public is ready to seize upon any likely scapegoat that has some association with Ottawa upon which to vent their frustration. It is just such a dissociation of cause and effect that explains the rise and persistence of freight rates as a regional issue. It has all the attributes of a good regional issue and if it didn't exist it might be necessary to invent it. At that, a good deal of invention has actually taken place in the most recent years of its history. These curious circumstances, I think, we must attribute to the faulty political hygiene in our society. Grievances arise of a type which our federal branch of government is able neither to dissipate nor resolve. In its monolithic form any concession that it may be driven to make may neither be put to its credit nor serve to mitigate the sense of grievance, for the pattern of attitudes toward monolithic government is quite different from those where the complainer himself feels both responsibility and some sense of being involved in the government's action at the same time. The freight rate issue is thus of importance in measuring the growth of such attitudes of irresponsibility and detachment. Subsidies may be proposed whose efficacy is highly dubious but this is disregarded because it is believed the money is coming from Ottawa, that is, from the wealthy citizens and industries of Central Canada. People who will go so far as to demand "postage-stamp" freight rates will still pay their electricity bills without a murmur.

The moral of the story is that we must look conscientiously and objectively for the true source of our difficulties and we must be sharp to recognize scapegoats when we see them and not waste our ammunition on them. If it is true, as I suggest, that at the bottom of our regional problem lies, not regional economic disparity, but the brittle and unresponding nature of the federal branch of our government, then some changes are in order. While certain features of the American system seem to have worked better in this respect, we must avoid getting into the sterile argument of either one or the other. A constitutional transplant would be as little viable as a head transplant and could be recommended seriously by no one. But this should not turn us away from investigating those areas which do seem to offer some hope of alleviating our own problem. Keeping a venerable object like a constitution roadworthy is like keeping an old car in trim. Newness in constitution is not always regarded as a virtue. Any part that will do the job and fit in with what is already there might be acceptable. But because a particular Rolls Royce part might serve the purpose does not mean that we need a Rolls Royce car. We should be interested only in keeping our old car on the road.

The immediate objective should be to turn the discussion into this area, for no federal constitution can survive for long a state of affairs that brings federal and provincial governments in continuous confrontation. George Drew, when he moved from Premier of Ontario to leader of the Opposition at Ottawa, found that his new position required him to take a stand on the freight rate issue. Western members offered some ironical comments on his attacks on the Board of Transport Commissioners, for when he was Premier of Ontario, his province and Quebec were the only provinces that failed to appeal against freight rate increases. His new attitude seemed inconsistent, to say the least. Drew's answer is interesting, not in whether it got him off the hook or not, but because in it he outlined clearly the way the constitution should work and at the same time conceded its failure to work properly. He stated that "in relation to dominion affairs every part of Canada is represented in this house by the members sent here from the different constituencies. . . . We thought that Ontario, in relation to dominion matters, is fully represented in this house by members of the different parties who have been elected to represent the constituencies of Ontario." Therefore, as provincial premier he saw no reason to intervene in a matter under federal jurisdiction. However, he added, "I do not want any word that I have said to imply criticism of provinces which have launched appeals, because I recognize that they were in a most unfavourable position in relation to the central provinces." These remarks, made in 1950, are relevant to the point I have tried to establish here. It is thought-provoking to note that even up to today we have not brought ourselves face to face with this aspect of our constitutional problem.

Notes

Notes to Part I, Introduction

1. See, among more recent studies, A.W. Currie, *Canadian Transportation Economics* (Toronto, 1967); and H.L. Purdy, *Transportation Competition and Public Policy* (Vancouver, 1972).

2. Joseph A. Schumpeter, "Science and Ideology," Presidential Address to the American Economic Association, December 28, 1948, *American Economic Review*, 39 (March, 1949).

Notes to Chapter 2

1. This quotation is taken from "The Freight Rate Structure of Canada," vol. II, pp. 23-4, an undated and unsigned report prepared for the Turgeon Royal Commission (the removal of the Mountain Differential in July of 1949 is referred to as an impending event) which contains much useful information, not all of which is readily available in other sources. I have drawn heavily on this source for this particular chapter. The Turgeon Royal Commission Papers, Public Archives of Canada (PAC), RG 33-49, vol. 16. There were seven special classes of rates in addition to the four general classes: grain; flour; salt; cement and plaster; lumber; livestock; agricultural implements and wooden building materials; and coal, coke, sand, stone, and pig iron. These classes conform with the conditions peculiar to the West – lower rates on settlers' basic needs.

2. A.W. Currie, "Freight Rates on Grain in Western Canada", *Canadian Historical Review*, 21 (1940), 40.

3. A study of the Crow's Nest Pass Rates is that of E. W. Tyrchniewicz, C.W. Nactyall, and G.F. Skinner; "Crow's Nest Pass Grain Rates: Time for a Change?" in *Proceedings of the Sixteenth Annual Meeting of the Transportation Research Forum*, November, 1975. This study contains further bibliographical references. Others have followed.

4. House of Commons, *Debates*, June 18, 1897, pp. 4568-9.

5. S.L. McLean, *Report on Railway Commissions* (1899); and McLean, *Report on Railway Rate Grievances and Regulative Legislation* (1902).

6. In time, his views came to be identified with the rather rigid mould into which the Board's precedents finally settled. Innis, in notes made during his membership on the Turgeon Royal Commission, speaks of the need for breaking with the "McLean tradition and the domination of traffic officers." PAC, RG 33-27, vol. 72.

7. [Exact reference to a Board document missing. Eds.]

8. Board of Railway Commissioners, Order No. 3258, July 6, 1907, "International Rates Case."

9. Regina Board of Trade vs. Canadian Pacific and Canadian Northern Railway Companies (The Regina Toll Case), Canadian Railway Cases (CRC), 11 CRC 386 (1910).

10. Canadian Pacific Railway vs. Regina Board of Trade, 13 CRC 203 to 216 (December 6, 1911).

11. In re Western Tolls (The Western Freight Rates Case), Judgement of April 16, 1914, 17 CRC 123.

12. 17 CRC 123 to 127.

13. *Ibid.*, 128.

14. *Ibid.*, 130.

15. *Canadian Annual Review* (1912), 209.

16. *Ibid.*, 196.

17. H.F. Angus, "Notes Suggested by the Regional Hearings," draft of an article contained in the Turgeon Royal Commission Papers, PAC, RG 33-27, vol. 70.

Notes to Chapter 3

1. Letter of H.J. Symington to Premier Martin, August 4, 1920. The W.M. Martin Papers, 38558. Saskatchewan Provincial Archives (SPA).

2. Letter to Gerald Graham, Commissioner, Saskatoon Board of Trade, August 4, 1920. Martin Papers, 38558. SPA.

3. P.C. 2434, October 6, 1920. Quoted in "Re Freight Toll – 1922," Judgements, Orders, and Rulings (JORR), Board of Railway Commissioners for Canada, vol. XII, No. 8, p. 61, July 5, 1922.

4. Letter to Robert Whiteside, Dirsay, Saskatchewan, October 7, 1920. Martin Papers, 38596. SPA.

5. Letter to G.G. McGeer, December 12, 1921. Martin Papers, 38825-38828. SPA.

6. *Canadian Annual Review* (1921).

7. Letter of April 13, 1921, in reply to Symington's letter of March 22. Martin Papers. SPA.

8. Martin expressed concern with branch line construction in a speech on the railway situation delivered November 18, 1920. Martin Papers, 30077. SPA.

9. W.L. Morton, *The Progressive Party in Canada* (Toronto, 1950), 299.

10. *Ibid.*, 301.

11. *Ibid.*, 305.

12. Letter to W. M. Martin, February 20, 1919. Martin Papers, SPA.

13. It is of interest to note that George H. Miller, in *Railroads and the Granger Laws*, states that in the period of American farmers' greatest interest in freight rates during the 1870's, leadership in both eastern and the midwestern states was provided by merchants and businessmen, particularly in the towns that were competing gateways across the main rivers. "Because of the unusual competitive nature of the railway enterprise in the Upper Mississippi Valley and because of the high concentration of absentee control in that area, the Granger states became major centers of political experimentation with the railroad question. The great distances between these states and their eastern markets, the newness of the burgeoning economies, and the immaturity of their political life undoubtedly intensified the difficulties they experienced. The strong sense of sectionalism in the West was another factor that gave a distinct character to the movement to reform in the Mississippi Valley, but the Farmers' Movement of the 1870's was not a major force in the shaping of this regulatory legislation. The so-called Granger laws dealt with issues that were national in scope, and in almost every case, the leaders of the movement for reform were merchants. . . ."

14. Russell R. Walker, *Politicians in a Pioneering Province* (Vancouver, 1969).

15. Excerpt from a letter to one J.A. Campbell of Vancouver, February 12, 1924, in reply to his request for a "brief memo re railway transportation rates." This was apparently to serve as ammunition against the Conservative H.H. Stevens, to forestall any

attempt to appropriate the credit for freight rate achievements for his party. Oliver Papers, Archives of British Columbia (ABC).

16. Attorney-General of British Columbia vs. Canadian Pacific Railway. Heard March 1, 1909. Judgement April 15, 1909. 8 CRC 346.

17. Letter to Campbell, February 12, 1924.

18. *Ibid.*

19. J.A. Argo, "Historical Review of the Canadian Railway Freight Rate Structure, 1876 to 1938," in R.A.C. Henry and Associates, "Freight Rates in Canada," a study made for the Royal Commission on Dominion-Provincial Relations, p. 78.

20. Judgement in Equalization of Rates Case, October 10, 1923, JORR, 13 at 173.

21. Letter to Campbell, February 12, 1924.

22. Letter of July 29, 1922. The C.A. Dunning Papers, 35010. SPA.

23. See letter of Oliver to Greenfield, December 19, 1921. Premiers' Papers file 385, 1921-1934. Provincial Archives of Alberta (PAA).

24. Telegram of Greenfield to Chard, February 13, 1922. Premiers' Papers file 385. PAA.

25. Premiers's Papers file 385, 1921-1934. PAA.

26. Dunning Papers, 35044-051. SPA.

27. As all this exchange of correspondence has been made public, Canadian Pacific reproduced it *in extenso* in its submission to the Cabinet in the appeal, pointing out at the same time that although Alberta had joined the appeal it had taken no part whatever in the original case. Submission of Canadian Pacific Railway Company re appeal of Board's decision of June 1922, dated May 9, 1923. (Copy in the Pitblado Papers, Manitoba Archives [MA].)

28. The telegrams are reproduced in McGeer's letter to Chard, March 27, 1923. Premiers' Papers file 384, 1921-34. PAA.

29. McGeer to Chard, March 27, 1923.

30. Letter of McKeown to Oliver, October 24, 1924. Oliver Papers. ABC.

31. Letter of Oliver to King, November 8, 1923. The McGeer Papers, file 2-10, Western Freight Rates correspondence, 1921-23. Archives of the University of British Columbia (AUBC).

32. McGeer Papers, *ibid.*

33. McGeer Papers, *ibid.*

34. McGeer Papers, *ibid.*

35. *The Vancouver Sun*, March 5, 1924.

36. BRC Transcripts, vol. 464, p. 7408, June 21, 1926. Quoted in JORR, Board of Railway Commissioners, vol. XVII, p. 132, September 12, 1927.

37. Order-in-Council No. 886, June 5, 1925.

38. Statutes of Canada, 15-16 Geo. V, p. 52.

39. BRC Transcripts, vol. 507, pp. 6701-4, April 8, 1927.

40. *Ibid.*, vol. 506, p. 6376, April 5, 1927.

41. *Ibid.*, p. 6404.

42. *Ibid.*, p. 6495.

43. *Ibid.*, vol. 507, p. 6603, April 8, 1927.

44. *Ibid.*, pp. 6701-4.

45. *Ibid.*, vol. 509, p. 7518, April 21, 1927.

46. *Ibid.*, p. 7677.

47. *Ibid.*, vol. 510, p. 7750, April 26, 1927. Quoted by Canadian National Counsel, Alister Fraser.

48. *Ibid.*, vol. 495, p. 1714. Also quoted with approval by Pitblado, Winnipeg Board of Trade, in Argument in vol. 509, p. 7335.

49. See General Order 448, August 26, 1927.

50. The McGeer Papers, file 2-15, letter to Premier of April 10, 1928.

51. The McGeer Papers, file 2-15.

52. *Ibid.*

53. S.F. Tolmie Papers, file 10 (Freight Rates), AUBC.

54. The McGeer Papers, file 2-15, October 19, 1929.

55. *Ibid.*

56. This information is contained in reports of Ladner to Tolmie found in the Tolmie Papers.

57. *Canadian Annual Review* (1934), 91; and *ibid.* (1935-36), 623.

Notes to Chapter 4

1. A recent example — an editorial in the *Halifax Chronicle-Herald*, December 16, 1974, entitled "Strangulation," begins "Freight rates have strangled Maritime industry for generations."

2. House of Commons, *Debates*, 1877, p.1528.

3. See Colin Howel, "Repeal, Reciprocity and Commercial Union in Nova Scotia Politics, 1886-87," M.A. thesis, Dalhousie University, 1967.

4. House of Commons, *Debates*, 1880, p. 877.

5. *Ibid.*, p. 498.

6. In terms to which we have later become accustomed, the record of the Intercolonial does not look that bad - a net accumulated operating deficit of $6.5 million over the 28 years from 1889 to 1916.

7. House of Commons, *Debates*, May 4, 1888, p. 1228.

8. For example, see the statement of Railways Minister H.R. Emmerson in House of Commons, *Debates*, 1906-07, p. 5210.

9. House of Commons, *Debates*, March 1, 1905, p. 1891.

10. *Ibid.*, 1906-07, p. 5209.

11. *Ibid.*, 1906, p. 135.

12. *Ibid.*, 1887, vol. 2, p. 768.

13. *Ibid.*, February 29, 1912, pp. 4131-2.

14. Drayton-Acworth Commission Report, 1917, p. xci.

15. Report of the Royal Commission on Maritime Claims, 1927, pp. 24-6.

16. *Canadian Annual Review* (1913), 693.

Notes to Chapter 5

1. W.C. Milner, in an article on the Maritime Provinces in the *Canadian Annual Review* (1924), points out that "a lesser cause [than the claims of Portland, Maine, to be Canada's national port] gave even greater offense. The cutting up of the Intercolonial into regional districts, and striking the section from Riviere du Loup to Montreal from the main section, was a blow at the *amour propre* of the people in the East, which they resented." (p. 333)

2. *Canadian Annual Review* (1925), 397.

3. This had worked for Premier Oliver when he scraped back into office in British Columbia in 1924, but it was not enough to save the Armstrong government in Nova Scotia in the following year.

4. *Canadian Annual Review* (1921), 394.

5. *Ibid.*, 699.

6. Patterson's papers are to be found in the Archives Section of the New Brunswick Museum in Saint John. His views are best summarized in three documents: (1) "Maritime Memorandum" is not dated nor is the authorship shown, but that it should be in his papers and repeat his main arguments makes it plausible to ascribe at least a share of the authorship to him. It seems to have been the brief presented by the Maritime Boards of Trade delegation to Ottawa in 1925. (2) *The True Story of Confederation* (2nd ed., 1926) contains an elaboration of his constitutional arguments. (3) "The Problems of the Maritime Provinces Within Confederation" (1930) is a lengthy paper presented to the Saint John Board of Trade in his capacity as President of the Transportation Commission of the Maritime Board of Trade.

7. Quoted in Patterson, *True Story*, 26.

8. Quoted in *ibid.*, 29.

9. Quoted in *ibid.*

10. Quoted in *ibid.*, 16.

11. Quoted in *ibid.*, 27; emphasis added.

12. *Ibid.*, 30.

13. The Report of the Royal Commission on Dominion-Provincial Relations, 1937, Book II, Recommendations. In Particular, see the section "The Transportation Provisions of Confederation," pp. 249-53.

14. *Ibid.*

15. Even Patterson was a bit coy on this point. It was safer to present it to the federal government as its obligation and problem rather than to try to spell out precisely what it meant. In "The Problems of the Maritime Provinces" (p. 31), he states: "If the Confederation means anything, it means that the Federal Parliament, as representing Canada, is obliged to provide transportation improvements which include a freight rate structure which will ensure the Maritime seaboard being the Atlantic trade terminus of Canada throughout the year and the fair regulation of trade between the Provinces."

16. Patterson, *The True Story*, 36.

17. *Ibid.*, 22.

18. See Michael Hatfield, "J.B.M. Baxter and the Maritime Rights Movement," M.A. thesis, Mount Allison University, 1970, pp. 36-9.

19. *Ibid.*, 39.

20. This is taken from my "Structure of Railroad Subsidies in Canada," York/University of Toronto Joint Program in Transportation, 1974.

21. House of Commons, *Debates* (1925), vol. I, p. 220.

22. The Armstrong Papers, Box 667, Public Archives of Nova Scotia.

23. Nova Scotia Brief to the Duncan Commission, 1926, p. 51.

24. *Canadian Annual Review* (1925), 396.

25. Nova Scotia Brief to the Duncan Commission.

26. Board of Transport Commissioners, JORR, vol. 17, p. 294.

27. *Canadian Annual Review* (1925), 397-9.

28. *Ibid.*

29. *Ibid.*

30. *Ibid.*

31. *Ibid.*

32. House of Commons, *Debates*, 1926-27, vol. II, p. 1827 (April 4, 1927).

33. For our purposes the relevant section of Order 505 reads: "Such representations relate more particularly to the alleged failure to use Canadian ports for Canadian trade to the extent to which they might be utilized, and to the handicaps said to result from the operation of the schedules of rates chargeable for the carriage of goods on the railways uniting the Maritime Provinces with the other provinces of Canada and to the

manner of administering that part of the Canadian National Railways System which was formerly known as the Intercolonial Railway by methods and conditions alleged to be inconsistent with the pledges given at the time of Confederation in regard thereto and with the practice followed from the time of construction of the railway until December 1918."

34. The Motherwell Papers, SPA.

35. Maritime opinion appreciated the job that Cornell had done in giving substance to their freight rate case. Mr. D. R. Turnbull, president of the Halifax Board of Trade and a member of the Committee of Freight Rates set up after the Moncton Conference in 1925, paid the following tribute after the Maritime Freight Rates Act was on the statute books: "The services of Mr. F. C. Cornell (who was formally recommended to the Committee as a freight rate expert) were secured and it is not too much to say that had this action not been taken and the work promptly and vigorously prosecuted, it is doubtful if we would have been able to have presented a proper case before the Duncan Commission. I would indeed go so far as to say that I believe the 20% reduction in freight rates which has meant so much to the people of the Maritime Provinces can be credited directly to the work done by Mr. Cornell under the direction of the Maritime Freight Rates Committee." Quoted in *The Commercial Laws*, Halifax Board of Trade, vol. 7, no. 7 (January, 1928).

36. First prize for the most inconsequential remark on the problem of the Canadian National deficits must go to Prime Minister Mackenzie King, who told the *Globe* in Toronto on January 12, 1926, that the problem could be solved through an equalization of rates! This must be regarded either as a confession of ignorance or as a master stroke by the Great Obfuscator. See *Canadian Annual Review* (1925), 119.

37. Report of the Royal Commission on Maritime Claims, p. 22.

38. *Ibid.*, pp. 24-6.

39. *Ibid.*, p. 236.

40. 17 George V, 1927, Chapter 44.

41. House of Commons, *Debates* (1926-27), vol. II, p. 1831.

42. "The Problems of the Maritime Provinces," p. 11.

43. *Ibid.*, p. 27.

44. *Ibid.*, p. 53.

45. *Ibid.*, p. 35.

46. *The Commercial Times,* Halifax Board of Trade (December, 1930).

Notes to Chapter 6

1. Maritime Transportation Commission vs. Canadian National Railways, 44 CRC 279, January 3, 1936.

2. Province of Nova Scotia vs. Canadian National Railways, 44 CRC 161, April 21, 1937.

3. 44 CRC 289 (p. 298). The long-standing influence of Assistant Chief Commissioner S.J. McLean in formulating regulatory doctrine seems apparent in this language – he was a member of the panel that heard the case. Compare it with the Regina Tolls Case.

4. The Commission in its early stages was known as the Rowell Commission after its first chairman, who was forced to retire by reason of illness, after which the Commission was referred to as the Sirois Commission after its second chairman. As so many years later there may be some doubt as to whether one and the same Commission is being referred to, I have used the hyphenated name throughout.

5. Report of the Royal Commission on Dominion-Provincial Relations, Book II, p. 189.

6. *Ibid.*, p. 198.

7. *Ibid.*, pp. 247-59.

8. *Ibid.*, p. 253.

9. *Ibid.*, p. 254.

10. *Ibid.*, p. 259.

11. In the Patterson papers there is a copy of a very bitter letter written to J.R. Dudley, Commissioner of the Saint John Board of Trade, undated and with no indication of whether it was actually sent, but which is obviously of a late date since it is basically a criticism of his successor in Cabinet. Here Patterson asserts the prominence of his role in the founding and activities of the Maritime Transportation Commission and considers the abolition of the provincial Department of Federal Relations as one of the "greatest tragedies in the political history of New Brunswick."

12. Report of the Royal Commission on Transportation, 1951, p. 27.

13. *Ibid.*, p. 191.

14. *Ibid.*, p. 199.

15. The telegrams, letters, memoranda, and newspaper clippings used in the reconstruction of this story have been obtained from the British Columbia Attorney-General's department records, files R 315-3 and R 318-3.

16. Quoted in *Vancouver Province*, January 31, 1941.

17. These remarks, taken from an undated editorial, appear from the context to have been contained in Wismer's remarks to the press upon his return from Ottawa.

18. Letter to Campney, copy to Wismer, February 20, 1941.

Notes to Chapter 7

1. *The Vancouver Sun*, February 15, 1945.

2. *Ibid.*, March 8, 1945.

3. *Ibid.*, March 22, 1945.

4. *Ibid.*, June 8, 1945.

5. *Ibid.*, May 26, 1945.

6. *The Calgary Albertan*, May 26, 1945.

7. *The Vancouver Sun*, June 26, 1945.

8. Letter of July 10, 1945, PAA, file 89289. Quotations from these letters were included in the Premier's opening remarks to the regional hearings in Edmonton on the 30 Per Cent Case. See Board of Transport Commissioners Transcripts, vol. 763, p. 8906.

9. *The Vancouver Sun*, July 6, 1945.

10. *Ibid.*, August 13, 1945.

11. *Ibid.*, August 22, 1945.

12. *Ibid.*, October 11, 1946.

13. PAA, Premiers' Papers, 69.289. Letter of July 16, 1945, to M.H.C. Nichols, Secretary, Alberta Farmers Union.

14. *Winnipeg Free Press*, October 11, 1946.

15. *The Globe and Mail*, October 11, 1946.

16. The Province of Manitoba congratulated itself on the success of the provincial delaying tactics in a "blue book" issued for the information of the public in January, 1948. Premier Garson, in his letter of introduction, said: "Had the province not opposed the railways' case the increased freight rates would undoubtedly have been made effective at least as early as the spring of 1947 [the 21 per cent increase took effect April 8, 1948] thus the money saved to the people of Manitoba because of a provincial intervention in this case has already amounted to a substantial sum." Quoted in Manitoba's Submissions in Opposition to an Increase in Freight Rates.

17. BTC Transcripts, 30 Per Cent Case, vol. 736, p. 3271.

18. 60 CRC 255.

19. See BTC Transcripts, vol. 777, pp. 14051-75, September, 29, 1947.

20. 61 CRC 65, The Provinces (except Ontario and Quebec) *et al.* vs. The Railway Association of Canada *et al.*

21. BTC Transcripts, pp. 17661-2; cited by Pitblado in vol. 779, p. 18731. See also vol. 817, p. 4310.

22. *Ibid.*, p. 16887; cited by Pitblado in vol. 789, p. 18715.

23. *Ibid.*, p. 17048; cited by Pitblado in vol. 789, p. 18715.

24. 62 CTC 1 (1948).

25. A very useful chronology of the main events to mid-September is given by C.F.H. Carson, KC, CPR counsel, in his statement to the Board at the hearings in a provincial motion for a stay of proceedings in the 30 Per Cent Increase Case, September 21, 1948. BTC Transcripts, vol. 796, pp. 2223-34. This is amplified and brought to April, 1950, in the Report of the Turgeon Commission in 1951, Appendix A to Chapter II, Section 3, "Delays in Freight Rate Revenue Cases," pp. 72-4.

26. House of Commons, *Debates*, 1950, vol. IV, p. 4266.

27. House of Commons, *Debates*, 1948, vol. III, p. 2652.

28. British Columbia Attorney-General's Papers, R 315-3.

29. House of Commons, *Debates*, 1948, vol. III, p. 2541.

30. *Ibid.*, p. 2625.

31. *Ibid.*, p. 2652.

32. *Ibid.*

33. *Ibid.*, p. 2653.

34. *Ibid.*, p. 2656.

35. *Ibid.*, p. 2657.

36. *Ibid.*, p. 2912.

37. *Ibid.*, p. 2638.

38. *Ibid.*, pp. 2916-7.

39. *Ibid.*, p. 2750.

40. The provincial brief stated that "our concern is that an understanding may be reached which will obviate the necessity of formal appeal."

41. Brief of the Provinces to the Governor-in-Council, April 26, 1948, retained in Turgeon Royal Commission Papers, PAC, RG 33-27, vol. 101.

42. Parts of the latter are reproduced in BTC Transcripts, vol. 796, pp. 2231-4.

43. Excerpts of this resolution are quoted in the Report of the Turgeon Commission, 1951, p. 48.

44. In the meantime a face-saving reason had been found for the change of position – the Public Inquiries Act was found to exclude from its operations any inquiries subject to any special law. The Board's investigation would have to have been under the Railway Act.

45. Quoted in the Report of the Turgeon Commission, p. 48.

46. Paragraph 18, Application of the Railway Association of Canada to the Board of Transport Commissioners for a 20 Per Cent Increase in Freight Rates.

47. The reader is warned to keep his critical faculties at the alert since I was mainly responsible for the composition and presentation of the Alberta brief on the Mountain Differential Case and of the brief on equalization to the Turgeon Royal Commission.

48. 63 CRC 214, Province of British Columbia, vs CPR, CNR *et al.*, April 23, 1949.

Notes to Chapter 8

1. There were actually two Turgeon Commissions on transportation. In 1955 he was appointed to deal with provincial complaints against the railways' use of agreed changes. The Commission recommended a relaxation of control over agreed changes, which was accepted by the government, the Railway Act being amended accordingly.

2. There had always been competition between the provinces over who could display the most fearsome wounds. British Columbia disputed Alberta's claim to be at the apex of the freight rate structure (see BTC Transcripts, vol. 817, p. 4315) and M.A. MacPherson, Saskatchewan counsel, is reported to have told the Board: "I want to point out that so far as my province is concerned we are at the freight shed of Canada" (BTC Transcripts, vol. 818, p. 4635). One sees what he meant but cannot help wondering whether he might put it even more strongly had he said "wood shed"!

3. Report of the Turgeon Royal Commission on Transportation, pp. 125-7. Hereafter cited as Turgeon Report.

4. Brief of the Transportation Commission of the Maritime Board of Trade to the Turgeon Royal Commission, p. 9.

5. *Ibid.*, p. 52.

6. Cited in Turgeon Report, p. 124.

7. The Chief Commissioner stated in his judgement: "Insofar as the Province of Manitoba's opposition to the removal of the Mountain Differential is based on the arguments advanced by the railways, effect cannot be given to the position it takes for the reasons I have already given respecting the contentions advanced by the railways." Province of British Columbia vs. CPR, CNR *et al.*, 63 CRTC 214 at 226. April 23, 1949.

8. Turgeon Report, pp. 30, 25.

9. *Ibid.*, p. 33.

10. *Ibid.*, p. 86.

11. *Ibid.*, p. 124.

12. References are to pages in the "Submission of the Province of Saskatchewan to the Royal Commission on Transportation." Regina, September 12, 1949. Emphasis has been added in every case.

13. There was some belated satisfaction to be felt in discovering recently an endorsement of this approach buried in the notes made by Innis during the Turgeon Commission: "Frawley's argument that the Board was set up to deal chiefly with personal discrimination and that the Act as it stands does not give the Board an effective means of dealing with regional discrimination seems to me to be sound." PAC, RG 33-27, vol. 70.

14. Turgeon Report, p. 100.

15. PAC, RG 33-27, vol. 70.

16. Turgeon Report, p. 285.

17. This was said at the conclusion of his course in Canadian economic history at the University of Toronto in 1934. James W. Carry called him a "technological determinist." See Carry, "Harold Adams Innis and Marshall McLuhan," in *McLuhan, Pro and Con* (Toronto: Penguin, 1969).

18. Marshall McLuhan, an acknowledged disciple of Innis, seems to have pushed this impression close to its logical conclusion in complete unintelligibility.

19. A further insight into Innis's scientism in his assessment of the freight rate problem is provided by the final sentences of his memorandum in the Report (p. 307): "A reorganization of the regulatory bodies concerned with transportation will facilitate collection of vital statistical facts and offset the most serious effects of a duopoly in its control of information. In this way more precise methods can be devised to meet the problems of transportation."

20. Turgeon Report, p. 306.

21. And yet, of course, it was repeated every time a new commodity, such as rapeseed, was brought in under the statutory umbrella.

22. See my *The Structure of Railway Subsidies in Canada*, (Downsview, Ontario: York University Transport Centre, 1974), 26-8.

23. House of Commons, *Debates*, October 26, 1951, p. 434.

Notes to Chapter 9

1. I am indebted for this concept to David Braybrooke and Charles E. Lindblom, *A Strategy of Decision; Policy Evaluation as a Social Process* (New York: Free Press, 1970), 240-4. Their example of an excessive enlargement of the reference group is that of the people of America being asked to decide whether Yale University should have a department of astronomy. The only popular description of such a situation is for it to be said that a certain matter has become involved in "politics."

2. *Ibid.*, 243.

3. Board of Transport Commissioners, RTC Transcript, vol. 916, February 5, 1953, p. 1764.

4. *Ibid.*, vol. 987, October 18, 1956, p. 6235.

5. *Ibid.*, p. 6266.

6. *Ibid.*, p. 6329.

7. *Ibid.*, October 19, 1956, pp. 6371, 6376.

8. *Ibid.*, pp. 6386, 6389.

9. *Ibid.*, vol. 988, October 24, 1956, p. 6462.

10. *Ibid.*, p. 6571.

11. BTC Transcripts, "9% Case," vol. 910, December 15, 1952, p. 7578.

12. House of Commons, *Debates*, 1949, vol. II, p. 1076, October 24, 1949. One should recall that almost contemporaneously with these remarks, the Province of Saskatchewan was submitting its brief to the Turgeon Royal Commission in which it stated that the mere removal of these differences in the respective scales would have insignificant effects.

13. House of Commons, *Debates*, 1950, vol. III, p. 3138, June 1, 1950. There is this to be said for Mr. Diefenbaker's confusion between percentages and percentage points that he may here have somewhat rashly followed the line of the *Winnipeg Free Press*. In the same speech he quoted with approval from an editorial committing the same mistake: "Thus the old discrimination against the West not only remains but is worsened. The latest flat increase of 7.4 per cent applied to an eastern rate of, say, 85 cents is one thing. Applied to a western rate on the identical commodity of one dollar, it is another. The present differential of 15 per cent is increased." (*Winnipeg Free Press*, March 3, 1950, quoted at *ibid.*, p. 3140.)

14. *Ibid.*, 1950, vol. IV, p. 4284, June 28, 1950.

15. *Ibid.*, 1951, vol. II, p. 1958, April 12, 1951.

16. *Ibid.*, 1951, Second Session, vol. II, p. 1383, November 27, 1951.

17. The new equalized class rate scale was made effective March 1, 1955, and a large number of equalized commodity mileage scales were made effective January 1, 1958.

18. House of Commons, *Debates*, 1957, vol. I, p. 1640, March 25, 1957.

19. *Ibid.*, 1957-58, vol. I, p. 1003, November 12, 1957.

20. *Ibid.*, vol. III, p. 1776, January 3, 1958. These interventions were to needle the new Conservative government facing its first freight rate increase since taking office after having spent the previous ten years making similar interventions.

21. *Ibid.*, 1959, vol. I, p. 64, January 19, 1959. This statement was made with the equalization program all but completed.

22. *Ibid.*, vol. II, p. 2208, March 24, 1959. This statement was made in introducing the Freight Rates Reduction Act and refers to the Government's intention "of proceeding with a comprehensive inquiry into matters affecting the railway."

23. *Ibid.*, 1957-58, vol. III, p. 2797, January 3, 1958.

24. *Ibid.*, p. 1798.

25. Under P.C. 1958-24, March 1, 1958.

26. P.C. 1958-305, February 18, 1958, and P.C. 1958-601, April 29, 1958.

27. House of Commons, *Debates*, 1959, vol. I, p. 64, January 19, 1959.

28. *Ibid.*

29. BTC Transcripts, vol. 1030, p. 8625, October 9, 1958.

30. *Ibid.*, p. 8650, October 8, 1958. Frawley stated: "I am not quarrelling with whether they give these men more wages or not. The Province of Alberta is not being drawn into the question of whether or not these men should have these extra wages or not. That is for the men and the railways and it is not for the Board and it is not indirectly for the Province of Alberta to have to say anything at all about whether these men should or should not have these extra wages."

31. *Ibid.*, p. 8703.

32. *Globe and Mail*, November 27, 1958.

33. "We said before we were in power that freight rates were unjustifiably high when raised horizontally. Did we act? When the board allowed the increase we held it up because it couldn't be justifiably brought into existence on the basis the increase was provided." (Press report of a speech made in Windsor during the March, 1958, election campaign, and quoted by Lionel Chevrier in House of Commons, *Debates*, 1959, vol. II, p. 2333, April 7, 1959.)

34. *Globe and Mail*, December 12, 1958.

35. House of Commons, *Debates*, 1959, vol. I, p. 3, January 15, 1959.

36. In its final argument to the MacPherson Royal Commission, Saskatchewan, while conceding some benefit from the equalization of the class rates, also stated: "there is every indication that equalization of commodity rates will, with some exceptions, raise rather than lower the costs to Western Canada of such movements." Royal Commission Transcripts, Summations, and Arguments, vol. II, p. 62, February 14, 1961.

37. Quoted in a speech by Hazen Argue (CCF, Assiniboia) on the Freight Rates Reduction Act. House of Commons, *Debates*, 1959, vol. II, p. 2232, March 25, 1959.

38. Typical of his success is the response to his readings from a (perhaps too enthusiastic) "Report on Equalization" of the Board of Transport Commissioners, dated September 27, 1957: "The equalized class rates have now been in effect for two and one half years and have cured the complaints that existed for so many years concerning the higher class rates in Western Canada compared with Eastern Canada." To which Mr. Broome (PC, Vancouver South) replied: "Nonsense." House of Commons, *Debates*. 1959, vol. II, p. 2381, April 9, 1959.

39. *Ibid.*, p. 2207, March 24, 1959.

40. *Ibid.*, p. 2208.

41. Except for one contract, 1966-1968, which was for a three-year period.

Notes to Chapter 10

1. Order-in-Council PC 1959-557, May 13, 1959.

2. House of Commons, *Debates*, May, 1959, vol. 3, p. 3749.

3. *Ibid.*, p. 3750.

4. *Ibid.*, p. 3752.

5. See the proceedings of the Commission's pre-hearing conference, contained in pp. 1-137 of *Transcripts* of the Royal Commission on Transportation, 1959.

6. *Transcripts*, vol. 5, p. 523ff.

7. *Ibid.*, p. 533.

8. *Ibid.*, p. 546.

9. *Ibid.*, vol. 6, p. 636.

10. *Ibid.*, 642.

11. *Ibid.*

12. *Ibid.*, p. 693.

13. There had been other cost hearings of a more limited nature, especially those conducted by the Board in the course of rate increase applications. A. W. Currie also cites grain cost studies prepared for, but largely ignored by, the Turgeon Commission. See Currie's presentation to the 1970 Conference on Transportation and Regional Development published by the Center for Transportation Studies, University of Manitoba. At the MacPherson Commission, cost studies account for almost half of the 25,000 pages of transcripts.

14. Due to time pressures, the MacPherson Commission recommendations were split between two volumes of a *Report.* The first, dated March, 1961, contains the essence of the regulatory philosophy. The second, dated in December, contains further details on the Commission's proposals. A third volume of background studies was published a few years later.

15. *Report* of the Royal Commission on Transportation, vol. 1, p. 19. (All references are to the typewritten edition.)

16. *Ibid.*, p. 21.

17. *Ibid.*, pp. 28-30.

18. *Ibid.*, pp. 68-70.

19. *Ibid.*, pp. 49-50.

20. *Ibid.*, p. 51.

21. *Ibid.*, p. 76, "Reservation and Observations."

22. *Ibid.*, pp. 77-8, "Reservation on Grain."

23. Edition of April 12, 1961.

24. Quoted in a Canadian Press story carried in various western newspapers in the week following the release of the *Report.*

25. When the Commission referred to costs in rate-making, it was probably using costs as a lower end such as that recommended in its section on minimum rates, rather than as basis for all rates. On page 65 of volume 2 of its *Report*, the Commission states, ". . . It should be left with management of all firms in all modes to decide, in the light of potential traffic, whether to carry it at the lowest possible prices, i.e., out-of-pocket costs, or at some price which contributes to overheads sparingly or abundantly."

26. House of Commons, *Debates,* 1961, vol. 2, p. 3506.

27. Editorial in the *Winnipeg Free Press*, July 20, 1963.

28. The one major difference between the two proposed acts was that Bill C-231 required the railways to pass on to "captive" shippers one half of the cost savings between the key weight (30,000 pounds) used to calculate the minimum rate and the actual rate. Bill C-120 contained no such provision.

Index